The Chronicles of Dubya

Volume 1

The Defeat of Saddam

by

Frank J. Fleming

edited by Sarah C. Fleming

Cover image by Brian Tiemann, grotto11.com/blog

Author photo by Sarah C. Fleming

For information, contact NTM Publishing, Inc., at info@ntmpublishing.com
or visit ntmpublishing.com.

ISBN-10: 0-9786832-0-X
ISBN-13: 978-0-9786832-0-7
$19.95 paperback

Printed in the United States of America

FIRST EDITION

Dedicated to my readers.
I've never heard you laugh,
but I've always taken your
LOLs at face value.

FOREWORD

In July of 2002, I started a blog called IMAO so I could share my opinions with the world. To protect my daytime identity as a mild-mannered gun nut, I came up with the clever pseudonym "Frank J." (Who would ever have thought to use their first name and middle initial as a pseudonym? NONE before me, that's who!) As happens with many beginning bloggers, I soon realized I had absolutely nothing worthwhile to add to an intelligent debate on any issue. Thus, I instead focused on writing stupid things that at least were interesting. While the number of intelligent and unique opinions one can have about an issue is finite, the number of stupid things to say in any situation has no such boundaries.

This strategy gave me some success in the emerging world of the blogosphere. My inane posts soon gained me respect, but I lacked that which is the goal of every blogger: to be worshipped like a god. On October 26th, 2002, upon hearing that the United Nations was once again stalling efforts to do anything about Iraq, I imagined what then White House Press Secretary Ari Fleischer would say about the UN if he were unrestrained by any need to be diplomatic. So I wrote a post entitled "In My World" of Fleischer swearing out the press and then storming off. It wasn't very clever—even by my own standards—but it did make me realize that, if I wanted to fill my blog with new material, instead of writing opinions about events, I could just make stuff up.

Thus started the "In My World" series where the Bush administration reacted to world events in a more satisfying and, frankly, more interesting way. I started by imitating the style of AP news stories reporting press conferences, but later the format broke out into full short stories—a sort of political fan-fiction that always bordered laughing at and laughing with the Bush administration. Soon the readership to my blog swelled in size, and the godlike power I desired was in my grasp!

So while President Bush never actually joined a biker gang and clashed with the Hell's Democrats, dealt with inter-dimensional alien warlords, fought a Japanese demon who entered the Democratic Primaries, or had to handle the backlash from Secretary of Defense Donald Rumsfeld constantly strangling people, don't these stories reflect their own truth since they involved the common wisdom of the times in which they were written? The answer to that, of course, is no. This book is in fact completely useless. But it is funny, and isn't that worth something?

Well, you tell me; you bought the book. Enjoy!

ACKNOWLEDGMENTS

I am a super-smart, brilliant man and never, ever needed the help of others. I should really only acknowledge myself, and you should thank your many gods that I share my genius with anyone. Still, I let others shoulder some of the burden for me just so they can be thankful to be a part of my greatness.

First, I should acknowledge my lovely and talented wife, SarahK, as otherwise she would yell at me and possibly strike me. She was first the t-shirt model for my site and then my wife. More importantly, she did the editing for this book. I was fine with being "close enough" with grammar and spelling, because any smart reader should be able to figure out what I mean, but she wanted the book to be accessible to dumb readers as well. She spent many hours editing this project with nary a complaint (except for the constant ones). She wants it noted, though, that she disapproves of my occasional use of the blasphemes "golly," "gosh," and "jeepers."

Second, I would like to thank my parents. They provided genetic material I needed to exist. Since that process is over, I have no further use for them. I also have two siblings: my older brother, Joe foo' the Marine, who fights for freedom (though, frankly, he could do a better job at it), and my younger sister, Silly Sister Sarah, who is a costume designer in Hollywood. I don't particularly care for either.

Third, I would like to thank the other *IMAO* bloggers: Cadet Happy, Harvey, Laurence Simon, RightWingDuck, and spacemonkey. I wouldn't trade you guys for anyone else... unless I could find some harder working people.

Fourth, I would like to thank all the other bloggers I have used at one point or another during my rise to success. Thanks to John Hawkins of *Right Wing News* for some of my blog's earliest traffic. Thanks to Misha of *The Anti-Idiotarian Rottweiler* and Rachel Lucas for early encouragement. Thanks to Scott Ott of *Scrappleface* since I stole the warning about not reproducing any part of this book without permission from his book without permission. Thanks to Bill Whittle of *Eject! Eject! Eject!* for being cool and helping me make this book (if only he could learn to be pithy). Thanks to Serenity of *Serenity's Journal* for helping me to at least try and be useful. Thanks to Michelle Malkin... though I'm not allowed to talk about her. Thanks to Jonah Goldberg, even though I hate him and will steal his job out of spite. And thanks to Glenn Reynolds of *Instapundit* for letting me have a sip of his puppy smoothies to help bring me power. May he continue to metaphorically murder the hobos that are ignorance and worship the Satan that is our progress toward the future.

Finally, I would like to thank the Bush administration, because they've been lots of fun, if nothing else.

Oh, and I'd like to thank Jesus, because I think He's cool.

If you feel like I should have thanked you but didn't, I didn't forget. I left you out on purpose, because I'm mad at you for some reason.

And you who bought this book. That gave me money and makes you a good person. I thank you.

But woe unto thee who reads this book without payment; ye are the product of pigs and monkeys and worth nothing but contempt and scorn!

TABLE OF CONTENTS

TABLE OF CONTENTS

TABLE OF CONTENTS

The Chronicles of Dubya
Volume 1
The Defeat of Saddam

October 26, 2002

In My World

The White House now says it can build a coalition against Iraq without the help of the UN. Ari Fleischer recently said at a press conference:

> [expletive deleted] them. [expletive deleted] them all. Why the hell do we need the UN's help? Give me a .22 target pistol, and I could invade France, so why do we need those [blasphemy and vulgar sexual act deleted] backing our military? We're America! We're one bad [expletive deleted]! If we need other countries to back us, we'll just conquer some areas and set up our own friendly countries. We can do that. We can do whatever the [expletive deleted] we want. Just to make things clear and make sure that I'm not misquoted, we have complete contempt for other countries and their opinions. Come to think of it, why am I explaining myself to the press? I hate you [expletive deleted]! I'm outta here.

France and Russia stated they were unhappy with the US position. France has been especially uneasy with America since Donald Rumsfeld tried to strangle their ambassador for "looking at him funny." They want war with Iraq to be the last option, while America wants it as the first option and diplomacy only as a final option. In the US resolution, the ordering of steps taken against Iraq will be war, then a nuclear strike, then biological warfare, then childish name-calling, then an embargo, and finally diplomacy if none of the previous efforts worked. France's resolution was diplomacy, followed by surrender to Iraq. War would only be allowed if unconditional surrender was not accepted. "France will attack with unholy vengeance anyone who prevents us from surrendering," said a French diplomat, probably named Pierre, before being strangled by Donald Rumsfeld.

November 12, 2002

Iraq Defiantly Refuses to Give Opinion on UN Resolution

Today the Iraqi parliament was scheduled to vote on whether to accept the UN resolution, but just before the vote, they were all killed by a US bomb attack. This bombing came just hours after an influential Iraqi diplomat who was about to give his opinion on the resolution was killed by a sniper bullet.

"This is an outrage," Ari Fleischer told the press with poorly faked anger. "No one in Iraq has yet even mentioned the UN resolution. This is pure defiance, and I think the only solution is to start fire-bombing Iraq and the countries near it." He then took a few casual sips from a martini.

"Isn't the reason we haven't heard a decision from Iraq because the US keeps killing anyone who is about to say something regarding it?" asked a reporter just before being jumped on and pummeled by Fleischer. There were no more questions, though there was some crying.

Saddam is said to soon be giving his decision on the UN Resolution, but no exact timetable has been given, as he is "very scared" and "in need of a new pair of pants."

"If we do not hear a decision soon," Bush said in a speech from the White House lawn, "we will have no choice but to kill Arafat."

When asked why Arafat, Bush responded, "Isn't he the leader of Iraq?"

Seeing confused looks from the crowd, he then asked, "So, if I were to kill Arafat in a hail of gun fire in vengeance for him trying to assassinate my father, I'd look kind of stupid?"

Bush then looked agitated. "On an unrelated matter, I need to very quickly make some phone calls." He then turned to leave but suddenly stopped, saying, "Ah, forget it. I'm going to go play some golf."

November 15, 2002

Rumsfeld: Iraqi 'Bastards' Will Be Nuked

Rumsfeld said that if the United States goes to war over weapons of mass destruction in Iraq, the American military would move to "finish it fast." When asked to clarify what that means, he said, "We're going to nuke the bastards."

When asked by a reporter if he meant the US would use a nuclear strike against Iraq if WMDs were used on US troops, Rumsfeld replied, "We'll probably claim that's what happened when we nuke them, just to calm the nancy-boys in Europe, but I'm pretty set on nuking them no matter what. As soon as some Iraqi passes gas near one of our troops, we'll cry 'Biological warfare!' and then nuke the bastards."

Rumsfeld was then asked how they will minimize collateral damage, and he immediately started laughing. "Minimize?! I want to maximize it! I don't like many of the countries near Iraq and am hoping we can spill some of the carnage into them and just tell them, 'Oops, sorry about that one.' Stupid bastards."

When asked if he was concerned about many innocent people being killed, Rumsfeld stated that the US position is one of "complete unconcern" and that "all the bastards have it coming."

"Won't using nuclear weapons cause even greater problems by turning all civilized nations against the US? It almost seems idiotic to settle on using nuclear weapons at this point," said a hysterical reporter.

Rumsfeld looked extremely perturbed to have his methods questioned. "Know what? I have a problem: my gun has too many bullets in it." He then pulled out a Luger and shot the reporter. "There; problem solved."

The French ambassador to America—replacing the one who was recently strangled—expressed displeasure at the Defense Secretary's "combative" attitude. "We should at least wait until inspections are done before we talk about the possibility of discussing whether or not we will talk about putting war on the table as a possible but unlikely option." The ambassador was then interrupted by automatic gunfire tearing through the embassy walls. A glance out the window showed that Rumsfeld was the gunman, Rumsfeld giving the startled ambassador the finger before speeding off in his Buick.

Soon after, Bush said he disagreed with Rumsfeld doing a drive-by shooting of the French embassy but also said, "There is room for all sorts of opinions in my administration."

November 26, 2002

White House Scoffs at Daschle's Criticism of Radio Commentators

Taking issue with Democratic Senator Tom Daschle, the White House spokesman said Monday that it's not right to compare violent religious fundamentalists overseas to American commentators who sound off on the air.

"For one thing, when we come after Daschle, we're not going to do something retarded like blow ourselves up," said President Bush's press secretary, Ari Fleischer. "Plus, our beating of him will have nothing to do with religion and everything to do with him being a slimy weasel."

When asked if the White House condemned anyone who would threaten Senator Daschle and his family, Fleischer responded, "That would be quite hypocritical since I myself have threatened Daschle and his family on many occasions. Once, I killed his cat and placed it in a shoebox with a letter telling him he was next. The president believes in the Constitutional right to threats, and he will kill the household pets of anyone who would threaten that right to threats."

On the topic of whether there was any sympathy for Daschle and his plight, Fleischer remarked, "Aww, the po' wittle Daschle doesn't like people to say mean things to him on the radio. Why don't I get the baby his bottle? Seriously, though, I want Daschle to know that if he brings up this topic again, I will harm him and his family."

A reporter then asked if making such threats against Daschle was actually legal. Fleischer casually produced a baseball bat from behind the podium, and the question was withdrawn.

When asked for comment, Daschle hid behind his chair in his office and started crying. Despite reporters threatening him and his family, the only statement they were able to get from him was, "I want my mommy!"

November 30, 2002

Dead Man Jeffords Slams Bush's Environmental Record

"The Bush administration has continued its pattern of sacrificing our environment to the demands of special interests," said Senator James Jeffords in the Democrats' weekly radio response as he tried to ignore the grim specter of death that floated above him.

"This year the power industry is getting a nice Christmas gift..." Jeffords continued, stopping momentarily as he was transfixed by the ghost's glowing red eyes. He forced himself to look away. "...the biggest weakening of the Clean Air Act in history."

"You betrayed the Republican party," the wraith said, its words seeming to echo within Jeffords's own head. "You handed the majority to the Democrats." It floated closer to Jeffords, setting itself inches before Jeffords's quivering face. "But now the Republicans will have the majority again, and I am here... for you!"

"I made a decision based on my conscience!" Jeffords screamed, and then realized he was still on the air. "Hopefully, moderates in both parties can do what we've done before," he said as he glanced at a book he'd bought about Japanese ritual suicide. "Do I really have to disembowel myself before my eldest son cuts off my head?" he wondered aloud before he was finally cut off the air.

When the White House was asked for a response, President Bush's press secretary Ari Fleischer refused to give one, saying there was nothing to respond to, since "dead men do not speak."

On whether there would be a backlash against Jeffords when the Republicans take the majority in the Senate, Fleischer said, "Are you reporters all 'tards? Of course we'll seek vengeance. We have a mandate from the people to hand out punishment to all our enemies. Little Jimmy Jeffords is going to wish he was never elected to public office. Originally, we were going to have Trent Lott beat him up on the floor of the Senate until the president pro tempore would finally yell, 'Finish him!' Then Lott would rip Jeffords's head out, along with his spine, and hold it up for a nice photo op as a warning to all other potential Judases. Unfortunately, we found out we would need a two-thirds majority in the Senate to do that. Instead, we'll find a slow torture for him, one that will make decapitation seem merciful." He then laughed maniacally, shouted, "No more questions from you fools!" and pulled his cloak around himself before storming away.

December 04, 2002

US Unimpressed with Iraqi Inspections

The US has been expressing concern that the Iraqi weapons inspections have been too easy. "This is absurd," Hans Blix responded to reporters. "Now let me continue to inspect this box of chocolates for WMDs. The top row seems clean... but what about the bottom row?!"

"That Hans Blix loves his chocolate!" Saddam laughed. "Now excuse me while I go use up all my chemical weapons on the Kurds before the Americans find them."

Kofi Annan said he was happy with the inspections so far and with the Iraqi cooperation, but Donald Rumsfeld was not so impressed, saying the Americans should "murder them all." When asked for clarification of who "them" was, Rumsfeld said, "The UN members and their families.

"I've been telling Bush for a long time that we should finally cut through the crap and kill everyone involved with the UN, but he keeps saying that's too harsh," Rumsfeld explained. "I'm starting to think that guy is a fruit. Just let it be known, though, that if Blix and his inspections get in the way of our war with Iraq, I will personally gut him like a fish. I'm telling you this now so that if he is found gutted in the future, you'll know I did it, and no one else can take credit."

Rumsfeld expressed his frustration about how long he has gone without a new war. "Do you know how much fun war with Iraq will be?" Rumsfeld said. "We'll be killing those Iraqis left and right, as they practically have Stone Age technology compared to our modern military." Rumsfeld then produced a small handheld computer. "See this? This is a PDA." He took out the stylus and touched a few points on the screen. "I just had some place bombed." When asked where he had bombed, Rumsfeld became irritated. "How the heck would I know? What do I look like, some computer geek? We'd still be using a telegraph to give troops orders if I had my way."

When a reporter questioned Rumsfeld's recent belligerent attitude toward the press, Rumsfeld responded by grabbing the reporter by his neck and lifting him into the air. The press conference ended abruptly as everyone fled in terror.

December 09, 2002

White House: US Must Get to War with Iraq Before Rumsfeld Hurts Someone

Washington has obtained a copy of Iraq's twelve thousand-page arms declaration. President Bush himself was seen to sit down and start reading it, but, after getting a quarter of the way through the first page, exclaimed, "This is boring!" and tossed it into a nearby fireplace. He then turned on a television while musing aloud, "I wonder what's on Comedy Central?"

"President Bush was unaware the job of presidency would ever involve heavy reading," White House Press Secretary Ari Fleischer later explained to reporters. "He, like most Americans, couldn't care less about the inspections and wants to get to the important business of bombing the crap out of Iraq and stealing their oil, which we will either use to lower gas prices or dump it all on France and set it on fire."

On the topic of when to expect war, Fleischer said, "I hope it will be as soon as possible, because every time the president and I have to tell Rumsfeld of a delay, it looks like he is going to hit us. All his plans for Christmas presents involve having a large supply of Iraqi skulls, so he's going to be royally pissed if we don't get moving soon. Right now, everyone except Condoleezza Rice is too afraid to face him, so we have to use her as a go-between."

When asked whether he was concerned by Rumsfeld's recent behavior of causing bomb scares at the French embassy, sending persistent death threats to Colin Powell, and suggesting he might start a military coup if the "nancy-boys at the White House don't get their butts in gear," Ari Fleischer told the press that "this was exactly the sort of behavior we expected when we hired him.

"Actually, it isn't me who should be worried about him instigating a military coup," Fleischer explained to the gathered reporters. "Guess who are going to be among the first people he executes if he actually goes through with it?

"What we need to do is quickly get through all this paperwork and begin our war with Iraq," Fleischer added, "before Rumsfeld decides to do something rash."

When asked if there were worries that, in the rush to war, they might not find out about any chemical or biological weapons Iraq has in its possession that it could then use against the US, Fleischer assured the press that the White House was "much more scared of Rumsfeld."

December 23, 2002

Wussy, Whiny Liberal Powell Asks for Mercy for America's Enemies

Secretary of State Colin Powell declared a few days ago that Iraq was in a "material breach," seemingly indicating America's willingness to go to war. When asked further about the issue, he said, "Obviously, there is a practical limit to just how long you can go down the road of non-cooperation," and then added, "though I don't match the bellicose nature of some of my colleagues," probably referring to Secretary of Defense Donald Rumsfeld. "The suggestion that we capture our Iraqi enemies and force them to watch their wives and children be burned alive in their own homes before we then torture the Iraqis to death is just too extreme. I don't see any reason why the wives and children of our enemies can't just be smothered to death and a videotape then be shown to each Iraqi before we commence torture."

Rumsfeld was outraged by the suggestion. He first paused to vomit in disgust at the mention of Colin Powell's name and then shouted at the reporters, "That weak-kneed, whiny liberal! Why don't we just take America's enemies and buy them a room at the Hilton? He should be branded a traitor for suggesting such mercy. I don't know why Bush hired that pinko. I swear I'll knock Bush down and stomp on him the next time I see him, and don't think his Secret Service will stop me. They do rigorous psychological tests before hiring those people, so you can be sure that they're all sane and thus scared of me."

A reporter asked Rumsfeld's opinion on Trent Lott's statements and the change in Republican leadership. Rumsfeld produced a Luger from under his coat and shot the reporter and then also shot the reporter behind him.

"Let this be a lesson to you!" Rumsfeld announced. "If you ask me a question that doesn't involve war with Iraq, I will kill you and the reporter next to you."

President Bush seemed unconcerned with the feud between his two cabinet members. "The reason I hired them was for a diversity of opinions. On one hand, I have the laughable opinion of an annoying, useless liberal, and on the other hand, I have that balanced by the opinion of a psychotic warmonger who wants nothing more than to hurt me."

In response to Rumsfeld's threats, Bush said, "I'm not too worried, though personally I would feel better if Cheney weren't hogging the undisclosed location all the time."

January 08, 2003

North Koreans Say Sanctions Means They Will Commit a Violent Suicide

North Koreans have upped their rhetoric, saying that sanctions against them would mean war. This immediately caused Secretary of Defense Donald Rumsfeld to inquire, "What kind of crack are they smoking?

"I know their leader Kim Jong-Il is some sort of nut, but even the insane show a pain-avoidance response. Does he not understand the violence we will perpetrate against him and his people if they even look like they may attack us? We will kill them all in such a cruel and painful manner that even *I* will feel sorry for the dumb Commie bastards. That doesn't mean I won't laugh as it happens, though."

When asked to clarify if America had anything to fear from a war with North Korea, Rumsfeld said that "the only thing to fear from them is that their radioactive, ashen remains are somehow blown over to the American mainland."

On whether there was a worry that a conflict with North Korea would be impossible while engaging Iraq, Rumsfeld stated, "We are capable of fighting two major regional conflicts. We're capable of winning decisively in one and swiftly defeating in the case of the other, and let there be no doubt about it."

Asked whether this belligerent attitude may turn off our European allies, Rumsfeld responded, "Let me restate that: we're capable of winning decisively in one and swiftly defeating in the case of the other while still having enough manpower left over to slap around a bunch of whiny girls." He then added sarcastically, "But don't take that as a suggestion of war. I'm just stating the facts.

"All I'm saying," he continued more seriously, "is if you wake up one morning to find the Iraqi deserts stained red with blood while at the same time North Korea is nothing but a smoldering ruin, and then you turn on the TV to find German Chancellor Gerhard Schroeder dancing for our amusement at gunpoint, don't act all surprised."

When repeatedly questioned as to whether America really did have the military capabilities to engage Iraq and North Korea at the same time, Rumsfeld initially looked supremely angry at not being immediately believed, but then he seemed to calm down and said, "I assure you we can do two things at once. As a demonstration of that, I will not rub my stomach and shoot reporters at the same time."

By the time he had drawn his Luger, the press had already cleared the room.

January 09, 2003

Senator Murray Defends Bin Laden Comments and Calls for Death to America

Outrage followed Senator Patty Murray's remarks in which she praised Osama bin Laden by saying:

> He's been out in these countries for decades building schools, building roads, building infrastructure, building daycare facilities, and building health care facilities, and people are extremely grateful. He's made their lives better. We have not done that.

Senator Murray has now defended her remarks, accusing people of twisting her words and stating that injustices like that are exactly why she now supports Osama bin Laden's goal of destroying America.

"There wouldn't be so much controversy if it weren't for the Zionist-controlled media," Senator Murray told reporters as she fiddled with what looked like a bomb. "Soon they and all the Crusaders will taste the just wrath of Osama bin Laden... as soon as he is done building The Terror Tots daycare center and filling in the potholes on Suicide Bomber Boulevard." She concluded with a shout of "Death to America!" and ululated for a minute straight, impressing the press in attendance.

Senator Patty Murray had previously tried to destroy America only by supporting liberal policies, but now she vows more direct means such as violent acts of terrorism. If you see Senator Murray, consider her armed, dangerous, and unapologetic. Do not approach her, but instead contact the FBI.

January 15, 2003

Rumsfeld Wants Talks with North Korean Leader

The White House softened its tone on North Korea by hinting that a sweeter energy and food deal may be made in exchange for disarmament, but Pyongyang hasn't let up on its militaristic tone toward Washington, threatening the US with undefined "options."

"Unless that option is to starve to death while we watch and laugh, I'm not sure what they're talking about," Defense Secretary Donald Rumsfeld said at a press conference. "Frankly, I'm getting tired of these retarded Commies. I keep trying to concentrate on the demise of the Iraqis, and then North Korea interrupts my train of thought by screaming, 'Kill us! Kill us horribly!'"

Surprisingly, Rumsfeld agreed with the idea of opening up talks with North Korea. "I think it's a great idea. We should have talks immediately and see if we can get Kim Jong-Il himself to attend. Then, as soon as we meet, I can strangle that freak myself while Condoleezza takes care of any guards." Rumsfeld savored the thought for a moment. "As soon as I saw that reject with his puffed-up hair, I said there was nothing I wanted more than to squeeze his neck until he is dead. Remember when I told you that?"

Most of the press in attendance nodded.

"Well, if Kim Jong-Il finds out about my new plans, I'll know who ratted me out," Rumsfeld told the reporters threateningly.

When asked whether murdering the leader of the North Koreans was the best course of action, Rumsfeld responded indignantly, "Are you questioning me?"

The reporter shook his head and shrank away from the podium.

"What do you say to reports that you are mentally unstable?" asked a reporter who was new to these press conferences.

"I'm sorry," Rumsfeld said, "I'm getting hard of hearing in my old age. Did you say something about wanting to be stabbed repeatedly in the neck with a ballpoint pen?"

Rumsfeld looked ready for violence but then calmed down. "My doctor says killing reporters is bad for my heart. He also had the gall to tell me to stop eating my steaks raw and instead cook them to at least medium rare like I'm some sort of fruit. I thought about giving him a good throttling, but I don't know if my health insurance covers that. Anyway, one more question."

The revered Helen Thomas stood up and asked, "Where am I? Has anyone seen my pills?"

Rumsfeld then frantically searched under his jacket, where he usually kept his Luger, but eventually gave up and announced, "This press conference is over," punched the nearest reporter, and left.

A North Korean diplomat immediately responded to Rumsfeld's statements, saying, "The super might of our country will knock the flying fortress of our enemy beneath the sea using the magic winds of our flutes." He went on a while longer, but, by all accounts, the rest of his statement was just random words strung together in imitations of sentences. The same diplomat was later found strangled to death, seemingly another victim of the serial killer known as the "Rumsfeld Strangler." He apparently only kills foreign diplomats and gets his name from his calling card he leaves on each body: the statement, "I'm Donald Rumsfeld. I strangled this guy" on a piece of the Defense Secretary's official stationery that is signed by Donald Rumsfeld and stamped by a notary public. DC police are baffled.

January 19, 2003

Stupid People No Like War

This weekend anti-war whack jobs took to the streets in a last push to preserve murderous regimes.

"War argh gurgle oil ergh BAD!" one of the more coherent protestors was heard to say.

The White House seemed unperturbed by all the demonstrations.

"I think the president welcomes the fact that we are a democracy and that people in the United States, unlike those in Iraq, are free to protest and to make their case known," said White House Press Secretary Ari Fleischer at a press conference, never once looking up from the Game Boy Advance in his hands.

"But what about the protestors who were beaten with their own 'No Blood for Oil' signs by men who claimed to have been paid by the White House?" asked one reporter.

"I think the president welcomes the fact that we are a democracy and that people in the United States, unlike those in Iraq, are free to yadda yadda yadda," Fleischer responded, now staring at the Game Boy quite intensely, apparently fighting a boss monster in the game *Metroid Fusion* that he was playing.

"You're not even paying attention to us!" shouted another reporter.

Fleischer then angrily chucked his Game Boy at the reporter, striking him in the head. "There, I paid you some attention."

"Ow! That hurt!" cried the reporter.

"Ow! That hurt!" Fleischer repeated in a high-pitched, mocking voice.

"You're the meanest press secretary ever!" the man yelled before running out of the press conference crying.

"Anyone else want to waste my time with one of your idiotic questions?" Fleischer asked angrily.

Helen Thomas then stood up.

"Merciful God, please kill me now," Fleischer was heard muttering.

"Why does Bush want to kill Iraqi children?" Helen Thomas asked. "What did Iraqi children ever do to him?"

"Here, I have a question for you," Fleischer responded. "Why won't you die, you shriveled old hag? What sort of unholy agreement do you have with Satan to keep your body living long after your mind has expired?"

"Where's my cat?" Thomas demanded. "Your talk of war has scared away my cat!"

"For the last time, Helen, your cat died thirty years ago!" said an exasperated Fleischer. "Someone please watch her. Any other questions?"

"Do you ever find it intimidating working with such a brilliant strategist as President Bush?" asked President Bush, poorly disguised with a porn star mustache.

"What are you doing here?"

"I'm trying to hide from Rumsfeld," whispered Bush. "I'm afraid that once he finds out we haven't started war yet, he's going to break my legs."

"I did see him walking around earlier with his leg-breaking sledgehammer."

"So, Ari, can we go 'debate' the protestors like you said we would?"

"Sure, did you bring your 'argument'?"

Bush held up a metal pipe. "Sure did... but I flooded the bathroom getting it."

Fleischer pulled out a baseball bat from behind the podium. "Let's roll."

"But we still have more questions!" protested one reporter. He was then struck with a bat, which surprised no one.

January 22, 2003

Bush Running Short on Patience That Rumsfeld Never Had

President Bush told reporters Tuesday that he is running short on patience with Iraq.

"It appears to be a re-run of a bad movie," Bush said. "Saddam Hussein is delaying. He's deceiving. He's asking for time. He's playing hide-and-seek with inspectors. One thing is for certain—he's not disarming.

"On the other hand, if he had woken up one day and couldn't remember what he did with all his WMDs, that would be like a re-run of a good movie, because that would be like *Dude, Where's My Car?*" Bush then chuckled to himself. "'Dude, where are my WMDs?' That crazy Saddam; what trouble is he going to get into next?"

The reporters just stared at him.

Bush then got angry. "You guys suck; I'm outta here."

In a later press conference, Secretary of Defense Donald Rumsfeld responded to Bush's comments. "I'm not sure what kind of movie Iraq is now," he said, "but as soon I get this war started, it's going to become the *Texas Chainsaw Massacre*. Generations from now, they will still be trying to scrub all the blood off the walls in Baghdad."

When asked whether there still might be any negotiations with Iraq to get them to disarm, Rumsfeld replied, "In my mind, the only thing still on the table is whether the spoon I will personally gut Saddam with is dull or sharpened. If he thinks that there is any way he can avoid a painful death at this point, then he is extremely high."

"Don't you ever feel ashamed about declaring war on innocent people just so you can get oil to make yourself richer?" asked a hippy who had somehow broken into the press conference.

The reporters immediately jumped away from the hippy, hoping to avoid any resultant splash damage. Surprisingly, Rumsfeld hadn't leapt on the dirty hippy to tear him limb from limb, but instead just stood behind the podium, glaring at the fool. Eventually, a low rumbling sound was heard, and the hippy started choking and then fell to the ground. The reporters didn't seem too surprised by the incident; although none of them had before seen Rumsfeld kill someone just by looking at them, they always assumed he could do something like that.

"Any other questions?" Rumsfeld demanded.

"Is he going to explode?" asked a reporter, looking at the hippy lying there in spasms.

"Eventually." Rumsfeld looked at his watch. "Laura Bush talked me into reading to school children, so someone film it for me."

In a nearby kindergarten class, Rumsfeld read some excerpts from *Jane's Guide to Guns* and then took questions from the children.

"My mom says guns are bad," said little Suzy, age five.

"Your mom is obviously a stupid whore," Rumsfeld responded.

Some of the children then started crying, asking that the "mean man go away."

"You children are weak!" Rumsfeld shouted in full rage, startling the children from their tears. "When I was your age, I had to help my village fight off roaming samurai with nothing but a pitch fork. And then I was in bed by six and never complained to my parents. I bet you children couldn't even pierce bamboo armor! You disgust me!"

That night, most of the children had trouble sleeping, fearing that Rumsfeld was hiding under their beds. They took little solace from the fact that Rumsfeld hardly ever waits in the dark to strangle someone in their sleep, instead preferring more direct approaches to killing.

January 27, 2003

White House Dismissive of Whiny "Allies"

The push for war has grown ever stronger, with even the more "moderate" members of the Bush administration, such as Colin Powell, raising the idea of unilateralism. Plus, some relations with allies have been harmed by Rumsfeld's characterizing France and Germany as "Old Europe" and dismissing them as irrelevant.

Even Republican Senator Chuck Hagel criticized the remarks, saying that the United States must assure the world it is patient and responsible and that "you don't do that with glancing blow, condescending remarks." Later that day, Hagel wound up in the hospital with most of his bones broken, as he had fallen down a long flight of stairs and then climbed up the stairs and fallen again four more times—at least according to the sole witness, Donald Rumsfeld. When he was asked whether that was just a lame story to cover up the fact that he had in reality severely beaten Hagel for his impudence, Rumsfeld responded, "Yes," and then raced off in his Buick, laughing.

White House Press Secretary Ari Fleischer did not seem eager to answer questions about the incident.

"I'm reading," he told questioning reporters at a press conference as he held up an advance copy of *Harry Potter and the Order of the Phoenix.*

"But these are important issues that need—"

"I'm almost done with this chapter," Ari said angrily and continued reading. "Harry Potter, you scamp, what trouble are you going to get into next?" he said to himself while chuckling. He then closed the book and looked at the reporters. "What the hell do you guys want?"

"Couldn't you find a different time to read?" asked one reporter.

"Hey, if you paid more attention in my previous press conferences, you could just guess what I'm going to say now and we wouldn't have to do these stupid things."

"So are you going to condemn Rumsfeld for his actions?"

Fleischer slapped his hand to his forehead. "How stupid are you people? No, I am not going to condemn Rumsfeld, because—other than when I'm giving press conferences with you idiots—I enjoy life. The official position of the White House on France's and Germany's stance against war is '@#$% them and the horses they rode in on.' We'd launch cruise missiles at them, but they are so irrelevant we don't even have their latitudes and longitudes written down anywhere."

A reporter then asked about the refusal of Iraqi scientists to have private meetings with UN weapons inspectors.

"Oh, I know this one," Fleischer exclaimed and searched his jacket, finally producing a small card. "President Bush believes that Iraq's refusal to allow Iraqi scientists to submit to private interviews with UN inspectors is unacceptable. Under UN Resolution 1441, Iraq has an obligation to comply."

"What are you going to do if they continue not to comply?" asked another reporter.

"Well, uh... according to UN Resolution... uh... 1234, if you keep asking me questions about this, I have to kick you in the nuts."

"Resolution 1234? Never heard of it."

"It's right here," Fleischer said, holding open his book so the reporter could see. When the reporter leaned close for a look, Fleischer slammed it shut on his face, and the reporter ran off crying.

"Idiot," Fleischer laughed. "Any other questions?"

Helen Thomas stood up.

"What did I do to deserve this?" Fleischer muttered to himself. "Did I murder the Pope in a previous life?"

"Now Jim, why—"

"Let me stop you right there, Helen," Fleischer interrupted. "For the last time, my name is Ari Fleischer, President George W. Bush's press secretary, not James Hagerty, Dwight D. Eisenhower's press secretary, you senile old bat."

Helen paused a moment to reflect. "Now Jim, is the White House aware that most people are against your war for oil?"

"Most *Americans* are not against fighting Iraq, because we're not a bunch of irrelevant pansies like that collection of countries they call the EU. While there are some incoherent, nitwit peaceniks out there, their numbers are now dwindling due to our secret assassins' efforts to poison bong water. One more question."

"Due to the president's extreme masculinity, do you, despite your heterosexuality, sometimes find yourself physically attracted to him?" asked President Bush, poorly disguised with a sombrero.

"Is Rumsfeld after you again?"

"He says I'm going to wind up like Hagel if I don't get France and Germany to shut up. What did he look like the last time you saw him, Ari?"

"He had a murderous glare in his eyes... but just the same one he normally has."

"Cool. Anyway, I was talking to Fuzzy the janitor, and he says he can get me into the Capitol building tonight. I was thinking you and I could go trash Daschle's office. I got a big bag of poo!"

"Well, don't tell all these people!" Fleischer shouted, pointing at the reporters.

"Oh yeah." Bush turned to the reporters with his "threatening face." "Don't any of you cross me, because I know some powerful people! I even know me, the president!"

The next morning, Daschle found his office had been vandalized. He then held an impromptu press conference in which he blamed it on "right-wing talk radio." During his statement, he was struck in the head with a beer bottle, which he blamed on "aliens."

January 29, 2003

Rumsfeld Finds Call to War Not Nearly Loud Enough

At President Bush's State of the Union Address, he came just short of declaring war against Iraq. This seemed to displease Defense Secretary Donald Rumsfeld, who sat watching, all the while looking ready to kill everyone around him.

At a press conference afterward, instead of the usual curtain behind Rumsfeld, there was a wall of flame. No one was sure, though, whether it was set up earlier for atmosphere or if it simply manifested itself as a physical representation of Rumsfeld's tremendous rage.

"Cower before me!" he yelled at the beginning of the conference. The reporters in attendance quickly complied. "The fact that we are not at war yet angers me greatly. Each time an Iraqi soldier takes a breath of air, it is an insult to all American people!"

He then grabbed one reporter by the collar and placed his Luger against the guy's head. "You look like you wish to question me!"

"Uh... when you get your war, what sort of post-war government do you plan to set up in Iraq?"

Rumsfeld stared him in the eyes for a short while. He finally dropped him and said, "I have decided that instead of killing you, I will answer the question. There will be no post-war government; everyone will have perished. Next question."

"What are your reactions to Saddam's alleged plans to burn his oil fields?" asked another reporter timidly.

"WHAT?!" Rumsfeld shouted angrily, causing the flames behind him to leap higher into the air. "Burning those oil fields was to be MY pleasure! What idea of mine is he going to steal next? Is he going to blow up his military complexes? Kill his soldiers with cluster bombs? Shoot himself in the head from a thousand yards out?"

After a moment's silence, a reporter bravely stepped forward. "We have reports that you and a group of mercenaries sneaked into both France and Germany and set bombs on a number of their landmarks. Are you going to ask for a ransom, or are you just saving their destruction for a special occasion?"

"I'm not going to stand here and answer questions about my personal life," Rumsfeld answered curtly.

"Why do you want to harm France and Germany?" piped in one reporter. "Don't you understand that they're just trying to bravely stand against America's imperial impulses?"

Rumsfeld just stared at the man for a moment. "Mother of mercy, am I going to hurt you," he finally said and then rolled up his sleeves. "My doctor says I need more aerobic exercise, so I'm going to give you a head start."

The reporter took the hint and started running. "This press conference is over," Rumsfeld announced before giving chase.

In unrelated news, another reporter was found dead, an apparent victim of the "Rumsfeld Strangler." This time the strangler left a new calling card, a Polaroid of Defense Secretary Donald Rumsfeld strangling the victim with the message, "Here's me, Donald Rumsfeld, strangling this guy" written on it. Police profilers say the culprit is probably a nineteen year-old Latino woman. DC police said they will not investigate, though, because "murderers are scary."

January 30, 2003

White House Demands Death of "Nutjob" Mandela

Escaping from handlers, former South African President Nelson Mandela has gone completely insane. Speaking of the US's stance on Iraq, he flailed his arms around and exclaimed, "One power with a president who has no foresight, who cannot think properly, is now wanting to plunge the world into a holocaust." He also said, "If there is a country that has committed unspeakable atrocities in the world, it is the United States of America," and "...Iraq produces 64% of the oil in the world. What Bush wants is to get hold of that oil." (Iraq produces 5% of the world's oil.) Mandela also accused America of racism, saying, "They do not care. Is it because the Secretary-General of the United Nations is now a black man?" He then ended his tirade by kung-fu-fighting invisible ninjas.

White House Press Secretary Ari Fleischer was surprisingly reserved, given the circumstances. "HE'S A DEAD MAN!" he screamed at a press conference held today. "Dead, you hear me? DEAD! No one says things like that about America and lives! No one! And I don't care if he is a complete nutjob. There's no excuse for that. He's dead!!!"

"Won't the international community be in an uproar if you assassinate Mandela?" asked a reporter.

"Ooh, the international community," Ari Fleischer said in a mocking high-pitched voice. "@#$% the international community. If other countries want their opinions to matter, they shouldn't be so small and weak."

"So you have no reservations about killing a Nobel Peace Prize winner?"

"The Nobel Peace Prize don't make you bulletproof," Fleischer answered. "It's not like anyone will get angry at us when we finally kill Arafat. And I doubt there will be any protest when the car bomb that kills Jimmy Carter is traced back to us."

"You're going to kill a former president?" asked one reporter in disbelief.

Fleischer looked confused. "Jimmy Carter was president? Of *this country*? How can that be? We have this whole Electoral College thing to ensure that brain-dead appeasers like him can never get into the White House. Anyway, it doesn't matter. He's dead. Arafat's dead. And Mandela is extra dead. He is a dead man, and nothing in this universe can save him. You make sure you print that in your papers: He is a dead man, and nothing can save him."

"This is for broadcast, actually," a reporter corrected him.

Fleischer punched him hard in the face. "Don't mess with me today!"

"So what do you say to Daschle's demands for an apology?" asked another reporter.

"That slimy weasel is still asking for an apology for our trashing his office?" Ari inquired.

"No, I believe he wants an apology for how you and Bush beat the crap out of him when he first came to you for an apology for the office vandalism."

"Hey, we beat him up fair and square," Fleischer said indignantly. "No one can walk up to us and act like a little weenie and then expect to not be severely beaten. All foreign diplomats know this now, and so should he."

President Bush then came running into the press conference. "Hey Ari! I found a book of matches!" he exclaimed. "Want to go burn things?"

"Cool!" Fleischer answered and then told reporters, "No more questions," as he quickly exited with Bush.

Helen Thomas was notably absent from the press conference. Apparently she had become confused and was outside asking inappropriately combative questions to a painting of Gerald Ford, which then tripped and fell on her.

In unrelated news, a number of melted Star Wars action figures were found near the White House. DC police say there is no evidence that the incident is terrorist-related, but they will continue to investigate.

February 03, 2003

God Denies Charges of Vengeance

Opinions in the Middle East about the Space Shuttle Columbia tragedy have been mixed. The official word from the Palestinian territories was one of condolence.

"President Arafat and the Palestinian Authority offer their condolences to the six American families and the Israeli family who lost their loved ones in the catastrophe," said Saeb Erekat, a senior Palestinian official and spokesman.

"Wow, I always said that Arafat's a nice guy," Bush responded. "That's why I told the Israelis that, when they kill him, to do it quickly and painlessly."

"They said no," he added.

In Iraq, loyalists to Saddam offered no such sorrow.

"We are happy that it broke up," government employee Abdul Jabbar al-Quraishi said. "God wants to show that His might is greater than the Americans'. They have encroached on our country. God is avenging us.

"Sure the Americans are extremely prosperous," he continued, "have access to vast technology and a standard of living that I can't even imagine. And maybe a homeless man begging on the streets in American could earn more money in a year than we can slaving away for a ruthless dictator. And perhaps the Americans have put men on the moon and have made huge leaps in science and technology based on their space program while, during the same time, our best accomplishment was learning a new way to cook a goat. But now they have lost seven astronauts in the heroic pursuit of science and must realize whom God really favors! Now please excuse while I go fester in my diseases."

Many in Iraq expressed similar notions that the Columbia tragedy was God's vengeance. Heaven Press Secretary Gabriel was on hand to answer these charges. "Now, I'll answer what I can, but obviously, a lot of this involves confidential information."

"What's the one true religion?" asked the first reporter.

Gabriel rolled his eyes. "I dunno... Scientology. Now please don't ask another question you know I can't answer."

"Was the destruction of the Columbia shuttle an act of God's vengeance?"

"Of course not. More than four billion people died in the past century, and it's not like anyone would think that's all in vengeance. Space travel is a dangerous pursuit, and the people involved knew that. That's what makes it heroism."

"So God admits to murdering more than four billion people in the past century? Does He plan on turning Himself in to authorities?"

Gabriel sighed and shook his head. "This is why we don't do these very often."

"What about when a celebration of Columbia's destruction in Iraq was broken up by a rain of angry monkeys?" asked another reporter. "That was pretty improbable, and some are pointing fingers at God."

"No comment."

"So does God ever hate anyone and thus destroy them with His wrathful fury and whatnot?"

"No, God doesn't hate anyone... He just smites some people from time to time. But really, that is rare, because human life is a sacred thing since man was created in His image."

"So does God closely resemble a monkey?"

Gabriel looked frustrated. "I... meant that in more of a metaphysical sense. One more question."

"Many say Saddam is quite an evil person. Can we expect some sort of unilateral action from the Almighty?"

"No, I wouldn't expect that. It's not God's place to constantly seek out violent retribution, as He has infinite mercy. In this world, Saddam has much more to fear from the Americans who, despite their best intentions, are not quite so infinite in their mercy."

February 05, 2003

US Troops to be Led by Haunted Robot

Secretary of State Colin Powell plans to present evidence to the UN today that Saddam has weapons of mass destruction and is mocking the rest of the world. On one audio tape, Saddam reportedly says, "I have weapons of mass destruction! Stupid world; I mock them! And I am so glad the UN will never hear me say this!"

Defense Secretary Rumsfeld showed his support for Colin Powell. "That weak-willed fool better not fail!" Rumsfeld shouted at a press conference, shaking his fist in the air.

"Chirac seems to say that he will not join the war plans no matter what," said one reporter. "How much do you plan on hurting him?"

"You must be from FOX News," Rumsfeld stated. "As for Chirac, just having other people see him after I'm done with him will be considered a crime against humanity."

"Is there any way you could agree on just having more inspections instead of war, in which innocent people will be killed?" asked another reporter.

Rumsfeld pulled out his Luger and shot the man in the knee. "Next question."

"Can we get him medical attention?" asked a reporter who watched the man roll around on the ground in pain.

"No."

Rumsfeld glanced behind him to see National Security Advisor Condoleezza Rice waiting impatiently. "Oh, yeah; we're now going to unveil some of the technology we are going to use in this war to slaughter our enemies and our lesser allies," Rumsfeld said. "Now, since I tend to stay away from anything more complicated than a semi-automatic, I'm going to turn this over to Dr. Condoleezza Rice."

Rumsfeld took a seat nearby, and Rice took the floor. "We wanted to have the ultimate leader to take our troops into battle," she announced. "We researched a number of ways to create this leader, such as cybernetic enhancements and gene splicing, but then we heard that a number of hippies claimed to have been severely beaten by a spectral entity. Upon further investigation, we determined it to be none other than the ghost of General George S. Patton. We used secret federal dark sorcerers to capture and contain the spirit—"

"There are dark sorcerers paid by the government?" one reporter interrupted.

"QUIET!" Rice screamed. "I will tell you when it is time for questions!" She then composed herself and smiled. "As I was saying, we captured the spirit of the General. Now all we needed is a container for it. So we've decided to use brand-new technology to unite the ways of the old with the ways of the new. Thus we have created Robo-Patton."

Projected onto a screen behind her was a picture of a hulking robot with ivory accents.

"Robo-Patton will have the power to inspire our troops to a quick and decisive victory, but he will not be some general giving orders from afar. Robo-Patton has hydraulic strength enough to slap the head clean off a man. He also has a built-in rocket launcher, rail gun, and Gatling gun, allowing him to dispatch threats of hardware and personnel. Robo-Patton will slaughter the enemy by the thousands."

She smiled a while, savoring the thought. Finally, she said, "Now you may ask questions."

"Do you really expect our troops to be led by this monstrous cyborg?"

"A cyborg is part human and part machine," Rice answered. "Robo-Patton is a pure robot being controlled by the spirit of General Patton. That makes him an android. Next question."

"Is there any chance Robo-Patton will go on an insane killing spree?"

"Is there any chance he won't?" Rumsfeld laughed.

Rice said, "There does seem to be some chance that Robo-Patton will not follow orders and will instead select his own targets. Most likely, though, he'll only kill people no one likes anyway, such as liberals or you."

"How do you people sleep at night when all you deal in is death and destruction?"

Rice looked unamused. "Your questions tire me." She pulled a remote out of her pocket and pressed a button. A transparent shield then came down from the ceiling, blocking Rice and Rumsfeld off from the reporters. "You have ten seconds before this room fills with poisonous gas," Rice announced. The press conference quickly ended.

In unrelated news, a large robot answering to the name General Patton is on the loose killing hippies in Berkeley, California. Government officials say they don't plan to do anything at this point, because the robot "will eventually tire himself out."

February 10, 2003

Bush Likened to Cowboy

President Bush seemed to signal war was approaching, saying Saddam "wants the world to think that hide-and-seek is a game that we should play. And it's over." He then added, "And the way we play hide-and-seek in Texas, after we find him, we beat him with sticks."

Bush then had a meeting with French President Jacques Chirac in a last-ditch effort to make the French president see his point of view. It did not go well.

"After the meeting, Chirac described you as being a cowboy. How do you respond?" asked a reporter at a press conference held afterwards.

"I object to that."

"Well, couldn't you admit that the way you lassoed Chirac, shot those accompanying him with a single-action revolver, and then yelled, 'Yee-haw!' while riding a horse off into the sunset with a bunch of stolen French cattle could be construed as the actions of a 'cowboy'?"

"Well, yeah," Bush admitted. "I was just objecting to the way he said it—like it was a bad thing. Who in the world doesn't like being a cowboy? I'm starting to think that Chirac may be... what's the word... homosexual. And I don't mean that in that he is 'happy and merry.' I mean that in that he's gay." Karl Rove then whispered in his ear. "But I don't mean that in a bad way."

"So are you factoring in France's and Germany's opinions?"

"Nah, honestly I just went to France to steal me some French cattle. I hate those guys. They make me think of that kid in class who would remind the teacher to give us homework. I beat that kid up, and that's still my policy."

"Are you pretty set on war, then?"

"Hells yeah. I hate that Osama and want to finally kill that bastard."

"Don't you mean Saddam, the leader of Iraq?" one reporter corrected.

Bush looked more confused than usual. "Shoot, I dunno. Bad people are going to die, so be happy!" He then shook his fist at the reporters. "Rumsfeld and Condi are in charge of this anyway. What they want is going to happen, because they're much smarter and more powerful than me; they're like Darth Sidious and Darth Maul."

"And would that make you Jar Jar Binks?" a reporter quipped.

Bush looked enraged. Karl Rove then whispered in his ear, and he calmed down and smiled. "That's pretty clever of you... Jar Jar Binks... that's a funny one... going to be laughing about that one for..."

"I'LL MURDER YOU DEAD!" Bush finally screamed and leapt on the hapless reporter. "I'm the President of the United States of America! The most powerful man in the world!" he yelled as he pounded the man's head into the ground. "I can have you declared an enemy combatant and deport your family to Syria!"

The Secret Service wrestled Bush away from the man, but as Bush was pulled to his feet, he quickly calmed down, straightened his tie and jacket, and tossed the reporter a blank pardon before walking off.

"He was just playing around," White House Press Secretary Ari Fleischer later told the press, "so there is no reason to sue him, unless you're some sort of crybaby... or hate not being injected with a drug that makes it look like you had a heart attack." He then glared at the press threateningly.

"What about when the president allegedly beat up Senator John Edwards and threw his shoes onto a telephone wire? Was he just playing then?"

Fleischer laughed. "I guess Mr. 'Regular Guy' caught a regular beating." Fleischer then glanced at his watch. "*The Simpsons* are coming on; I'm outta here."

February 12, 2003

Rumsfeld: I'd Rather be Killing Commies

Osama bin Laden is said to have released a new tape calling evil terrorist retards to arms if the US attacks Iraq. In his taped message, he instructed terrorists in battle strategies aimed at causing the highest number of American casualties. This involved telling them the best ways of splattering one's blood when shot so that Americans may later slip on it.

At a press conference, Defense Secretary Donald Rumsfeld seemed to be amused by the tape. "It's fun for them to pretend that Iraq could actually be a worthy opponent to the US, but according to our analysts, the difference in length of an invasion with them using their best weaponry available and the best fighting strategies, opposed to them just standing there letting us shoot them is about eight minutes."

Rumsfeld then took questions.

"Do you regret lumping Germany in with Cuba and Libya?"

"Would I have said it if I didn't mean it?" Rumsfeld asked, glowering at the man.

"Uh... no, sir. Of course not," the reporter said, slinking away.

"Germany, Libya, and Cuba are all alike. They won't help us with Iraq, they are evil countries, and we are currently working on plans to assassinate their leadership."

"Actually," National Security Advisor Condoleezza Rice interrupted, "we don't have plans for Libya."

Rumsfeld grumbled to himself as he snatched a nearby napkin and pulled out a pen. He then quickly jotted a few things down. "Tying timed explosives to monkeys is easy enough," he mused to himself, "but teaching them the subtleties of ninjitsu will take time." He tucked the napkin into his breast pocket. "I'll file this later. Next question."

"What is your reaction to your German relatives who disowned you?"

"Of course, I can't have fools like that claiming my bloodline. I will hunt them down, kill them, and burn their bodies, then bury their ashes in a dank bog. Nothing too surprising. Anyway, I'm going to now let Dr. Rice tell you about some more of our new technology to help with our fighting."

Rice then stepped forward. "For a possible conflict with North Korea, we've created a new firearm safety feature that will help avoid friendly fire incidents." Rice held up a handgun with some sort of optical attachment under the barrel. "The firing pin is blocked until the gun detects that it is pointed at a Communist."

"How can it tell if someone is a Communist?"

"Could you do me a favor?" Rice asked the reporter as she pointed the gun at him. "Could you say 'dictatorship of the proletariat'?"

"Potato chip... of the polar... chariot?" the reporter said with confusion as Rice pulled the trigger to empty clicks.

"Wow!" Rice exclaimed. "Too dumb to even be a Communist; didn't think that was possible."

"I would point out," said another reporter, "that just because someone has a Communist viewpoint doesn't mean they should be shot."

Rice then pointed the gun at him and pulled the trigger. "It works!"

"One less Commie," Rumsfeld laughed. "I hope we finish this Iraq thing soon; I miss killing Commies. Remember when I strangled one in 'Nam?"

"Yeah, that was last year," Rice answered. "Caused a bit of a media firestorm."

"Hey, if God didn't want us killing Commies, he wouldn't have given them necks fit for strangling."

"We still have questions," interrupted one reporter.

Rice pointed the gun at the reporter and pulled the trigger—an empty click. "Fine, what?"

"Diplomats for both the French and the Germans are in town right now. Do you and Rumsfeld plan on meeting with them?"

"Yes, we do," Rumsfeld said with a sinister laugh and then ended the press conference.

In unrelated news, the "Rumsfeld Strangler" has struck again, killing French and German diplomats. This time, a videotape was left on the scene. On it, one can see Defense Secretary Donald Rumsfeld strangling a diplomat while he says, "I'm Donald Rumsfeld. I'm strangling you." The end credits seem to indicate he had help in the act, as the cinematography is credited to "Condoleezza Rice." DC police are tired and confused. Cracking an easier case, they arrested a seventy year-old woman who tried to defend herself with a handgun when an assailant broke into her apartment. That assailant, who has numerous assault and drug convictions, was immediately elected mayor.

February 14, 2003

Clinton Visited by Ghosts of Founding Fathers

For the benefit of those wondering what the opinion of a self-indulged, immoral scumbag is about war with Iraq, Clinton spoke at a synagogue Thursday. He said the Bush administration should not take action without guidance from cartoon space monkey Hans Blix. Clinton also said any "pre-emptive strike" against Iraq by the United States should come only with the support of Europe, including inconsequential, impotent NATO members France, Belgium, and Germany.

To the surprise of everyone in attendance, once Clinton finished speaking, the ghosts of George Washington, Thomas Jefferson, James Madison, and Benjamin Franklin materialized in front of him. "Wow, what an honor!" Clinton exclaimed. "Now you can explain to everyone how great a legacy my presidency made and maybe convince them to make me president again."

A smile formed on Washington's ethereal face. "We've watched you for a long time."

"Pretty impressive, huh?" Clinton beamed. "I knew you guys wouldn't care about a few little scandals here and there when my heart was into making America great. Well, I just want you to know I humbly accept you bowing before me."

Washington chuckled a bit. "Yeah... that's what we're here for. As we said, we've watched you for a long time, and we've always wanted to meet you in person like this so we could tell you something."

"Sure, what?"

Washington floated closer, his translucent face seemingly bearing a grave matter. "Now, I want you to listen to this and remember it well."

The ghosts of the founding fathers then beat Clinton savagely for three hours straight. Clinton supporters fled the synagogue in terror, but soon other people crowded inside when they heard a fight going on. And it was quite spectacular, the poltergeist rage of the founding fathers flinging Clinton against the walls and ceilings and then ripping objects off the walls to beat him with.

"It was so cool!" exclaimed Sean Cooper, 17, who witnessed the event. "They were totally, like, railing on the guy. I started feeling sorry for Clinton, but then he started talking again, which just ticked off everyone even more, especially the ghost dudes. Franklin then held him from behind while Madison whaled on him, yelling, 'Feel your pain!' I don't know much about James Madison, but I'm going to have to look him up in a history book; that guy rocks!"

"Clinton may not know what 'is' is," said Jeremy Mitchell, 26, who ran into the synagogue after hearing the commotion and applause, "but we all sure now know the definition of an ass-kicking."

After the ghosts finally departed, Clinton himself was nowhere to be seen, possibly having been pulled into a ghost world to suffer eternal torments. A while later, though, he turned up in a nearby dumpster, disappointing many. Historians are now debating whether to add a new asterisk to Clinton's name on the list of presidents, making it read, "William Jefferson Clinton *impeached **savagely beaten by founding fathers."

February 17, 2003

Benevolent Bush Does Not Slaughter Protestors

Hundreds of thousands of Commie, pinko, anti-American retards took to the streets world-wide Saturday, thinking that if people see how a bunch of morons are able to both march and hold signs at the same time, then those people will forget their own welfare and the welfare of others and decide to mindlessly oppose war. There is no exact count of how many protestors attended, but census takers said there was enough incoherence for at least a million schizophrenics. In one place, the protesting got rowdy enough that hoses were used to keep the protestors back. People then had a second thought about it, stopped the hoses, sprayed the protestors with soap, and turned on the hoses again.

President Bush, though not agreeing with their viewpoints, expressed his happiness that they all lived in a society where differing ideas could be expressed.

"STUPID FILTHY SMELLY HIPPIES!" he screamed at the beginning of his press conference.

"So will all the protests have any effect on your stance on Iraq?" asked a reporter.

Bush rolled his eyes. "Yeah, Saddam can gas whomever he wants; the mangy hippies have spoken. I just wish there was a way America could save the world for all the serious people and leave the drooling, scummy hippies still vulnerable to terrorists."

"So you want the protestors dead?"

Bush smiled. "Wouldn't that be cool? All of them in hippy hell, where there are no signs to carry, no tie-dye shirts to wear, everyone has to have short hair and be clean-shaven, everyone has to work a regular job, and there's no pot smoking. And I could make it happen, too. Just one phone call, and I could have helicopters strafing these protesters, killing them by the thousands. And no idiotic slogan they could chant could stop a bullet." He continued to smile quietly for a moment but then changed to a more serious expression. "But I don't, because I'm just that tolerant and kind. They do everything they can to make me want to slaughter them, but I leave them un-killed. Do they understand how much will that takes? Do they ever say, 'Hey, thanks for not having me killed, President Bush, even though I'm a filthy, scummy, worthless hippy, deserving of a violent hippy death'? No, they never give me any credit." Bush stewed in his anger for a few moments. "It makes me want to murder them!"

"So you think the protestors should be more grateful to you?"

"Of course! Do you know I even had Condi distract Rumsfeld with a World War II movie marathon so he wouldn't spend all day strangling hippies? He's going to have crippling arthritis if we don't keep him from doing all that strangling.

"Anyway, my point is, I just want those protestors to stop for one moment and think that if America really is as evil and imperialistic as they say, then why aren't they dead? If they think we just want oil, hell, we could take over the entire world and have not just all the oil in the world, but all the gold, all the diamonds, all the chimpanzees and orangutans, and all the corndogs. And who could stop us? France? We could be nuking away while those dinguses would be trying to negotiate with us. Those weenies in Europe could never mobilize in time to stop us from world conquest. But we don't take over the world, and you know why?"

"Hadn't thought of it until now?" ventured one reporter.

"No, because we're just that benevolent. We have all this power, and we don't just slaughter everyone we dislike even though it would be a simple thing to do so. We even try to help other countries instead of just conquering them. All these smelly hippies should bow before us and thank us daily for allowing them the privilege of their filthy hippiness. But they just yell at me, and it makes me just want to beat them. I wish one were here right now so I—"

"No blood for oil!" shouted a mangy hippy who had sneaked into the press conference.

"Thank you, God," Bush said, looking skyward before jumping toward the man and screaming, "HIPPY!!!" He then pounded him soundly, finishing him off with a Texas two-step. "Hope that was a learning experience for the young man," Bush said as he ambled back to the podium.

"So is your policy to injure but not kill hippies?"

"Why are you guys always grilling me? Can't we just talk friendly-like for a change? So, did everyone see the 300th episode of *The Simpsons* last night?"

No one responded.

"You guys are freaks," Bush said with disgust. He pulled out a revolver and started firing at their feet. "Now dance!" The reporters quickly fled.

"Bush was just a little high-strung by the congregation of all those filthy, stinking hippies," Press Secretary Ari Fleischer explained at a later press conference. "His firing a gun at you was all in good fun."

"Was the gun loaded with real bullets or just blanks?" asked a reporter.

Fleischer sighed. "Yeah, Bush carries a gun filled with blanks; that makes lots of sense," Fleisher responded in a mocking tone. "Man, you guys ask the dumbest questions."

February 19, 2003

Somewhere There is a Very Angry Universe with Two Belgiums

"Impudent nations!" French President Jacques Chirac exclaimed at a press conference in his stronghold. He was greatly angered by the east European candidates for EU membership who issued pro-American statements, and he wished nothing more than to chide them publicly. "What you have done goes against the views of France, the most civilized nation of all! You must shut up if you wish to join the EU, of which France declares itself leader!"

"We have an intruder!" screamed his head of security. "He's described as an angry-looking old man."

"Must be that fool Rumsfeld!" Chirac responded. "Well, we're prepared for him! Send out the assault force!" Armed troops quickly rushed out of the press conference. "Now you die, Rumsfeld!" Chirac exclaimed. "No one keeps me from being extremely rude and arrogant! No one!" He laughed in an evil and effeminate way.

He turned back to the press. "Now, where was I? Oh yes... Silly little nations! How dare you defy France, the pinnacle of humanity?! We're too smart and sophisticated to fight in any wars. We just surrender and wait for everything to turn out all right in the end. America and their infantile talk about good and evil, morality, and justice will mess up the sophisticated business ventures we have with Saddam."

Automatic gunfire sounded nearby. It lasted a few seconds, and then there was silence. Chirac smiled. "Pierre," he said into his radio, "I assume Rumsfeld is no more."

"Pierre's not available right now," answered a familiar voice.

"This press conference is over!" Chirac yelled before fleeing. He entered a secure room with one entrance and took a machine gun off the wall.

"'Old Europe,' eh?" he said to himself as he pointed the gun at the door. "Well, we'll see who outlives whom." He heard noises outside and then pulled the trigger. Laughing wildly, he unloaded the gun at the door, turning the wall in front of him into swiss cheese. When the gun clicked empty, he crept forward but stopped when he saw a bright light shining through the bullet holes.

A Buick crashed through the wall, flinging Chirac backward. Through the dust and the bright headlights, he could see the figure of Donald Rumsfeld walking toward him.

"Don't hurt me! I surrender!" Chirac squealed as he tried to squirm away.

Rumsfeld grabbed him by his collar and lifted him into the air.

"I'm just an impotent Frenchman!" Chirac pleaded. "My country is old and irrelevant. You gain nothing from harming me!"

Rumsfeld just stared at him.

"You can invade Iraq! I support that now! You can invade any country you want, and we'll cheer you on! You can even invade us! Well put up more of a fight than we did with the Germans so it's not too boring for your troops."

Rumsfeld squinted.

"Please. I have a wife and children and a mistress. They're the ones saying bad things about you! Kill them!"

Rumsfeld tightened his grip.

"What do you want?" Chirac cried.

"My pen."

"What?!"

"Last time I was here, I left a pen."

Chirac looked to his side to see a cardboard box labeled, "Lost and Found" on a table next to him. He reached in and pulled out a metal pen. "Is this it?"

"That's it." Rumsfeld took the pen and dropped Chirac on the ground. He then got back into his Buick.

"Nice seeing you again, Rumsfeld!" Chirac called to him as he drove away. "Come back any time! I love America!"

* * * *

"So can we expect war soon?" asked a reporter.

"I hope so," National Security Advisor Condoleezza Rice answered. "The troops are restless, and they're running out of desert rats to shoot while they wait."

"We've heard Donald Rumsfeld has taken his vacation in France. Seems an odd choice, given all the recent controversy."

"If Rumsfeld wanted you to know about his vacation, he would have told you about it himself," Rice said with annoyance. "Anyway, on to the tech demos." On a screen behind her appeared a picture of a small electronic device with a drill. "This is a special projectile that homes onto a target's head, slowly drills into his skull, and then explodes. Honestly, it offers no tactical advantage over just shooting a target with normal bullets, but we all thought it was pretty cool and can't wait to see it work on some actual enemy combatants. By the way, if someone has a use for a dozen headless monkeys, talk to me after the press conference."

"Wouldn't a weapon like that violate the Geneva Conventions?" asked a disgusted-looking reporter.

"The what?" Rice asked, appearing confused. She pressed a button on her remote, and the picture on screen changed to show a new, extremely complex-looking device. "This new weapon twists the space-time continuum to completely remove its target from existence."

"What do you say to scientists who warn that use of this device could destroy the universe?"

"Current theories say that there are at least millions of different universes," Rice responded, "so losing one or two of them isn't of much concern. Anyway, we've found a nice, isolated place to test this out."

In unrelated news, Belgium seems to be missing, completely having disappeared from the face of the earth. Investigators can't say exactly how long it has been gone, since no one has really paid much attention to it.

February 26, 2003

Happy Children Equals Angry Rumsfeld

Saddam challenged Bush to a debate, and he readily accepted. The start of the Bush-Saddam debate was quite rocky, with Saddam making objections to the format early on.

"Bush has a bat!" Saddam exclaimed. "No one said he could bring a baseball bat!"

"Uh-uh," Bush responded, "I said I was going to wear a cowboy hat and carry a baseball bat for the debate, and you said it was okay."

"I remember agreeing to the cowboy hat... but not the bat. You're going to use that to break my kneecaps!"

"That's crazy talk! You're a crazy dictator! All that comes out of your mouth is crazy." Bush then started up an electric razor.

"Now he's got an electric shaver!" Saddam yelled. "He's going to break my knee caps and then shave off my mustache as a trophy!"

"You really should be named Crazy McCrazy, you crazy dictator," Bush responded indignantly. "When you talk, all you do is heap crazy upon crazy."

"In Saddam's defense, President Bush," piped in the debate's moderator, Jim Lehrer, "you do have a box labeled 'Trophy Saddam Mustache' sitting next to you, and you did just open it as if you're anticipating placing a trophy Saddam mustache inside it."

"That box is just a good luck charm I was given by my father. Can't we get on with the debate?"

"Okay. You get the first opening statement, President Saddam."

"Fine." Saddam pulled out some index cards. "You imperialist Yankee scum, why do you oppress—AHH! MY KNEECAPS!"

In other war news, Secretary of Defense Donald Rumsfeld appears to be growing more and more impatient with the delays over an attack on Iraq. Close associates describe his anger as "great" and his wrath as "terrible."

"These are pictures of happy Iraqis," Rumsfeld said as he showed some slides of an Iraqi family sitting down for dinner and smiling children playing in the streets. "Do you know what happy Iraqis mean?" Rumsfeld asked the clueless reporters. He paused a moment so they could stare back at him like deer trapped in headlights. "It means THEY ARE NOT BEING BOMBED!" He put up new slides of the ceiling collapsing on the family and children running from explosions in terror. "These are artists' renderings of what the Iraqis should look like. These are pictures of glorious war."

"Isn't one of the reasons for war with Iraq to help the Iraqi people?" ventured one of the reporters.

"WHAT?!" Rumsfeld yelled. "That's the most ridiculous thing I ever heard. Who gave you such an idiotic notion?" He then pointed an accusing finger at National Security Advisor Condoleezza Rice. "Was it you?"

"Oh, come on, Donald," Rice sighed, "I was just telling you this morning how much I hate Iraqi children."

"I know. It must have been the nancy-boy Colin Powell." Rumsfeld shook his fist in the air. "He wants to do nothing but coddle the enemy. Do you know he approved bombing of just one of the five orphanages I had on my list? If he were here, I could just strangle him!" He then eyed the reporter who asked the question. "Maybe I'll just strangle you instead!" He grabbed the reporter by the neck but dropped him after a second. "It's just not the same."

"Why are you so anxious to get to war?" asked a frustrated reporter. "Don't you worry about all the uncertainties?"

Rumsfeld rolled his eyes. "Everything is an uncertainty. How can I be certain this gun is loaded?" He pulled out his Luger and shot the reporter. "Guess it was loaded... but can I be certain it's still loaded?" He looked at the reporter lying on the ground. "Hey, I asked you a question! For pete's sake, reporters these days don't know how to take a bullet. I once saw Teddy Roosevelt shoot a reporter five times, and the guy still came back with a follow-up question."

Rumsfeld's eyes grew distant. "Of course, we were all tougher back then, because at any moment, a press conference could be broken up by a Mongol horde. I remember that's how my eighth birthday party ended—everyone fleeing as sword-wielding Mongols cut at our party hats. After a horse hoof destroyed my cake before I even got to blow out the candles, I vowed that day I would see all the Mongols dead." A small tear fell from his eye. "Ah, the innocence of youth." Rumsfeld then regained his composure. "Any other questions?"

"You scare me," remarked a reporter.

"That's not a question, but it is very perceptive of you. Now, I believe Dr. Rice had some new hardware to tell you about."

On screen appeared a giant mech armed to the teeth. Also, an American flag was prominently painted on its front. "We call this our War Machine,"

Rice explained. "It stands about ten stories tall. You'll notice we've drawn a hapless foreigner about to be crushed by its foot to give it scale. Its function will be to smash through villages, crushing buildings as it blares 'God Bless America' on its giant speakers. This is all part of our effort to make lesser cultures fear America in the same way they would fear the gods."

"Who would drive such a monstrosity?"

"No one. It has a programmed AI to make sure it only attacks the enemy."

"Are you sure it won't someday turn against us?" asked a reporter, looking frightened.

"The two programmers who hacked out the code over a weekend-long programming marathon assured me that would never happen." Rice smiled for a moment but then heard a beeping sound. She pulled a PDA out of her pocket and looked at the screen. "Apparently the War Machine has gone berserk and destroyed most of Massachusetts. Those programmers better pay me back for the box of chocolate donuts I gave them."

"Actually, I told the War Machine to do that," Rumsfeld said. "I hate Massachusetts. So did it get all the Kennedys?"

Rice checked the PDA. "No, it says here that Ted Kennedy escaped."

"We'll have to take him down ourselves. Get me my Ted Kennedy gun."

Rice opened the gun cabinet that Rumsfeld always had on hand at his press conferences. She pulled out a large rifle. "Is this it?"

"No! That little thing is an elephant gun. I need something that can bring down a Ted Kennedy."

She then took out an even larger rifle and handed it to Rumsfeld. "Here you go."

Rumsfeld smiled. "The hunt is on."

In unrelated news, Ted Kennedy, his natural habitat destroyed, is roaming the countryside confused and angry. Reports are that he's ransacking households looking for food to consume and money to steal for liberal boondoggles. One area man reported that his liquor cabinet was completed decimated. Police warn that Ted Kennedy is crazed and extremely liberal and that no one should accept a ride home from him under any circumstances.

March 03, 2003

President Bush to Do Own Lawn Care

Khalid Shaikh Mohammed, allegedly the planner of the September 11 terrorist attacks, is now in US custody, having been captured in Pakistan. President Bush was quick to give a statement about the victory.

"Yeah, we got that sucka!" Bush announced to the press. "I have plans to personally question Mohammed to find out what other evil terrorist secrets he is hiding."

When asked if he would be willing to use torture to extract information from Mohammed, Bush answered, "Absolutely not. Torture is bad, and we is a civilized nation."

"So why do you have a rubber hose with you?" a reporter asked.

"Uh... because I plan on watering the White House lawn after questioning Mohammed."

"Don't you have a lawn service to do that?"

"Hey, I'm just trying to save the tax payers money!" Bush answered angrily. "Now stop asking me so many questions, or I'll beat you with this hose just like I'm about to beat Khalid Shaikh Mohammed!"

White House Press Secretary Ari Fleischer soon gave a press conference to once again explain that Bush didn't mean what he said. He didn't seem in the mood for taking questions today, though.

"Why do we have to tell you idiots anything?" Fleischer asked. "Everyone hates you people. We're the government of the United States of America. We don't have to explain ourselves to anyone!"

"Don't you owe explanations of your actions to the American people?" answered a reporter.

"That's an interesting theory," Fleischer stated, "and I will respond to it by throwing a beer bottle at your head." Fleischer was true to his word.

"Do you have to drink during these press conferences?" asked another reporter, one who was not currently bleeding.

Fleischer saw Helen Thomas preparing to ask a question. "Yes."

"Why does President Harding want an illegal war for oil?" Thomas asked. "Why does he want to kill innocent Iraqi children?"

"Helen, please, if there is any decency in you, just lie down on the ground and stop breathing," Fleischer urged.

"You stole my pills earlier today!" Thomas yelled at him. "You give them back."

"No. And I don't want any more questions about this 'Blood for Oil' nonsense. As I keep explaining to you people, we already stole all of Iraq's oil while we were distracting Saddam with the inspections. This war with Iraq is pure bloodlust, plain and simple, and oil has nothing to do with it."

"What is the White House's response to the increasing rhetoric from North Korea? They claim that the CIA is plotting to blow up their reactors and that they will respond with a nuclear war."

"Nuclear war against whom?" Fleischer laughed. "Pasadena? Their nukes are pathetic."

"But they could hit South Korea and Japan."

Fleischer shrugged his shoulders. "So what? We don't live there. I say let the CIA blow up their reactors. President Bush's official opinion is that the CIA can do whatever they want as long as they don't assassinate him like they did JFK."

"Is there any truth to the rumor that you and President Bush secretly met with Jimmy Carter under the pretenses of asking him to negotiate with North Korea but then proceeded to beat him up and steal his lunch money?"

Fleischer pounded his fist into his palm. "That little squealer! Uh... I mean... I want the press to know that Jimmy Carter is a dirty liar and that all the cool politicians hate him."

President Bush ran into the room. "Hey Ari, can I borrow your hose? I need it to go spray some protestors."

"What happened to yours?"

"I broke it on a Muslim. Come on, I hear Martin Sheen is among them. Maybe I can give him some up close and personal lessons on how a *real* president beats up a protestor."

"Sweet!" Fleischer exclaimed, running off with Bush.

"But we have questions about the state of current affairs that are important to the American people!" one reporter protested, but Fleischer and Bush were already gone. "Who am I kidding? We would have more viewers if we were questioning Zora from *Joe Millionaire*."

March 05, 2003

Rumsfeld Reveals His Evil Plans

"WAR!" Rumsfeld shouted and then resumed in a whisper, "I can feel it nearing... growing closer... and as war approaches, my strength grows..."

He noticed the press starting to back away toward the exit.

"The doors are locked," he told them. "Ask your questions."

"So you're not worried that the US will not have the votes it needs in the UN?"

"The UN is weak! This world is for the strong! The UN serves no purpose anymore."

"What about the UN's own plan for a post-war Iraq?"

Rumsfeld laughed heartily, striking fear in the hearts of all the reporters. "After Iraq is obliterated, we will turn our vengeance on the UN and all those unfaithful to America. Most of Europe will be strip-mined and Canada changed into a prison camp."

"So all those protesters who said that America has imperialistic intentions..."

"Were absolutely right... and will be killed."

"So why do you tell us this now?" asked one reporter, cowering.

"Because it is too late to stop us!" Rumsfeld declared triumphantly. "No filthy hippy, no matter how cleverly worded his placard, can prevent America's war machine now that the gears are turning. Soon all of the world will rest under America's thumb, and it will be a glorious new era of prosperity... except for those who don't live in America. They will wail mournfully the rest of their short lives, cursing the day they ever spoke against the USA."

"Don't you think the American people won't stand for such imperialism?"

Rumsfeld grabbed the reporter by his collar. "You will report none of this!" He then tossed him across the room. "Freedom of the press has been abolished!" He threw a bunch of papers to the press. "Here are the stories you will report."

"But we have integrity as news correspondents—"

"Rarr!" Rumsfeld yelled as he shook his fists in the air threateningly.

"Yes, master!"

* * * *

"In our top story tonight, the cause of cancer has been discovered: listening to liberals. Experts have found that their ideas are actually so idiotic that they're carcinogenic."

"Hey Ari, you gotta see this!" Bush shouted as he sat watching TV. "They're reporting... ack... cough... erk..."

Ari Fleischer ran over and gave Bush the Heimlich maneuver, popping a pretzel out of his mouth. "What is it?"

"Rumsfeld convinced reporters he ended freedom of the press again. It's hilarious!"

"Experts say to shun peace rallies at all cost," the report continued, "and recommend quarantining all liberal college professors. Also, they say if you see Michael Moore, you should beat him with an axe handle before he has a chance to speak."

"Hell," Bush remarked, "I already knew to do that."

March 10, 2003

Bush and Chirac Personally Supervise Inspections

In an effort to prove whether Iraq is actually disarming, President Bush and President Chirac went to Iraq to personally watch Saddam as he destroyed his weapons of mass destruction.

"You aren't going to get anything past me, Saddam," Bush warned. "I know you're not disarming."

"Why are you Americans so mean?" Saddam asked, sounding quite hurt. "Here I am, clearly destroying my anthrax." He then threw another bag labeled "Anthrax" into the furnace.

"Did I hear that bag meow?" Bush asked. He then opened one of the bags. "These bags aren't full of anthrax! They're full of cute little kittens!"

"Whaaaat?!" Saddam exclaimed, slapping his hands to his face a la Macaulay Culkin. "I thought those bags were full of anthrax!"

"I knew Saddam would do everything he could to undermine this disarmament! He's so evil he's burning kittens alive!"

"Nonsense, you silly American; inspections are working!" Chirac declared. "Now that Saddam realized he is burning the wrong bags, he can get to destroying the real anthrax."

"Don't rush me," Saddam said, measuring some chemicals. "I'm not done making it yet."

"He's making biological weapons as we speak!" Bush yelled. "I told you this disarmament is bull."

"You stupid warmongering American; I spit on your mother," Chirac said as he put a flask on a Bunsen burner. "Why won't you let the inspections process take its course?"

"You're helping him make it!" Bush said, getting steaming mad. "I'll murder you both!"

Bush began to reach for the Colt .45 at his hip, but Karl Rove whispered, "Diplomacy! Diplomacy!" in his ear, and he settled down.

Saddam walked over to a nearby detonator. "Now I'm going to destroy my missiles just like I promised."

Chirac patted Saddam on the head. "What a good evil dictator. Not so crude like a certain current American president I won't mention." He then turned up his nose at Bush.

Saddam pressed the plunger, and there was an explosion nearby.

"Why are children running away from that explosion?" Bush asked as he squinted to get a better look. "Those aren't missiles! You're blowing up the playground equipment at the orphanage! You're a monster!"

"Whaaaat?! The orphanage?!" Saddam yelled, looking really, really surprised. "Who wired these explosives? This is the most ridiculous thing ever!"

"Inspections are working!" Chirac cheered, doing a little French dance. "I haven't yet come up with an explanation of why this means inspections are working, but just give me a minute more."

"You better destroy the real missiles right now!" Bush demanded.

"Alright," Saddam answered, "but then I think the UN should disarm America of its weapons of mass destruction, such as its nuclear missiles, its daisy cutters, and its Donald Rumsfeld."

Chirac shuddered. "Don't mention that name in front of me; such a rash and angry person. So how do you plan on destroying the missiles, Saddam?"

"I think I'll launch them at Israel."

"There is much support for that at the UN," Chirac stated. "Hey, I'm starting a new UN commission on hating America. You should head it after this silly disarmament thing is done with, and the Americans are laughed at like the fools they are."

"Diplomacy! Diplomacy!" Karl Rove shouted at Bush, but it was too late.

* * * *

"Bush's beating of Chirac and Saddam with a sack full of kittens has created an international incident; will any apologies be issued?" a reporter asked.

"The president has already sent a written apology to the kittens," White House Press Secretary Ari Fleischer stated.

"Kittens can't read."

Fleischer rolled his eyes. "The president is not a zoologist. He can't be expected to keep track of which animals can and cannot read."

"So does the president have anything else to say?"

"Nothing more than his usual weekly proclamation of his complete and utter contempt for the press. Oh, and he bet me five dollars I couldn't hit one of you in the eye with my pen." Fleischer then flicked his pen at the reporters.

"Ahh! My eye!"
"Bull's-eye!"

March 12, 2003

Robot Spiders Almost as Hostile to Questions as Rumsfeld

"War could be any day now," Secretary of Defense Donald Rumsfeld exclaimed. "I've told my troops to start killing a few Iraqis each day to warm up."

"Shouldn't you be solemn and reserved about the horrible prospect of war?" asked a reporter.

When the pistol-whipping was over, another reporter asked a question. "You seem to say you're willing to go to war without the help of the British. Is this true?"

"Iraqis continue to breathe air each day, and this is an insult to us all. I can't be expected to wait for anyone before I begin to end this atrocity. The way we kill them will probably be too bloody for those crumpet eaters to stand, anyway."

"Are you concerned about the UN Security Council vetoing the new resolution?"

"Let me be clear: the UN is dead to me, and if I have my way, it will soon be dead to everyone. That said, anyone who vetoes something the US supports vetoes their own life. The children of tomorrow will sing many sad songs about those who oppose us today."

"Did you see that 60 Minutes segment with President Clinton and Senator Dole on Sunday?"

"No, but I shot the first reporter who asked me about it," Rumsfeld said as he drew his Luger and shot the reporter. "For the last time, keep your questions about war!"

"Aren't you afraid that our new belligerent attitude might have a bad effect on kids these days?"

"Poppycock. Kids these days need to be tougher. I keep hearing about how kids can't even bring a knife into school anymore. Back in my day, we had a rifle club at our elementary school, well-stocked with ammo. Good thing, too, because it was the only way we survived that onslaught of ten thousand Zulu warriors who attacked us one year. We kept firing on them, and they kept coming as if there was no end to them. Eventually, we ran out of ammo and had to resort to pegging the Zulus with dodge balls. Lost my best friend that day when he chucked one, and a Zulu caught it. It was a horrible day, but the teacher still didn't delay the math test I hadn't studied for."

"Anyway, I think it's time for my presentation now," National Security Advisor Condoleezza Rice said, stepping forward. "I guess you have all now heard of our 21,000-pound MOAB." A picture of one of the bombs appeared on screen. "This is one that is about to be dropped on a real target in a new attempt to intimidate the Iraqis."

"Where is it being dropped?"

"That's classified."

"Why's it say 'Veto this, you frogs' on the front of it?"

"That's also classified." A dummy that looked like Saddam Hussein was brought out. "Here is our new assassination device," Rice explained, placing a spider-like robot on the ground. "It zooms in on the target's voice pattern."

Inside the dummy, a tape player was started. "I am Saddam. I like hiding weapons of mass destruction. The French are my friends." With a loud screech, the robot jumped onto the face of the dummy and exploded.

"I was the one who decided to make it screech," Rice said proudly. "So you can get a better look at these, we have now filled the press room floor with them." The reporters looked down, and indeed the floor was swarming with little spider robots.

"Is there any chance they could attack the wrong person?" asked a very frightened reporter.

Rice thought about that for a moment. "That's a good question. I'll look into it."

Another reporter started to speak, but a loud screech followed by an explosion was heard.

"Uh-oh," Rice uttered, "everyone better just keep real quiet right now."

Rumsfeld watched all the reporters standing completely still and silent. "This is the best press conference ever. Well, I'm going to go grab a scotch and see if my war's started yet. Condi, you try and clean this up without killing too many reporters."

"Cleaning is the janitor's job. Why don't I just lock the doors and call it a test case?"

"Have fun!" Rumsfeld said to the reporters as he and Rice went through the back exit of the room. "If you have any more questions about whether this war is unjust, ask them to the spiders."

March 17, 2003

One Last Chance

The moment of truth has arrived at the UN, as an informal Security Council meeting will finally decide the UN's position on Iraq. If the UN votes for military action, it will give further support to the US's war with Iraq. If the UN votes against attacking Iraq, it will lose its legitimacy, and the UN building will be immediately bulldozed to the ground.

"Actions will soon be taken," President Bush announced to the press. "This is our enemy's final chance. After today, they can talk to the cruise missiles, and the cruise missiles are not good conversationalists. They are prone to constant interruptions, often brash in their language, and are poor listeners. Plus, they incinerate you."

"Are you implying that there is a chance for Iraq to avoid war if they immediately disarm?" asked a reporter.

"Hell no—I promised the American people stolen Iraqi oil, and that's what they're going to get. What I was talking about was France. France better start shaping up, or America will rain its mighty wrath upon them."

"You're really angry enough about France's behavior to attack them?"

"Yes we are. We renamed the french fries and french toast in the cafeteria to 'freedom toast' and 'freedom fries,' since anything with 'french' as part of the name will cause someone to vomit. We've also now made it part of all sporting events that after our national anthem is played, a French flag is burned. Then a French tourist is publicly beaten."

President Jacques Chirac appeared unintimidated. "Silly Americans, you cannot harm the great and mighty France," he announced to the press. "We will veto your war, and then America will crumble, since it no longer has the support of the true powerhouse in this world: the UN. Then Saddam and I will find Dick Cheney's undisclosed location and defeat America from the inside. When America is gone, Saddam and I shall rule together, plunging the world into tyranny and rudeness." Chirac then laughed evilly and effeminately until a squirrel ran by. Then he ducked behind his podium and started crying.

March 19, 2003

Rumsfeld Vows Frog-a-cide

"Can we start bombing them now?" Rumsfeld asked impatiently.

"No, we still have to wait just a little bit more," Condoleezza Rice answered.

"If it weren't for that sissy little Texan," Rumsfeld declared angrily, "I could have demolished Iraq long ago, along with North Korea and most of Europe."

"The press," Rice reminded him, pointing to the reporters standing before them and cowering in fear.

"Ask your questions quickly," Rumsfeld commanded them. "As soon as this war starts, I'm lobbying to have you all killed as a precautionary matter."

"What is your reaction to France saying they may help the US if there is a chemical attack?"

"That's simply not enough to keep me from personally murdering all Frenchmen. They have shown no faith to the US, and they will pay with their blood."

"Are you really going to kill them all?" asked a reporter in disbelief.

"Yes, total frog-a-cide." He then stared the reporter in the eye. "Do you doubt that I can?"

"No, sir, no," the reporter answered, trying to back away.

"They'll probably surrender on sight of an angry American," Rumsfeld explained. "I'll then strangle them with their white flags."

"When will this occur?"

"Sometime after we demolish Iraq. I plan to put Saddam's head on a pole and then use it as a cudgel against Chirac."

"On account of your hatred of the French, are you in support of the renaming of french fries and french toast to 'freedom fries' and 'freedom toast'?"

Rumsfeld shrugged his shoulders. "I only eat meat." He then turned to Rice. "His question wasted my time. Teach him through pain."

Rice operated a remote control, and the reporter fell to the ground, twitching. "I forgot to mention to you all," Rice said, "that I had pain inducers surgically implanted in all of you."

"When did you do that?" asked a worried reporter.

Rice smiled. "That's classified."

"But that's against the law!" another reporter protested.

"I AM ABOVE THE LAW!" Rice screamed.

"Any more questions," Rumsfeld asked, "or do you all fully understand that Iraq and France will soon be destroyed?"

"What about the Iraqi children?" screeched Helen Thomas, who had somehow wandered into Rumsfeld's press conference.

"The Iraqi children will die, and so will you!" Rumsfeld yelled in full rage as he whipped out his Luger and started firing at her. Thomas ran out of the pressroom, cackling all the way.

"She's quicker than she looks," Rumsfeld said mournfully as he re-holstered his gun.

"You'll get her one day," Rice assured him, patting him on the shoulder.

"We're really scared now," said one reporter. "Can we go now?"

"Yes, flee in terror," Rumsfeld told them, and they quickly complied.

A French diplomat was scheduled to respond to Rumsfeld's remarks but was found murdered, seemingly yet another victim of the "Rumsfeld Strangler." DC police aren't sure, though, since the note left at the scene was written in some sort of crazy monkey language, reading, "*Je suis Donald Rumsfeld. J'ai étranglé cet homme.*" Authorities say if you have any information that could lead to the whereabouts of the Rumsfeld Strangler, keep it to yourself so he doesn't strangle you.

March 24, 2003

Rumsfeld Vows to Kill Everyone and Then Sing "Kum Ba Ya"

Last Thursday, demonstrators vandalized Secretary of Defense Donald Rumsfeld's New Mexico home to protest the war. Recently, protestors returned to Rumsfeld's home again, this time decorating the trees around his home with their own entrails.

"Was this new vandalism not actually a form of protest, but in fact the result of your viciously murdering the protesters and then dismembering their corpses as a warning to others?" asked a reporter at Rumsfeld's press conference.

"My lawyers told me not to answer questions about the matter," he answered gruffly.

"Then might we at least ask whose blood it is that you're currently caked in?"

"Again, my lawyers told me not to answer questions about that matter."

"Aren't your lawyers in fact dead?"

"They kept telling me what to do!" He clenched his hand into a fist. "I hate lawyers! So do any of you have questions about Operation Iraqi Murder Death Kill?"

"Don't you mean 'Operation Iraqi Freedom'?" corrected one reporter.

"I forgot what name we settled on, but you know what I mean."

"So are you satisfied with the current progress of the war?"

"Yes, we are making great progress. Our Shock and Aww and Shock campaign has been going especially well. That's where we first hit the Iraqis with a shock, .i.e., an initial bombing campaign. While they're dazed and confused, we then flood the city with cute little puppies to make them go, 'Aww.' Then while they're distracted by the puppies, we hit them with more shock, i.e., more bloody mayhem. I'm sure it won't be too long until Baghdad is ours, and Saddam is dead."

"You don't plan on capturing Saddam?"

"No, he will die."

"What if he surrenders?"

"Then he will die with his hands up. Next question."

"Now that some Americans have been killed and captured, will you admit the futility of this war and that its costs are too high?"

Rumsfeld thought about that for a moment. "I think the best way to answer that question would be to rip this podium out of the ground and then smash it over your head," Rumsfeld said, ripping the podium out of the ground and then smashing it over the reporter's head. "Any other questions?"

"How do you respond to reports that Marines are wantonly killing camels when lacking Iraqis to kill?"

"It's the US Marines' supreme right in this world to kill whatever the hell they want, and they shall not be questioned on that matter."

"Don't you think these actions in Iraq might lead to a broader war?"

"I hope so, for after Iraq, I have plans to continue into other countries in the Middle East, wiping out even more terrorists. Then we will start another campaign in Asia, beginning in North Korea and wiping out all other Asian enemies to America. Next we will start a front in Europe doing the same. Eventually, we will hunt down and kill everyone who is trying to harm America, everyone who is thinking of harming America, anyone who supports the harming of America, and anyone who is not vehemently opposed to harming America. In summary, anyone who wishes to terrorize America will die. Anyone who isn't against terrorism in America will die. Anyone who sees an American killed or captured on TV and cheers will die. Anyone who hates America will die. Anyone who spells America with a 'k' will die. Anyone who doesn't cheer every time they hear the name of America will die. And when all our enemies are finally dead, we will beckon in this newfound era of peace by sitting in a circle and singing 'Kum Ba Ya.'"

"Are you serious about all that?"

"Everything except for the 'Kum Ba Ya' part."

March 26, 2003

If Iraq Uses WMDs, the US May Respond with Happiness

President Bush decided to personally give a press conference to update everyone on the state of the war. "Despite all the negative reports, I want everyone to know that Operation Wacky Iraqi Attacky is doing tremendously," he announced. National Security Advisor Condoleezza Rice then whispered in his ear. "What?!" Bush responded. "That liar Colin Powell told me he was going with my name idea!" Bush looked back at the reporters. "So does anyone have questions about the boringly-titled Operation Iraqi Freedom?"

"If Iraq uses WMDs against US troops, will you consider striking back with nuclear weapons?"

"No, absolutely not. Karl Rove carefully explained to me that the diplomatic costs are too high." He looked around. "Where is he?"

"We have some new technology related to that," Rice told the press. "This is a new weapon to help us defeat our enemies but isn't as mean and scary as a nuclear weapon. It's a ten-megaton 'Happy Bomb.'" Rice then pulled back a sheet, revealing a large bomb with a smiley face displayed prominently on the front. "Look, it's smiling!" Rice exclaimed. "Isn't it happy?"

"Wow! It *is* smiling!" Bush said excitedly. "Let's use it now!"

"Isn't that actually a nuclear bomb with just a smile painted on it?" asked one reporter skeptically.

"Yeah, that's a good question," Bush said to Rice, getting suspicious. "Did you just paint a smile on a nuclear bomb?"

"No, of course not," Rice replied innocently. "There are also stencils of bunnies on the side."

"Hey, there *are* bunnies on the side!" Bush said happily. "Cute ones! We should use this bomb now!"

"So will this bomb have horrible radiation effects on wherever it is dropped?" asked another reporter.

"Not horrible radiation effects," Rice answered, smiling, "but lovely happiness effects... over a 150-mile radius."

"Wow! How happy will it make places?" Bush asked.

"Too happy for most people to stand—or plants or animals—and the happiness will last for decades."

"Holy cow! That sure sounds like a lot of happiness!" Bush said, getting psyched. "We should use this bomb now!"

"So will this 'happiness' cause gruesome mutative effects?" inquired an incredulous reporter.

"No, it's natural for this much happiness to... uh... change a creature into something... even happier—"

"Like in Pokemon?" Bush interrupted.

"Uh... yeah... like in... Pokemon," Rice answered, trying to keep a straight face.

"Cool! I want a Charizard. We should use this bomb now!"

"Aren't you afraid of the resultant protests?" asked a reporter.

"Wait," Bush said, turning to Rice, "there aren't going to be more smelly, hippy protesters bothering me about this, are there?"

"No," Rice assured him, "because the first thing the Happy Bomb does is make a giant mushroom, and hippies love mushrooms."

"Wow! A giant mushroom! Let's use this bomb now!"

"Great," Rice said, producing a map of Iraq. "I've marked with frowny faces a number of strategic locations that just aren't very happy."

"George!" called Laura Bush, walking into the press conference. "What are you doing?"

"Important strategic stuff."

"I thought I told you to stay away from Condoleezza," Laura chided him. "She's always trying to trick you into using nuclear weapons when Karl Rove isn't around."

"But she's changed," Bush answered. "She now wants to use a Happy Bomb instead."

Laura smacked Bush upside the head. "Don't be so gullible."

"Come on, dear, not in front of the press," Bush pleaded.

"Almost got away with it," Rice said angrily as she walked off.

"That Condoleezza and that Rumsfeld are bad influences on you," Laura told him. "They just keep trying to get you into more wars. You should instead consult with that nice Colin Powell."

"But everyone in my administration hates Colin Powell," Bush protested. "If they see me hanging out with him, they'll think I'm not cool."

"You can't spend all your time worrying what people think about you, or you'll end up like that Billy Clinton, whom I *definitely* don't want to see you talking to." She started pulling him out of the press conference. "Now come on. You promised me you would fix the closet door today."

Bush looked to see the press was chuckling at him. "Ari," Bush yelled, "make sure no one reports anything about this."

"On it!" White House Press Secretary Ari Fleischer said as he took the podium and faced the reporters. "Who here likes freedom of the press?" he asked and then surveyed the group in front of him. "Wow, that's everyone. Now here's a different question: who likes not getting hit in the head with a lead pipe? It's okay to think about it... Looks like it's everyone again." Fleischer fished for something hidden behind the podium. "Now let's say you could only choose one..."

March 31, 2003

Cleaning Staff Nearly Fed Up With Press Conferences

"Now that the war has lasted more than a week, will you admit that it's hopeless and apologize to the American people?"

The sound of a Luger firing was the immediate response. "I can't stand any more of these questions!" Rumsfeld shouted, frantically checking his pockets. "Where's that extra clip?!"

"Now that resistance is stronger than we reporters expected, is America starting to draw up plans to surrender to Saddam?"

"Rarrr!" Rumsfeld shouted as he tossed his gun at the reporter's head, knocking him unconscious. "I can't believe we involved you idiots in something as serious as a war. If they did it my way, we would never have told the press about the war. Would have just framed another celebrity for murder to distract you all while we invaded Iraq in secret."

"You wouldn't be able to keep something like that from the press!" declared a reporter proudly. "We're too smart and investigative for that!"

"Ha! Then how come none of the embedded reporters has figured out they're just being driven around in circles in a desert in Nevada? Has even one of them noticed that the 'Iraqis' they see surrendering are just Mexicans we hired?" Rumsfeld then slapped his head. "Darn, didn't mean to say that; I need more sleep." He turned to Condoleezza Rice. "Dr. Rice, give me that new memory eraser you were working on."

"It's not done yet. You'll have to use the old one." She handed him a baseball bat.

Rumsfeld held it over his head, ready to strike. "Now everyone stand still, or this won't work right."

"We didn't hear anything! We didn't hear anything!" pleaded the reporters.

"Fine," Rumsfeld said, dropping the bat and taking some pills out of his jacket pocket. "Dr. Rice, you take over. I'm going to take some of my rage medication."

Rice then took the floor. "I want to assure you that, despite your own idiotic opinions, this war is going according to plan. So, anymore questions?"

"Why are two press seats used up by a chimpanzee and a robot?"

"We're doing some preliminary testing of whether we can replace reporters with either monkeys or robots," Rice explained. "Please just ignore them."

"I don't like the robot idea," Rumsfeld commented. "It's bulletproof."

The chimpanzee then raised his hand. "Bobo, what's your question?" Rice asked.

Bobo then bit the reporter next to him.

"Bobo, that's not a question! Bad monkey!" Rice scolded as Rumsfeld laughed.

The robot then lifted one of its metal claws into the air. "Go ahead and ask your question, Killbot 4000," Rice urged.

"When will the weak humans be destroyed?" it asked in a synthesized voice.

"I keep telling you reporters that we're not putting a timetable on this war!" Rice answered angrily.

"I definitely like the monkey better," Rumsfeld commented.

"He's still attacking me!" yelled a reporter, fleeing from Bobo, who was now trying to beat the man with a folding chair.

"Monkey funny!" Rumsfeld laughed.

"The pills must have kicked in," Rice remarked.

"All humans must die!" the robot interjected.

"Hey!" protested another reporter. "It's no longer your turn to ask quest—"

He was cut short as the robot's claw clamped around his neck.

"Killbot destroy puny humans!" the robot declared as it lifted the reporter into the air.

"On second thought, I do like that robot's moxie," Rumsfeld commented. "Hey Condi, let's go hit some bars and plan more military operations."

"Alright," Rice said, watching the chaos on the press floor, "but we'd better give the cleaning staff a heads-up first."

April 01, 2003 (April Fool's Day)

France Replaces America as a Superpower

"You can't hide anything from us!" declared the intrepid reporter. "Tell us the truth!"

"Stop yelling at me!" cried Rumsfeld, slouching behind the podium.

"Admit you hadn't planned for resistance and your war is a failure!" the reporter demanded.

"You can't make me," Rumsfeld muttered, now almost completely hiding behind the podium. "Dr. Rice, please save me."

"No," Condoleezza Rice answered as she walked in front of the press. "I've now taken a political position more consistent with my race and gender, thus becoming a liberal democrat, a savior of humanity. And I want to announce that this war is evil and a Zionist plot! In fact, every member of this administration, including the president himself, is secretly Jewish!"

"Oy, vey! Our secret is out!" Rumsfeld exclaimed. "But it doesn't matter how ingenious you reporters all are, you can't stop our war now that it's started."

"But I can!" shouted a voice from the rear as the doors to the room burst open. In strode a hulk of a man, his clothing barely concealing his rippling muscles.

"Oh, it's Michael Moore!" swooned a female reporter. "The protector of truth and justice in this world... and I can't help but remark how great his hygiene is!"

"After my reasoned speech at the Academy Awards, support for this war has crumbled," Moore declared in a booming voice. "It has also emboldened the Iraqis to fight against the US imperialism, and now your troops flee."

"Don't hurt me, Michael Moore!" Rumsfeld pleaded as he tried to run. He was stopped at the door by none other than Jacques Chirac and Saddam Hussein.

"America is over as a superpower!" Chirac declared. "But France and Iraq have joined together to form a new superpower—Friaqi!"

"And you are under arrest for attacking me, a democratically elected leader, in your greedy pursuit of oil," Saddam said as he handcuffed Rumsfeld.

"And all Americans are in trouble for their crudeness! Except for a few of your wisest, such as the paragon of virtue, Michael Moore!" Chirac yelled. “And your democracy will be replaced with a much better system where France will tell you what to do and think!”

“And new dress code!” Saddam added. “Everyone must wear a beret and grow a bushy mustache!”

“And now the world will have peace at last,” Chirac announced, “for all conflicts will be solved with endless debate. Now, as a first order of business, let’s ship all those troublesome Jews in Israel into the sea and give the land to the peaceful Palestinians!”

“Hip, hip, hooray!” cried the reporters, ushering in this new era of peace and Frenchiness.

April 02, 2003

Cheney Wishes Undisclosed Location Was More Disclosed

"Nuke them!"

"We're not nuking Iraq, Rummy," Bush answered firmly.

"No, not Iraq—the annoying reporters. Trick them into thinking that we're having a press conference in the middle of a desert, then nuke them all."

"I think that's a great idea," Ari Fleischer remarked. "Reporters suck. I hate them."

"I will remind you," Condoleezza Rice told Bush, "that we could spare some nuclear weapons. We have enough nukes to blow the world up eight times, but our computer simulations show that even in the worst case scenario, we'd never need to blow up the world more than six times."

"We can't nuke the reporters," Bush said. "Everyone will get mad at me."

"How will anyone find out?" Fleischer said. "All the reporters will be dead."

"Someone might write something about it on the internet," Bush suggested.

"The only people who use the internet are pedophiles and crack addicts," Rumsfeld scoffed. "No one will care what they say."

"Nuking seems a bit harsh," Colin Powell said. "Can't we just injure some reporters and maybe threaten their families?"

"You weak-willed liberal!" Rumsfeld screamed. "Why don't you just sell us all out to the Communists? I'll kill you!!" He sprung toward Powell but was held in place by some chains.

"Will those chains hold him?" Powell asked, worried.

"The Secret Service assured me they would," Bush answered and then looked at Rumsfeld. "You have to control that temper, Rummy."

"I'll murder you for telling me to control my temper!" Rumsfeld shouted as he tried to reach for Bush's neck.

"There will be no murdering of the press," Karl Rove announced, his dark eyes meeting individually all those seated at the table. "The prophesied destruction of the Democrats grows near, and we must tread lightly. We simply must manipulate the foolish press into its own demise."

"Sounds good, Rover," Bush answered. "Now let's get to our main business: the war. I have Dick via satellite from his undisclosed location so he can give his opinions as well." A monitor turned on showing Dick Cheney. "What's up, Dick?"

"Yeah, Bush, I'm not doing so well. Have you gotten any closer to finding out where I am?"

"Sorry, Dick, not really a priority with the war going on, but as soon as we figure out where we filed that, we'll send a helicopter to come get you."

"I don't see why you couldn't have just told me where I was staying."

"We didn't tell you so that if you were tortured by terrorists, they wouldn't be able to find out where you are."

"But they would already have found me to be able to torture me!" Cheney shouted.

Bush thought about that. "Well, hindsight is 20/20, Dick; what do you want me to tell you?"

"Are you sure you can't remember where I am?"

"Honestly, I was watching an episode of *The Simpsons* when I was told, so I didn't really catch much of it." A thought then struck him. "Do you feel weightless, Dick? Like you could float through the air?"

"No," Cheney answered with annoyance.

"Then scratch that idea."

"I think I hear water flowing nearby," Cheney offered hopefully. "Does that help?"

"Maybe. Anyway, we got to get back to talking about war."

"At least tell me how my family is doing!" Cheney pleaded.

"Uh... who's your family again, Dick?"

"The Cheneys!" he answered angrily.

"Oh... they're cool. Now just chill out, Dick; this is no big emergency. You have a year's worth of food there and almost a week's worth of air." Bush looked at rest of the people seated at the table. "Now let's get back to discussing this war."

"Our precise bomb attacks have decimated Iraq's military with minimal civilian casualties," Rice stated proudly.

"This war is almost too clean," Rumsfeld said with disgust. "Our troops thirst for blood and decimation. Their morale will go down if they don't see misery inflicted upon others."

"Actually, I think our soldiers enjoy seeing Iraqis cheer them on," Powell said.

"Rarrr!" Rumsfeld shouted, trying to break his chains.

"I'll have to make your new nickname Mr. Angry," Bush said, chuckling.

"I'll rip your guts out for giving me a nickname!" Rumsfeld yelled, again reaching for Bush's neck.

"We have to be careful of public opinion, though," Rove warned. "Some people are thinking we weren't prepared for this level of resistance."

"Then people will die!" Rumsfeld shouted, trying once again to break his chains.

"You have to respect Rummy's enthusiasm," Bush commented. "So, are we all set on our main goal: getting that oil?"

"Actually, the purpose of the war is to rid Iraq of its weapons of mass destruction and liberate the Iraqi people," Powell corrected him.

"You're just falling for the protesters' propaganda," Bush answered. "They're trying to convince everyone that this war is about liberating Iraqis and destroying WMDs, even though we keep telling them it's about getting oil."

"You got that backwards," Powell asserted.

Bush looked confused. "We're giving them oil?"

"Forget Iraq," Rumsfeld said. "That's just our first stop on eliminating America's enemies. Did you get my list of other nations I think we should attack next?"

"Yeah," Bush answered, looking at a piece of paper. "It just says 'Non-English-speaking countries.'"

"I don't trust countries that don't speak English," Rumsfeld remarked. "Can't tell what they're saying. For all we know, they're constantly plotting against America."

"We can't get too mired in war," Rove warned. "We need a significant military victory to correspond with an economic upturn as a final blow to the Democrats, causing them to whither and die as maggots feast upon them."

"I will not have politics ruin something as good and pure as killing people and blowing stuff up!" Rumsfeld declared angrily.

"People, we have to remember what war is all about in the end," Bush said. "It's about people's sacrifice. Our military is composed of many great Americans who have sacrificed their time, some of their rights, and maybe their lives, all so they can kill evil foreigners. There is no more beautiful expression of the American spirit than the deaths of smelly, unshaven people who mean us harm."

"My left arm is tingling," Cheney said.

"I'm glad my speech touched you like that," Bush said happily.

Just then Laura Bush walked into the room. "I have Rice Krispies treats and Kool-Aid!" she announced as she began to hand them out.

"Awesome!" Fleischer exclaimed.

"Help me, Laura!" Cheney yelled. "I'm lost, and I'm having a heart attack!"

Laura turned off the monitor. "You're not going to get any work done if you're watching TV while you do it."

"Thanks for the Rice Krispies treats, Mrs. Bush," Powell said as Laura headed out of the room.

"Powell got a larger piece than me," Rumsfeld complained. "I'll kill you all!"

Just then the phone rang. "Shoot; it's Daschle," Bush exclaimed, answering the call. "What the hell do you want?"

"I just opened the door to my office to find a wall of solid concrete," Daschle whined.

"Why should I care?"

"I know you had something to do with it! You're always out to get me!"

"That's because you're a weasel, and I hate you."

"It also sounds like someone is pounding on the wall from the inside."

"Who cares?" Bush answered but then saw Fleischer motioning to him.

"I think I remember where we hid Cheney," Fleischer said, laughing.

"Oh yeah, now I remember!" Bush exclaimed. "We turned that jerk's office into an undisclosed location."

"Don't tell him!" Fleischer urged.

Bush put the phone to his ear. "I'm pretty sure I remember your office door always opening to a concrete wall."

"That's not true, and you know it!"

"All I guess I can say is that you failed so miserably at not being a prick that we were forced to fill your office with concrete." Bush then slammed the phone down. "Moron," he laughed as he took a bite of his Rice Krispies treat. He then noticed an empty chair covered in broken chains. "Ahh crap."

April 07, 2003

To the Victor Goes the Renaming

"So... any more questions about how brilliantly the war is going?" Rumsfeld asked the press.

"Why don't you just tell us how great the war is going, and you don't have to hurt any of us?" suggested one reporter.

"I'll tell you how well the war is going, but no promises on that second part. Operation Make Iraqis Dead and Take Their Oil is going great!"

Condoleezza Rice whispered into his ear. "I don't care what it's called as long as we get to kill evil foreigners!" Rumsfeld yelled. "Anyway, our forces are dominating the pathetic Iraqi resistance. We hardly even have to engage them anymore. Their vehicles explode upon sight of our tanks. Their troops spontaneously combust just thinking about having to fight us. We have completely surrounded Baghdad. Nothing can get past us now. Earlier, a monkey riding a camel tried to get past our blockade. I am proud to tell you that that monkey and that camel were so riddled with bullets as to be unidentifiable."

"Poor monkey," said one of the reporters.

"There will be no sympathy for the enemy!" Rumsfeld shouted angrily.

"What about reports that coalition forces have begun renaming buildings in Iraq?" a reporter asked.

"Yes, we have more appropriately named some buildings. The Saddam Hussein Airport is now the Baghdad Airport. The Saddam Hussein Theater is now the Baghdad Theater. The Saddam Hussein Hospital is now the Saddam Hussein Memorial Hospital. Also, we renamed Basra 'Funkytown.' And we started renaming the POWs; too many were named Mohammed. Also, I kinda find it funny to see an Iraqi soldier named 'Cody.'"

"You can't just rename whomever you please!" said a shocked reporter.

"Yes I can! Your name is now Polly Prissypants," Rumsfeld told the man. Rice then handed him his new social security card.

"I don't want a new name!" the reporter complained.

"Quiet, Polly Prissypants!" Rumsfeld shouted.

"So are you sure that Saddam is dead?" asked another reporter.

"We are not. He has too many of those dang look-alikes. Actually, there have been some suggestions that the original Saddam was a kindly man who loved puppies and wanted nothing more than peace in the Middle East, but then he was killed and replaced by an evil, warmongering look-alike. To make sure we stop him, we're killing everyone who looks like Saddam."

"You can't just discriminately kill people like that!" declared a reporter.

"You know, with a bushy mustache and a beret, you might look like Saddam," Rumsfeld said, reaching under his coat for his gun.

"Statement withdrawn!"

"There are reports that the smiling pictures of Saddam strewn throughout Iraq have been replaced with frowning pictures of you," said one reporter. "This has caused many children there to have nightmares. Will you assure the Iraqi children you are not hiding under their beds or in their closets waiting to strangle them?"

"I will not take any options off the table in this war," Rumsfeld declared. "Next question."

"Are you afraid of the door-to-door fighting as you try to further take control of Baghdad?"

"No, because for that operation we have a secret ninja task force I can't tell you anything about."

"What can you tell us about this secret ninja task force you can't tell us anything about?"

"Nothing."

"Hey, I think I see movement up in the rafters!" said one reporter, pointing upwards. "It's the secret ninjas!"

Rumsfeld turned to Rice. "Quick, do something before they find out about our secret ninjas!"

Rice held up a device that flashed in multiple colors and made strange noises. "This is a new invention of mine," she told the press. "Its purpose is to distract and then blind reporters."

"Wow! That is distracting!" exclaimed a reporter as he and everyone else stared at the device.

Suddenly a bright flash came from the device. "I'm blind!" yelled a number of reporters.

One reporter in the back raised his hand. "I'm still just distracted."

"Darn, it needs more adjustments," Rice uttered.

April 09, 2003

Laser-Guided Concrete Makes Great Practical Jokes

"Man, do I still got to do all these press conferences?" White House Press Secretary Ari Fleischer complained. "I thought I had all of you idiots embedded."

"Hey, we have important questions, and you should give us respect," complained one reporter.

"Just start asking your questions before I decide to embed my foot up your—"

"Was the tank attack against the journalists in the Palestine hotel on purpose?"

"Of course not. What idiot would think that?"

"Well, there is the transcript of the communications in the tank:

> VOICE1: Hey, there is that hotel full of journalists.
> VOICE2: Let us fire at it and kill some.
> VOICE1: What an excellent idea. (sound of tank firing)
> VOICE1: I bet that killed some.
> VOICE2: Hooray!"

"Whatever," Fleischer responded. "Evidence never proves anything. The coalition forces do their best to not harm non-combatants. We have even come up with this laser-guided concrete to help us avoid collateral damage. They just drop out of the sky, crushing the target with a huge piece of concrete and harming nothing else. It was adapted from the work of Professor Wile E. Coyote, who developed a laser-guided anvil for the purpose of hunting a variety of quick-moving desert bird."

"Will we be able to hear from this Professor Coyote?"

"Unfortunately, no. In an extremely tragic and unfunny turn of events, Professor Coyote was himself crushed by the anvil instead of the intended target. He left behind a wife and three kids.

"Anyhoo, the reason I am having the press conference out in this field is so I can demonstrate this concrete bomb. Just stare at the old building over yonder."

"Because that's where you are dropping the bomb?" inquired one reporter.

"Yeah... uh... because that is where I am dropping the bomb," Fleischer said, trying to hold back a laugh. "Now, make sure everyone watches it carefully and does not pay attention to what I am doing." Fleischer now aimed a laser on the group of reporters.

"Hey, he's targeting us!" one yelled. They all ran just in time for a large concrete bomb to drop in the center of the group.

"You tried to kill us all!" accused one reporter.

"No, as I explained to you, it's an inert bomb. It would have just crushed those directly beneath it... hopefully one being Helen Thomas." He saw her approaching with a question. "But no such luck."

"Are you happy now that you've killed Iraqi children?" Thomas asked.

"We didn't kill Iraqi children, you old bat. Actually, I have a drawing from a five year-old Iraqi boy I want you to see." He produced a crayon drawing. "See, here he drew you. And here he drew a bus that is running you over. Here he drew himself smiling while this happens. Iraqi children hate you, you old hag, just like I hate you."

"You stole my pills again!" Thomas yelled. "Give me back my pills!"

"NEVER!"

Just then President Bush ran up. "That concrete bomb gave me a great idea!" he exclaimed. "Let's go throw bricks through the windows at the Democrats' headquarters!"

"I'm there, dude!" Fleischer said, running off with Bush.

"But we have more questions!" yelled one reporter. "Wait a second... is he pointing another laser at us? Run!"

April 14, 2003

Suspicious-Looking Middle-Eastern Men Laugh at All the President's Jokes

"Mr. President, I just need you to sign these war plans for attacking Syria and a couple more countries to be named later."

"What countries?"

"You've never heard of them," Rumsfeld said irately. "Just sign the paper."

"Uh-uh, Rummy. No more wars until you finish your first one. You still have to secure Tikrit, and I need some WMDs to prove to everyone I'm right, and they're wrong." Bush then turned to the nearby monitor. "Isn't that right, Dick?"

"Some clear evidence of weapons of mass destruction will really help our cause," Cheney agreed.

"You will do as I tell you!" Rumsfeld shouted. "I'm the Secretary of War! Defy me, and I'll kill you both!"

Bush laughed. "You can't kill us both, silly; Dick's location is undisclosed."

"That's right. You kill Bush, I become president," Cheney said.

"Of course, since I am the only one who knows where he is," Bush muttered to himself, "if you killed me, he would eventually starve to death, so thus killing me would kill him indirectly."

"What?!" Cheney exclaimed. "You didn't tell anyone else where I am this time?"

"Undisclosed," Bush told him calmly. "Anyway, you're going to laugh and laugh when you find out where you are this time."

"Quit jabbering, and approve my war!" Rumsfeld shouted angrily.

"No, you finish your first war like a good Secretary of Defense, and then we'll talk."

"Rarr!" Rumsfeld yelled as he punched a large whole in the wall.

"Man," Bush sighed, "that's why I always hold these meetings in Daschle's office."

"Rarr!" Rumsfeld cried again as he picked up Daschle's desk and threw it out the window.

"I think I hear music," Cheney said. "Did you hide me at the carnival again?"

"No. Way off," Bush laughed. "Man, this one is so funny. The suspicious-looking Middle-Eastern men I told it to thought it was funny as well."

"Suspicious-looking Middle-Eastern men?!" Cheney exclaimed. "They could only be one thing: terrorists."

Just then, Bush watched on screen as two terrorists wielding AK-47s entered the room behind Cheney. "American infidel!" one shouted. "We will make you tell us nuclear secrets!"

"Not if I can help it!" Cheney declared, grabbing his chest and collapsing to the floor.

"We have to help Dick!" Bush cried.

"Where is he?" Rumsfeld asked.

"He's at the mall in the boarded up store that says 'Soon to be a Dunkin' Donuts.'"

"You almost hit me with my desk!" Daschle whined, entering his office.

"What are you going to do about it?" Bush asked. "Cry?"

"Yes!" Daschle yelled, starting to tear up.

"Rarr!" Rumsfeld yelled, tossing Daschle out the window.

"That was funny!" Bush said, pointing and laughing. "Uh... now, what were we doing?"

"You were signing my excessive war plans," Rumsfeld told him, handing him the paper.

"Okie-dokie," Bush said as he started to sign it. He then glanced at the monitor. "Man, those terrorists are doing some piss-poor CPR."

April 16, 2003

The Press is Getting Bored with Seeing Daschle Mauled by a Gorilla Every Year

"So is there any chance this war could expand out to Syria?"

"I'm not telling you guys," White House Press Secretary Ari Fleischer scoffed. "Stop asking me questions."

"But this is a press conference!" exclaimed the reporter.

"Whatever." Fleischer took a swig of his bottle of tequila.

"What about reports that the US will be meeting with North Korea in China?" asked another reporter.

"No way we're going there, dude," Fleisher exclaimed. "There's SARS there. Actually, that's the administration's position: let SARS take care of them."

"Is there any information you can give us on the new government you'll be setting up in Iraq?"

"Yes. We'll be organizing it similar to feudal Japan, with different Iraqis selected to be Samurai lords."

"You just made that up!" a reporter accused.

"Prove it," Fleischer challenged, taking another drink of tequila.

"Why aren't you giving us actual answers to our questions?"

"Because you're ugly and stupid; there's an actual answer to your question."

"Do you have any comment on progress toward catching the Rumsfeld Strangler?" asked another reporter.

Fleischer laughed. "The Rumsfeld Strangler is just an invention of the liberal media."

"Many believe otherwise. Some say the murderer is someone from your administration."

"Who?"

"Secretary of Labor Elaine Chao."

"That's ridiculous; she's barely ever strangled anyone."

"Hey! Another reporter has been strangled!" someone shouted at the back.

"Rumsfeld, did you see anything?" Fleischer asked.

"Why would I have seen anything?" Rumsfeld responded angrily as he stood next to the body. "I don't have time for this; I have wars to plan." He then sauntered off.

"Probably just strangled himself," Fleischer assured the press.

"Do you have anything else to tell us today?" asked a reporter.

Fleischer looked at his empty bottle of tequila. "Yes, I need help getting the worm out of the bottle." He then broke the bottle over the reporter's head.

"You're the meanest, drunkenest press secretary ever!" the reporter cried, running away.

"I have a question. What would you say is the better quality of the president: his fierce intellect or his superb leadership?" asked President Bush, poorly disguised in a gorilla costume.

"What are you doing here?"

"Trying to find out why you haven't been to the meetings lately," Bush responded.

"I got this new Zelda game; the pieces of the triforce aren't going to find themselves."

"Cool!" Bush exclaimed. "Can I play?"

"It's a single player game; you can watch. So why are you dressed as a gorilla?"

"I got Daschle a phony newspaper saying that a gorilla escaped from the zoo. Now I'm going to go to his office and maul that weasel. It'll be so funny! He'll be like, 'Ah! A gorilla is attacking me.'"

"He wasn't fooled last time you tried to maul him wearing a gorilla costume."

"Whatever. Just come and film it so I can show the tape at the White House Correspondents Dinner."

April 21, 2003

Bush Plans to Use Blasphemy Instead of War

"President Bush—"

"Just wait a sec, Condi," Bush said as he leaned out the window, waiting for the right moment. Finally, he released the water balloon. "Got him!"

"You got me all wet!" Senator Tom Daschle whined.

"Ha ha!" Bush laughed. "So what are you going to do about it?"

"I'm telling the press!" Daschle yelled.

Bush slammed the window shut. "Crybaby." He then turned to Condoleezza Rice. "If the press comes asking about this, I was here with you."

"You *are* here with me!" Rice said impatiently.

"Good, you know how to play the game," he answered smugly as he took a seat. "What's on your mind?"

"I wanted to talk about more about our military strategy."

"Again?!" Bush exclaimed. "But I wanted to watch TV now. You keep working me like this, and I'm going to have to complain to my union boss."

"There is no presidents' union!" Rice answered irately.

Bush looked confused. "But Ariel Sharon keeps taking my dues each week..." A thought then struck him, and his expression turned to anger. "That Jew bastard! If he just wanted more money to bulldoze Palestinian homes, he could have just asked. I hate those Palestinians, always blowing themselves up. Why don't they just kill themselves?"

Rice had a number of things she wanted to say in response, but she decided to let it go. "We need to talk about Syria."

"Why can't we just talk about Iraq?" Bush complained. "We kicked butt there. I thought for a moment there was going to be trouble, but then 'zip,' 'bang,' 'pow,' we took Baghdad. Now I just have to set up a new government there chock full of democracy, and people will be like, 'Hey Bush, you're the best president ever!' and I'll be like, 'Yes I am. Now get me a soda, bitch!'"

"But we have to move on the popularity of the Iraqi war to go on to other wars," Rice told him, "and the troops have about run out of people to kill; they're getting restless."

"I thought we were just going to use diplomacy and scare Syria, though."

"A relentless barrage of bombs and ground troops is scary," Rice assured him.

"I dunno. I'm gonna ask Dick." He turned on the monitor with the satellite connection to Cheney's undisclosed location. "You there?"

"*Sí, señor.*"

Bush stared at the man on screen for a moment and then turned to Rice. "Did we replace Dick with a Mexican?"

"I don't believe so."

Bush looked at the Mexican. "What are you doing there?"

"I see this place here, and there was food and a TV. So I sit down to watch TV but instead see American president."

"Is the vice president around there?"

"I know not of this vice president, *señor.*"

"He has white hair, is balding, tends to have heart attacks, and answers to the name of Dick."

"I would certainly have noticed such a *gringo* if he were here, *señor.*"

"Alrighty, then. Well, you stay put in case we have to kill you as part of some cover-up."

"*Sí, señor.*"

Bush turned off the monitor. "Dick Cheney is loose!" he exclaimed. "He could kill millions!"

Rice just stared at him.

"Sorry, I forgot why we locked him away in the first place," Bush admitted sheepishly.

"Let's just get to my war plans," Rice demanded. "We attack Syria, then we go on to Jordan. Next, we skip over Saudi Arabia, saying, 'Oh, you're our friends, Saudi Arabia; we won't attack you,' and then we attack Yemen. Now, when Saudi Arabia least expects it, POW! We hit them too."

Laura Bush then came in the room. "George! You're not letting that harlot talk you into more war again, are you?"

"Excuse me, Mrs. Bush," Rice said politely. "We have important matters of national security to talk about. Aren't there some books you need to order into the Dewey Decimal System?"

Laura just stared back angrily. "I have a mind to give you a good talking to one of these days," she threatened.

"Hey, let's not fight," Bush urged. "I have a great idea that doesn't involve any war. The problem with lots of those countries is that some people interpret the Koran to mean violence is okay. So let's steal their Korans and rewrite them!"

"I don't think that will work, sir," Rice said.

"It will. We'll just steal them the same as I stole Tom Daschle's Koran."

"That's the antenna to his car, dear," Laura told him.

"Whatever, same principle. We just take the Korans, put in bold letters, 'Don't kill people... especially Americans,' and there will be no more interpretations that violence is allowed. It's a great idea!"

* * * *

"Hello, Mr. Muslim," Tom Daschle said, opening his front door. "How can I help you?"

"I'm fulfilling my religious obligation," the man said and then kicked Daschle in the groin.

"That bastard rewrote the Koran again!" Daschle wheezed. "I'll get him... and his little tax cuts, too."

April 23, 2003

Rumsfeld Seemed Unhappy About Letting Inspectors Back Into Iraq, Though No Statement Was Given

"The destruction may seem to have ceased now, but do not be fooled. This is just the eye of the storm, and soon the true carnage begins as we unleash our fury once more on the enemy, hunting them down and painting their wretched cities red with their blood."

"So are you saying you have further plans for military action?" asked a reporter.

"Yes, you fool!" Rumsfeld shouted. "Your stupidity only increases my rage, rage which I will take out upon the children of lesser countries in your name."

"What about setting up a new government in Iraq?"

"Nuke them! Let their new government be airborne ash. No mercy for our enemies!"

"Is that the current position of the administration?"

"I care not for their opinions! Especially not the opinion of that whiny liberal Colin Powell!" Rumsfeld yelled. He then said in a mocking, high-pitched voice, "'You can't just indiscriminately kill everyone, Rumsfeld.'"

"Aren't you afraid that this preemptive strike against Iraq has set a bad precedent?"

"No, it's a good precedent. Now countries know that if we find them a threat, we will attack them."

"And what countries do you find to be a threat?"

"Countries that are foreign."

"But wait a second," a reporter said snidely. "Won't—"

The reporter was cut short by the sound of Rumsfeld's Luger firing. "See, I knew his question was going to be asinine, so I shot him for it. Preemptive strike."

"What do you think about the UN and Hans Blix's insistence that weapons inspectors be let back into Iraq?" asked a non-shot reporter.

Rumsfeld was just silent for a moment. Then his body started to shake as if the rage inside him was trying to escape in a huge explosion of carnage. Finally, he screamed, "Rarr!" and the reporters fled as he charged forward.

* * * *

"Goody goody!" Blix exclaimed. "I hope we can get the weapons inspectors back into Iraq, and then I can eat more chocolates."

"But what shall we do with the insolent Americans?" Kofi Annan asked. "I think we should ask the opinions of nations run by tyrannical dictators."

"Kill the Jews!" one diplomat shouted.

"That's six votes for 'kill the Jews,'" Kofi said proudly. "I think we're going to have a consensus!"

Suddenly a sound of "Rarr!" was heard, as two UN security guards went flying through the air.

"Oh no!" Blix shrieked in terror. "It's Rumsfeld!"

"Do as we all practiced, and hide under your desks," Kofi shouted.

Rumsfeld scanned the seemingly empty room, sniffing the air. "I know you're here," he said. "I can smell your fear." Then, with each swing of his arm, he knocked a table out of the way.

Colin Powell came running into the room. "I'm glad I found you," he said. "You forgot to take your pills to prevent your murderous rage."

"This isn't murderous rage," Rumsfeld insisted, "it's murderous clarity!"

Powell handed him his pills, and Rumsfeld grudgingly took them.

"Murderousness subsiding," Rumsfeld uttered. "Now all I want to do is severely beat everyone here."

He then spotted Blix and Kofi trying to escape. "Don't hurt us!" they pleaded.

"No!" Rumsfeld slammed their heads together.

"See," Powell said proudly. "Can't we all be much happier after compromise?"

"I'm still planning to strangle you later," Rumsfeld answered.

"Yeah... well... I'll meet you back in DC," Powell said, running off.

April 28, 2003

El VP

"Man, it's certainly been a stressing time, Dick. I have to worry about getting a good government set up in Iraq, and then I have to fight the Democrats to get tax cuts so I can improve the economy. But they don't want the economy to improve since they're weasels. You know what I mean, Dick?"

"*Sí, señor.*"

Bush looked at the monitor. "You're not Dick. You're still that Mexican."

"*Sí, señor.*"

"Why are you still at the undisclosed location?"

"I do not know, *señor*. One day people come and say, 'We have to take you to your new location, Vice President Cheney.' And I say, 'I am not this Cheney you speak of.' But still, they put a blindfold on me and take me away. Now I do not know where I am, *señor*."

"Sorry about that," Bush said, thinking hard. "Man, where could Dick be? If it gets out I lost the VP, you just know there is going to be more of those 'Bush is dumb' jokes."

"*Sí, señor*. I just came up with one myself."

"Anyway, I'm going to nickname you 'the Mexican', a'ight?"

"*Sí.*"

Bush thought for a while. "How would you like to be the vice president? It pays $192,600 a year... uh... I mean three bucks an hour."

"What do I have to do?"

"Just appear to do a speech, and then fake a heart attack to get out of it. Can you do that?"

"*Sí, señor.*"

"Sweet. You're a good American."

"I'm a Mexican, *señor*."

"Well... you're a good whatever you are."

"Shouldn't you be looking for this Cheney you speak of?"

"Hey!" Bush said angrily. "I'm the president. I'm the idea man, a'ight?"

"*Sí, señor.*"

Bush then saw his wife Laura enter the room. "Hey, can I ask you a question, honey?"

"Sure, dear."

"If the vice president suddenly looked more Mexican to you, how would you react?"

She just stared at Bush for a long while. Finally, she said, "Know what? I like to stay out of politics."

* * * *

"Has the vice president been replaced with a Mexican?" asked a reporter.

"That's crazy talk," White House Press Secretary Ari Fleischer responded. "Anyone who thinks that is as crazy as Helen Thomas."

"I heard that!" Thomas yelled.

"I know you did, you old hag!" Fleischer responded.

"If he wasn't a Mexican," said another reporter, "why did he keep referring to us reporters as 'stupid *gringos*'?"

"Because Vice President Cheney thought the phrase 'asshats' was getting overused in his press conferences."

"So what was up with the poncho and sombrero?"

Fleischer looked confused. "The vice president wasn't wearing a poncho and a sombrero."

"No, I mean Bush."

"Oh! Well, he had just watched some westerns," Fleischer explained. "You know how Bush is. Now can we have a question about serious policy issues?"

"There have been rumors that Syria has been harboring Iraqis and their chemical weapons. Why haven't we just marched in there and killed all of them? Is your administration a bunch of pansies?" asked a FOX News reporter.

"Hey, be fair," Fleischer said defensively. "We have to be diplomatic about things like—"

The reporter started making chicken sounds.

"That's not very professional!"

Bush and the Mexican then came running into the conference. "Hey! Me and my new best friend..." Bush noticed all the reporters. "...I mean my old friend, Dick Cheney, have a great idea. We just found Daschle's car and want to overturn it. It sure is going to be fun, isn't it, Mexican?"

"When do I get to go back to Mexico? I miss my family."

"You crack me up, dude," Bush said, laughing. "So, Ari, you want to help?"

"Sure," he answered, "but I get to wear the sombrero this time."

"But it's my sombrero!" the Mexican complained.

"Learn to share, dude," Bush chided him.

"I can't wait to see Daschle's face once he finds his car overturned!" Fleischer exclaimed.

"You'll get to see it right away," Bush chuckled. "He's still in the car!"

April 30, 2003

Career Day

"Now, I want this career day with these first graders to go well, so all of you be on your best behavior," Laura Bush warned. "And I swear, Donald, if you strangle anyone today, I'll give you a talking to you won't believe."

"Do I have to sit next to Tom Daschle?" Bush complained.

"Yes," Laura answered. "If Donald's going to make his best effort not to strangle anyone, then the least I can do is not put him next to Tom Daschle."

"I told you to bring Condi instead," Bush said.

"I don't like that woman," Laura shot back. "Now let's go into the classroom and meet the kids."

They entered the room as the teacher announced, "I have a special treat for you today, children. Laura Bush has brought four people from the government to talk to you about their jobs. So let's all be on our best behavior."

"That goes for all of you, too," Laura warned as the four of them, the Marine, Tom Daschle, George W. Bush, and Donald Rumsfeld, took seats in front of the class.

"I guess I'll start," said the Marine. "My name is Buck, Buck the Marine. My job is to kill for'ners. There are a lot of for'ners running around out there, so I have my work cut out for me. I just got back from Iraq. There were a lot of for'ners there, and there are now many less."

"So what do you like best about your job?" the teacher asked.

"I'd have to say the killin'. Now, you can't just kill any for'ners; you have to follow your orders and only kill certain ones. Like in Iraq, some were shooting at me, so I killed them. That was fun. Some threw down their weapons and raised their hands; I don't like that, because then I can't kill them... especially not with them embedded reporters watching. I thought of killing the embedded reporter, but he ain't foreign. I only kill for'ners."

"What was it like liberating an Iraqi town?" asked the teacher.

"That had its high points and low points. Some Iraqis sniped at me, so I killed them; that was fun. Some cheered me on; couldn't kill them. A little Iraqi girl walked up and said, 'I love America.' That made me happy... but not as much as killin'."

"Now children, do you have any questions for Buck?"

"How do you kill people?" asked a little boy.

"Usually with my M-16. Sometimes with my .45-caliber sidearm; 9mm is for fags."

"We don't use that kind of language in class, Buck," the teacher politely told him.

"Sorry, ma'am. Anyway, my favorite weapon for killin' is my KA-BAR. I sneak up behind someone, stab him in the kidneys, and hold it in; you can't scream with a blade in your kidneys. Then, when he finally goes into shock, I pull the blade out and slit his throat. It's a very effective method. I recommend you try it sometime."

"My mom came from another country; would you kill her?" a concerned little girl asked.

"If so ordered, yes, I would kill your mom. Any other questions?"

"What do you do now?"

"Right now I am on leave. I hang out with friends, drink, and talk about all my killin'. I'm hoping something will happen soon in North Korea, though; never killed a Korean. Anyway, right now I have killed more people than the SARS virus, but that could change if I don't get out in the field again soon."

"Buck, why don't you tell them what you have to do to become a Marine," the teacher suggested.

"Certainly. You have to go through boot camp. There they will put you through hell. They will break down your body. They will break down your mind. They will break down your spirit. You will beg for mercy. You will not get it. You will beg for death. It will not come. If you survive—and I mean 'if'—you will be a Marine. Then you can kill for'ners. So who wants to be a Marine?"

The kids just stared at him bewildered, none of them raising their hands.

"What are you all? Fags?"

"Buck, we don't use that kind of language here," the teacher warned again.

"Sorry, ma'am."

"Now, Tom Daschle, why don't you tell the class what you do."

"Certainly. First of all, I would like to say how grateful I am for Buck's service in our military."

Buck stared at Daschle for a moment. "I don't think I like you."

"I get that a lot," Daschle said, laughing. "Anyway, children, I am a US senator. I help vote for what becomes our laws."

"You're a devil man!" screamed one child.

"Yes, I seem to radiate off sort of sinister vibe that young children pick up on," Daschle explained. "Commonly, babies cry when I come near. Most people, though, as they grow older no longer sense my evil so easily and then may vote for me."

"My dad says you're a mean man who takes his money," said a little boy.

"I think that your dad is just being selfish to try and keep his money. As a senator, I'm better equipped to know how to spend people's money. And we'll be able to take even more money into our loving care if we Democrats can get a majority in 2004."

"Yeah, that will happen," Bush chuckled.

"It's not your turn, Mr. Bush," the teacher told him firmly. "Let Mr. Daschle speak. Now, Mr. Daschle, what does one have to do to become a senator?"

"I think it's a good idea to first become a lawyer. That helps erode away your soul, which is an obstacle in politics. Then I say you need to act concerned about lots of things and talk down to people. And it's good to have a believable smile." Daschle then smiled, causing the class to cry.

"Make the scary man go away!" cried one girl.

"Maybe it's time for George Bush to speak," the teacher said. "Tell the class what your job is."

"I'm the President of the United States, the most powerful man in the world," Bush said proudly. "Maybe the universe. Within at least a few light-years from here, for sure, though. It's a fun job. I miss signing off on all those executions like when I was governor, but instead I can declare wars now and kill even more bad people. You know that Iraqi war? That was my idea."

"And I would just like to say I supported the troops," Daschle added, "but I was saddened how your botched diplomacy forced us into conflict."

"Oh, and I always had something I wanted to say in response to that," Bush said. He then turned to his side and punched Daschle in the face.

"You broke my nose!" Daschle screamed.

"People say I sometimes garble my words, but I think I was pretty clear there," Bush chuckled.

"There is no hitting in class!" the teacher yelled. "Mr. Daschle, you can go to the nurse. President Bush, you're getting a demerit."

"I'm going to tell!" Daschle cried, running off.

"Crybaby," Bush uttered.

Laura smacked him on the back of the head. "You're embarrassing me."

The teacher added Bush's name to a list on the wall and put a frowny face next to it.

"Ha ha!" laughed a kid. "Bush got a demerit!"

"What's your name, kid?"

"Uh... Tommy."

"Tommy what?"

"Tommy... Anderson."

"Well, guess what? The Andersons are about to get audited. It's going to be so stressful for your parents that they'll get divorced, and it will be all your fault."

"George!" Laura yelled.

"What? He was making fun of me."

"Why don't you explain more of your job," the teacher told him.

"Alright. I have to keep the world from imploding, since the rest of the countries are a bunch of idiots. The worst is France. How can I describe this to you? Uh... France is kinda like that kid in class everyone hates who reminds the teacher to give out homework." He then pointed to a geeky-looking kid wearing glasses. "Probably that kid; he's France."

"But without homework," the kid responded, "how are we going—"

"Quiet, France. I'm tired of dealing with you."

"Do you have questions for Mr. Bush?" the teacher asked the class.

"My mom says you didn't really win the election," said one boy.

"She said that, huh?" Bush answered, looking a bit annoyed. "Well, I want you to go home and smack her in the face for me. And she can't ground you for it, because I pardon you."

"George!" Laura shouted.

"What?" Bush said innocently.

"You don't seem that powerful to me," said one kid.

"I am powerful."

"Are not."

"Are so!" Bush yelled, rising out of his seat.

The kid just stuck his tongue out.

"I'll show you!" Bush shouted, grabbing a nearby globe. "I'll just pick a country and bomb it."

"Whatever," the kid said dismissively.

"Don't do this, George!" Laura warned.

Bush spun the globe and then stopped it with his finger. "The United States! I'll bomb the... oh, better spin again." He spun the globe once more and stopped it. "Hmm... I don't know how to say this one, but I can just spell it for them," he said as he took out his cell phone. "Hey, I want you to bomb a country spelled K-Y-R-G-Y-Z-stan... Just do it... I don't have to give you a reason why..." Bush looked at the kid with a haughty expression. "I'm the president."

Laura just shook her head.

Bush turned on a TV in the corner of the room. "After the success of the Iraqi war, a new era of peace is spreading through the Middle East," the news anchor said. "Experts say democracy will soon flourish, and... This just in. The US has launched an unprovoked attack against Kyrgyzstan. Who knows what diplomatic damage this will do to the US and to how the US is viewed around the world. It could take years to repair..."

Bush turned off the TV. "Told ya!" he said and then stuck his tongue out at the kid.

"So what does someone have to do to become president?" the teacher asked, trying to take control again of the class.

"I think it helps if your father was president," Bush said, sitting back down, "and better make sure your stupid brother doesn't mess up the voting in his state."

"Could I one day be president?" asked a boy.

"No, you're too fat."

"George!" Laura yelled, hitting Bush on the head.

"Uh... I mean, if you work really hard, you could become president, despite your tubbiness."

"I think it's now Donald Rumsfeld's turn," the teacher said. "So what is your job?"

"I am the Secretary of War."

"Defense," Laura corrected him.

"Whatever they call it now," he said with annoyance, "my job is to make sure America strikes fear into the hearts of all other nations. It was through my lobbying that I made sure we had this Iraq war."

"I want to thank you for that," Buck said.

"Glad you enjoyed the war," Rumsfeld answered. "There will be more to come."

"My parents say you're an evil warmonger," said a little girl.

Rumsfeld stared at her for a few seconds. "After this, I'm going to follow you home and murder your family."

"Donald!" Laura yelled. "I told you no threatening the children!"

"Why don't you tell us more about what your job requires," the teacher urged.

"Certainly. A Secretary of Defense must thirst for blood. He must love nothing more than to see the enemy cower before him, begging for mercy. But you must not be merciful. The enemy will see that as weakness, and we must never show weakness, for we are the United States of America."

"Ooh-rah!" Buck added.

"Are you going to kill and eat us?" asked a scared little child.

Rumsfeld considered this for a little while. "Not at this time," he finally answered.

"So what exactly do you do at your job?" the teacher asked.

"Other than the war planning and the thirsting for blood, I have to give press conferences and talk to idiot reporters. I would like to kill them all, but then next week there would just be a new set of reporters, even dumber than the last. One time there was—"

"I like the reporter with the big mustache," said a little boy.

"That child spoke out of turn; have him beaten," Rumsfeld ordered the teacher.

"We don't 'beat' children anymore," the teacher responded. "That's child abuse."

"Poppycock! When I was their age, if you were bad, they had this large stick they would beat you with for hours. And if you were good, they had an even bigger stick to beat you with. Beatings made you tougher, so it was a privilege to be pummeled."

"I'm confused," said one kid. "You said before that you were a secretary, but I thought a secretary was the woman who gets people coffee."

"You children are insolent!" Rumsfeld shouted, pulling out his Luger. "Line up for execution!"

Laura grabbed the Luger away. "I told you no guns at career day."

"That's my Luger!" Rumsfeld protested.

"You'll get it back after class if you're good."

"Rarr!" Rumsfeld yelled, but Laura just kept staring back at him sternly.

"Why don't you tell the kids what they need to do if they want to be a Secretary of Defense," the teacher said.

"None of them can be Secretary of Defense; they are too weak and stupid."

"Don't say things like that," the teacher chided him. "Give them a positive message."

"Don't tell me what to do!" Rumsfeld yelled, reaching for the teacher's throat.

Laura pushed him back into his chair. "No strangling!" she yelled at him. "Not at an event I organized!"

"I think the children have learned enough for today," the teacher said. "I want to thank you all for giving us your time today. Certainly pass that message on to Mr. Daschle when you see him again."

"Yeah, I'll pass him a message," Bush chuckled, hitting his fist into his palm.

"We're all going to O'Malley's after this," Buck announced to the kids. "You can meet us there, have a few beers, and I can tell you more about killing for'ners."

"Cool!" Bush exclaimed. "We'll have a game of darts."

"Just make sure to drive Donald home if he gets tipsy," Laura told Bush.

"Are you saying I can't hold my liquor, woman?" Rumsfeld demanded angrily.

"You know he's a mean drunk," Laura whispered to Bush, "so be careful."

"Heck, he's a mean sober," Bush said. "Drunk, he's a WMD."

May 07, 2003

White House Denies Scaring Away France

"So why are we watching the stupid *gringo* Democrat get into his car?"

"Just wait for it," Bush answered, watching out the window with barely contained excitement. Below them, Tom Daschle sat down in his car and turned the ignition. Soon his car exploded into a ball of flame, and Daschle started screaming and running around the parking lot on fire.

"Stop, drop, and roll, jackass!" Bush shouted and closed the window. He then collapsed into his chair, laughing.

"Isn't that attempted murder?" the Mexican asked with some concern.

"What are you? Some legal scholar? Practical jokes aren't crimes."

"Anyway, *Señor* Bush, I watched the Democrats' debate and took some notes on who may be your challenger in 2004. First off—"

"Who cares?" Bush scoffed. "So the Democrats are fighting to find out which one of them gets to be the next Mondale. I'm a war president, yo; I'm untouchable."

"Whatever you say, *Señor* Bush."

"Yeah, that's right: whatever *I* say. Because I'm the president, and you're just the VP."

"About that," the Mexican said. "When I was just doing speeches now and then, three dollars an hour was fair pay, but now you have me putting budgets together. I was thinking maybe I should now get four dollars an hour to be the VP."

"A one dollar raise?!" Bush exclaimed. "Have you gone *loco*? Maybe I'll give you a quarter more an hour, but that's it."

"No way. I need a dollar more, or I just go back to Mexico to find work."

"$3.50."

The Mexican considered this. "$3.75."

"Okay, Mexican, you drive a hard bargain, but $3.75 it is. All those numbers in the budgets better add up, though."

The Mexican glanced out the door. "That crazy warmongering *señorita* is coming."

"Condi? Does she look mad?"

The Mexican didn't answer and instead hid in a closet.

Condoleezza Rice stormed into the room and tossed a folder at Bush. "What's this?"

"Oh, just a little exploratory thing-a-ma-jig," Bush said innocently.

"You're planning on replacing your entire cabinet with cheap Mexican labor! The only thing that stopped you is you couldn't find a Mexican violent enough to replace Rumsfeld."

"It was just an idea."

"The America people won't stand for the entire Executive Branch being replaced with illegal immigrants like the VP."

"I didn't immigrate," the Mexican said defensively as he emerged from the closet. "I was kidnapped."

"See, Condi, he was kidnapped," Bush said. "Stop getting so angry."

"You need to find Cheney and end this nonsense," Rice told him.

"But he could be anywhere!" Bush protested.

"Such as right here," answered a familiar voice. There in the doorway stood Dick Cheney, adorned in a poncho and a sombrero.

"Wow!" Bush exclaimed. "What happened to you?"

"Something led me from the undisclosed location in Mexico," Cheney explained in a somber voice. "I found myself in the middle of the desert, lost and alone. I thought I was done for, but then a coyote spirit brought me to an abandoned abode in which I found a poncho, a sombrero, and a pistol. I then knew my true calling and wandered Mexico, freeing poor towns from the oppression of banditos. They called me El Dicko, and evil learned to fear my name. Finally, having brought justice where there was none, my job in Mexico was done, and I returned here to continue my fight as vice president, renewed now in spirit."

"That's a great story, Dick," Bush exclaimed. "Oh, but I gotta tell you what happened yesterday when me and the Mexican were playing Mario Kart—"

"The Mexican?"

"Yeah, I now have this Mexican as VP, so I don't need you anymore," Bush explained. "He costs less, he listens to me more, and he smacks me in the back of the head while calling me stupid about half as much you. So you can just go back to Halliburton or whatever."

"You can't replace me with a Mexican!" Cheney yelled.

"The Mexican never yells at me."

"It doesn't matter. I was elected VP, and you can't just replace me." Cheney looked at the Mexican. "You have to go now."

"But what about my $3.75?" the Mexican shouted.

"Here's an advance on that," Bush said, handing the Mexican three dollars and seventy-five cents. "That should be enough to get you a cab ride to a couple blocks from here. Then I guess you'll have to walk the rest of the way back to Mexico."

"If I ever seen you again, *gringo*," the Mexican threatened as he walked out the door, "I cut you!"

"I'll miss you too, Mexican," Bush answered, tearing up.

"Man, you're an idiot," Cheney uttered.

Bush looked at Cheney with an angry glance. "Secret Service!" Bush called out. "Put the VP somewhere undisclosed."

Two Secret Service agents appeared and started dragging Cheney away. "You can't do this to me again!" Cheney shouted. "I'll find where I am, and then I'll find where you are, and then I'll have my revenge!"

"Anyway," Rice said, "let's get back to business." She placed a piece of paper in front of Bush. "Just sign this, and we'll get to nuking Finland."

"Alrighty," Bush said, taking out his pen. Suddenly he stopped. "Hey, you're not tricking me into nuking Finland again. What's the real business I'm supposed to do now?"

"You must speak to France," Karl Rove said, emerging from the shadows.

"What? But I hate those douche-bags."

"Yesss," Karl Rove hissed, "but they want to save face after the war, so Chirac is going to call you, as foretold. If you speak kindly to him, he will admit France's mistake, thus increasing the positive perception of you abroad. This will further lead to the downfall of the Democrats, as predicted in the books of the ancients."

"Sounds good, I guess," Bush said, "but could you stop wearing that black robe and hood? It's creeping me out." He then picked up his phone. "So is there a call from France waiting for me? ...What do you mean, Chirac already called?... Then who took the phone call? ... RUMSFELD?!"

They all rushed out of the room to find a nearby office where Donald Rumsfeld was shouting into a phone. "Blood! Death! Kill! PAIN! I will gouge out your eyes! I will feast upon your entrails! I will—"

Bush hung up the phone...

"I was talking to some frogs!" Rumsfeld shouted angrily. "And I wasn't done yet!"

"We were trying to talk nice to them, Rummy," Bush explained.

"This could be damaging," Rove said in an ominous voice.

The news was playing on a nearby TV. "This just in: tourists to France say they are now unable to find the country. Apparently it was so scared by something that the entire nation went into hiding. No one can be sure what caused this, but most are guessing it's Bush's botched diplomacy."

"Aww, dangit, Rummy," Bush complained. "You have to get that anger of yours under control."

"Rarr!" Rumsfeld shouted. "I'll kill you all for reasons I'll think of later!"

Rice grabbed Rumsfeld in a headlock as he tried to lunge forward. "We already tried sending him to an anger management class," she said as she tried to hold Rumsfeld back, "but they just sent him back with a note recommending he be put down."

"Can't you inject him with something to calm him now?" Bush asked.

"All I have is the stuff that kills someone and makes it look like it was a heart attack," Rice answered.

"I just got off my habit of that!" Rumsfeld yelled. "You're not getting me hooked again."

Ari Fleischer then entered the room. "I heard yelling, and then I thought, 'Hey, people are going to need Ari again.'"

"Yeah, Ari," Bush said, "Rumsfeld has gone psycho angry."

"Well, guess what I have with me," Ari said, holding up a rifle. "The tranquilizer gun from that time you accidentally let an elephant loose in the White House."

"Cool! Shoot Rumsfeld!" Bush exclaimed.

"Rarr!" Rumsfeld yelled, trying to shake free of Rice.

Ari fired a dart into him.

"Rar!"

"Hit him again!" Bush commanded.

Ari fired once more.

"Ra..." Rumsfeld started to shout, but then trailed off. "I'm feeling sleepy now. I'm going to go to bed and will kill you all in the morning." Rice then let him loose, and he went out the door.

"Now you better go explain why France being scared away isn't our fault," Bush told Ari.

"Why do I always have to do that?" Ari complained. "Can't for once I be president, and you have to go out and explain away my stupid mistakes?"

"Do not worry," Karl Rove told him. "I will summon help for you to cover up this problem. The less you know, the better." He then disappeared back into the shadows.

* * * *

"Why would we know anything about France?" Ari responded to the press. "We hate them."

"So the disappearance of France has nothing to do with any actions by the White House?" asked a reporter.

"No, of course not," Ari responded. "That's stupid to say. Why the heck would we have anything to do with those goobers? I bet they were all scared away by a bee or something."

"Then how do you respond to Senator Daschle's statement from his hospital room that he's 'saddened by how Bush's poor diplomacy scared away France'?"

"I would just like to remind Daschle that he is very vulnerable right now in that full-body cast."

"What about this one rumor," asked a reporter, "that you were going to have a diplomatic call with Chirac, but then Rumsfeld—"

The reporter was cut off as a demon appeared in a flash of fire, grabbed the reporter, and then disappeared in another burst of flame.

"Uh... why did a demon just take that reporter?" asked another member of the press.

"Hey, stick to policy questions," Ari told them. "I don't know anything about demons."

"Would you admit that it's from this administration's lack of balls that they've now lost their opportunity to bomb France for their insolence?" asked a FOX News reporter.

"Hey, bombing France was always on the table, but matters of diplomacy are more delicate than that."

"Why do you want to bomb the Syrian children?" asked Helen Thomas. "What have the Syrian children done to President Bush?"

"There are no plans to attack Syria, you crazy old hag."

"Yeah, there are no plans to attack Syria because the current administration is a bunch of eunuchs," said the FOX News reporter. "If you weren't all such homos, instead of the Syrian children reciting their ABCs right now, they'd be getting their last rites."

"I swear, if you weren't a woman..." Ari threatened, shaking his fist.

"Bring it on, baldo!"

"Hey, I found this stick, and I thought it would be great for breaking over the head of John Kerry," Bush said, running into the press conference. "That will teach him to be so French-looking." He then noticed the press. "I mean, I was going to talk to Kerry about how dangerous trees are, supplying people with deadly weapons in the form of sticks."

"When I hold Kerry, you'd better have better aim this time," Ari said, rubbing a bruise on his head.

"Why is your administration such a bunch of pansies?" the FOX News reporter asked Bush.

"Uh... I think that question is better answered by Colin Powell."

May 12, 2003

FOX & Friends Transcript—Interview with Buck the Marine

...

E.D. Hill: Why don't we just bomb France? I'm tired of hearing about them.

Brian Kilmeade: Some people say they have a right to disagree with us... but I'm not so sure.

Steve Doocy: Maybe we could just put out some weasel poison to take care of them.

E.D.: Anyway, our next guest, unlike the French, is a real hero. Just home from Iraq, here is Buck the Marine.

Buck: Thanks for the kind words, ma'am. But I am no more a hero than any other American who does his job day in and day out. Just like some people's jobs are to bake bread, other people's jobs are to build automobiles, and mine is to kill for'ners.

Brian: So how would you deal with the French?

Buck: If so ordered, I would go door-to-door eliminating any resistance with my trusty M-16.

Steve: No weasel poison?

Buck: No, sir. I believe that would be classified as a chemical weapon. Probably there would be an aerial strike before the ground fighting, though.

E.D.: Well, I would just like to thank you for your service overseas. You're the reason we have a free country.

Buck: Thank you, ma'am. You can be assured that while Buck the Marine is alive and kicking, I will see to it that America is a land of liberty, free to have entertaining yet informative morning shows such as this one.

Brian: So did you see a lot of action while in Iraq?

Buck: Yes, sir, I did. Many Iraqis shot at me, and many Iraqis were then killed. Some people from other countries also came to fight us, so I killed them as well.

Steve: Guess they saved you the trip of going to their countries to kill them.

Buck: There were no plans to invade their countries.

Steve: I was just joking, Buck.

Buck: Oh. Sorry to ruin your comic timing, sir.

Steve: It's okay, Buck; don't worry about it.

E.D.: I understand that you were once ambushed.

Buck: Yes, that is correct, ma'am. Some Iraqis came at us with their hands raised, as if to surrender. Then, as we came near, they attacked.

E.D.: That must have really upset you, seeing such deceitful tactics.

Buck: Actually, it made my day. I find taking for'ners prisoner to be quite boring, but killin' them is both my job and my favorite hobby. Soon as those Iraqis moved for their weapons, me and my buddies killed the whole lot of them and then shouted, "Ooh-rah!" Now those Iraqis can practice their phony surrendering in for'ner hell.

Brian: Were you ever scared when being attacked like that?

Buck: One must always keep a healthy amount of fear to stay on his toes, but those Iraqis can barely hit anything with their second-hand AK-47s. Plus, I've been shot so many times by 7.62x39 caliber rounds that I hardly even notice anymore.

E.D.: I'm just glad you're alright now. So, how is it to be back in the States?

Buck: As much as I like killin' for'ners, I did miss my home, the land I fought for in defense of its honor and its interests. Anyway, I have to leave some for'ners for the other Marines to kill; wouldn't be fair if I killed them all myself.

Steve: Don't have to worry so much about getting shot with an AK-47 here.

Buck: That is true. Still, those people staring at me through the windows at my six o'clock are making me nervous.

E.D.: That's just tourists. We have those windows so they can look in while we're filming. They're harmless.

Buck: I would like to trust you on that, ma'am, but it goes against my instincts to have unknown entities unwatched behind me. And I certainly cannot look at them and talk to you fine folks.

Brian: Not really sure how to make them go away, Buck.

Buck: I have a solution to that matter.

(gunshot)

Buck: See, they've scattered like pigeons. Ooh-rah!

Steve: I've always wanted to do that, but the producers would never let me. So what is that gun?

Buck: It's a 1911, .45 caliber. She's my trusty sidearm, and I always keep her with me.

E.D.: You're not actually supposed to have guns in the studio.

Buck: I was unaware of that, ma'am.

Brian: And we're not supposed to do shots during commercial breaks, but, hey, rules are made to be broken.

Buck: Not for Buck. I'll keep my gun in its holster for the remainder of the show.

E.D.: Now that you are in America, I've heard that you were approached by Laura Bush to help in educating children with your experience.

Buck: Yes, ma'am. First I participated in a Career Day, where I told children what it is like to be a Marine. I thought that was pretty successful, and at the age of six, a child has plenty of years to prepare him- or herself for boot camp. Now Mrs. Bush has me working on a new program to help stop child abductions.

Brian: And you are re-defining the way children should handle being approached by strangers.

Buck: Yes, before 9/11, children were told that, if approached by a stranger and told to get in a car, to run away and tell someone of authority. Now that 9/11 has redefined things, we are moving toward a more... uh... what's that psychobabble word...

Steve: Proactive?

Buck: Yeah, that's it. Proactive. We're teaching children a more proactive approach to strangers... principally to stab them. I call it "Taking a Stab at Preventing Child Abductions."

E.D.: Did you think of that name yourself? It's very clever.

Buck: Yes, I did. Thank you, ma'am.

Steve: So how is stabbing a stranger better than just running away from one?

Buck: Well, for one thing, it teaches wackos to fear children, as they should. Also, it makes the said strangers easier to identify to the police. Instead of just saying to look for a "strange-looking man," they can be told to look for a "strange-looking man with a hideous stab wound."

E.D.: And the kids love this.

Buck: Yes, ma'am. I've taught them my favorite stabbing method. That is to hold the knife such that the blade faces upwards. Then, after stabbing, the blade can be removed in an upwards, slicing motion, causing maximum damage.

Brian: That's great advice, but I hear that some school districts have given you trouble.

Buck: That is true, sir; many schools do not allow children to carry knives.

E.D.: It's almost like they want children to be abducted!

Buck: I do not know their motives, ma'am, but I will not teach children to break the rules. Instead, I've taught them ways to stab strangers while abiding by school policy. They can use a sharpened pencil or a key, both things they are allowed to bring to school. I've also taught children how to cut someone's throat with a credit card, but most elementary school children do not have credit cards, due to their lack of a credit history and steady jobs.

Steve: Sounds like you are doing some good work for the children.

Buck: If I can help kids have happy childhoods free of troubles, then I will be a happy Buck. Just as happy as when killin' for'ners.

E.D.: That's a beautiful sentiment.

Brian: Now, as clean-cut as you are, I hear you have run into some legal trouble.

Buck: Yes, sir. I had witnessed a flag-burning. Though it brought a tear to my eye to see such a travesty, I understand that it is considered free speech, something I have shed blood on more foreign lands than I can count in defense of. Then I thought, well I am allowed free speech as well. Since one sets fire to an American flag to protest the American flag, I thought I would set fire to a flag burner to protest the flag-burning. Ends up that was not considered speech, and I was brought to court over it.

E.D.: That is such a double standard!

Brian: Well, some might say that the difference is one is a flag, and the other a person.

Buck: Yes, sir, I understand that argument, but I ask, who do people respect more, the American flag, or a hippy? Seems more people respect that flag, so I don't see why burning a hippy would be a worse crime.

Steve: So what was the verdict?

Buck: In the state of Alabama, burning a hippy constitutes a fifty-dollar fine.

E.D.: But you're not going to pay it?

Buck: No, ma'am. I'm going to fight this all the way to the Supreme Court if I have to. I'm going to fight for my speech as well as others'.

E.D.: And we certainly wish you good luck with that.

Brian: Now we're going to take some calls from our viewers. Claire from Austin, Texas, do you have a question for Buck?

Claire: Yes, but first of all I want to say how thankful I am for him killing all those for'ners.

Buck: It was my pleasure, ma'am.

Claire: So, Buck, what do you think of all those anti-war protestors?

Buck: Well, I was killin' those for'ners for the protestors' freedom of speech as well. Even though I may not agree with them, that they can express their viewpoints is a beautiful thing. That said, I must remind protestors that, while it is legal for them to shout whatever epithets they want at me and to deride my military service, it is not legal to touch me, as learned one protestor who will no longer have the use of his left hand.

Steve: Conrad from San Francisco, California, you're on FOX & Friends.

Conrad: I just want to say I'm disgusted by a baby killer like Buck who fights for corporate oil interests!

E.D.: Oh my goodness! What a horrible person! It scares me to think that someone like that watches this channel.

Brian: Maybe he meant to watch CNN and accidentally hit the remote control buttons for this channel.

Steve: Or maybe he's an (shudder) MSNBC viewer.

E.D.: I keep telling the higher-ups that I don't want affiliates carrying our channel in places like San Francisco and Berkeley. I can't sleep at night thinking weirdos like those people were looking at me on TV.

Buck: Still, Conrad made a good point. One has to be careful with those babies. Once on an operation we encountered a baby in a crib. We stopped to say, "Aww, what a cute little baby." Then he attacked us. Ended up being a homicidal midget with a knife. A midget being so small, he was hard to shoot. Ended up losing four good men to that [expletive deleted] midget.

Steve: They prefer to be called "the vertically challenged."

Buck: Sorry, sir. I lost four good men and to that [expletive deleted] vertically challenged person. Now I look on all babies with suspicion.

E.D.: I know what you mean. Every once in a while, I'm scared my baby might have been replaced by a midget in disguise.

Buck: That's why someone should always have a gun in hand when checking on her newborn.

E.D.: Great advice for new mothers. Great advice.

Steve: That's all the time we have. I want to thank you, Buck, for stopping by and sharing your time with us.

Buck: It was my pleasure, sir. Ooh-rah!

May 14, 2003

US Claims to Have No Plans to Attack Britain, Australia, or Israel

In Rumsfeld's press conference, he quickly got to the issue of the Iraqi occupation.

"Our cleanup in Iraq is going well. Soon we will have hunted down and killed every Iraqi."

Condoleezza Rice whispered into his ear.

Rumsfeld rolled his eyes. "I mean, a stable government will soon be set up."

"The president keeps referring to Iraq as a 'battle,' thus implying it is part of a continuing war," said one reporter. "Who do you have plans to attack next?"

"Let's see." Rumsfeld pulled down a map of the world with the US at the center, where it's supposed to be. He looked at it for a while. "It would probably be easier to just list the countries we have no plans to attack. One is Britain. Another is Australia. Not attacking Israel. No plans for Canada... no, scratch that, I misspoke there. What are these islands up here, Dr. Rice?"

"Those are part of Norway," she answered. "We have plans."

"What about down here at the bottom?"

"That's not really a country," Rice told him. "That's Antarctica."

"But there are people there?"

"Scientists doing research."

"Well, I want to know what 'research' they are doing and have plans to eliminate them all if necessary," Rumsfeld said and then looked back at the map. "So what's left? Well, there's our own country, the United States."

Rice whispered in his ear.

"Sorry, there are plans to attack some parts of the United States, the parts that aren't being American enough. They may need a regime change."

"Are you allowed to attack parts of your own country?" asked a reporter skeptically.

"There is precedent," Rice explained. "The Civil War."

"But those states seceded."

"And this is a preemptive strike before places secede," Rice said.

"Or on places we wish would secede," Rumsfeld added.

"But what is most likely your next target? Is it Syria?"

"We don't want to reveal our planning," Rumsfeld answered. "Everyone except Britain, Australia, Israel, and most of the US should consider themselves equally likely to be attacked."

"Does the recruiting of more people who can read French to help translate intelligence give any evidence of who you plan on attacking next?" asked a reporter.

Rumsfeld pulled out a Colt Python, pointed it at the reporter, and pulled the trigger. It clicked empty. "I should probably explain this. I've decided to move to a revolver with only some of the chambers containing bullets. Thus, if your question displeases me, you may get shot, or you may get off with just a warning."

"How many chambers have bullets?"

"I don't remember. If I get asked five more idiotic questions, we'll find out."

"North Korea may have aimed a laser at one of our helicopters," said a reporter. "Will there be any repercussions?"

"I have discussed this with some visiting North Korean diplomats."

"The same ones that were later found dead, victims of the 'Rumsfeld Strangler'?" exclaimed the reporter. "Did you see anyone suspicious when you met with them?"

"I was too busy strangling Norks to notice anyone suspicious."

"Darnit," the reporter muttered, "I wanted to crack that case."

"Do the bombings in Saudi Arabia prove all the United States's efforts have been futile?" asked another reporter.

Rumsfeld seemed to think about this for a while. Finally, he shouted, "Rarr!" and punched through the reporter's chest, producing his heart. He put the heart in a plastic baggy and put it away in his pocket.

"Do you plan on eating that later?" asked a squeamish reporter.

"That would be disgusting," Rumsfeld answered. "It's a treat for my dog."

"Will the strike against the terrorists who committed these crimes involve wrath that is insane and disproportionate, or will the wrath be more tailored in its severity and less insane?" asked a FOX News reporter.

"Great question. I lobbied for the former. During the long, torturous deaths of the terrorists, I would have their families hunted down and their children gutted. Instead, that whiny liberal Colin Powell argued us down to just forcing the children to witness all their toys being smashed. The deaths of the terrorists will still be long and torturous though."

A phone rang, and Rumsfeld pulled out his cell phone. "What?... Tell them we won't accept a surrender until we at least get to kill a few people." Rumsfeld looked back at the reporters. "I need to go now."

"But I still have a ques—" one reporter started to say, but Rumsfeld pulled out his revolver and pulled the trigger five times at the reporter. All clicked empty.

"Ah, I forgot to put any bullets in," Rumsfeld grumbled. "That's old age for you."

May 19, 2003

White House Hopes Democrats Don't Flee to Canada (wink wink)

"But we need that tax cut to spur on the economy," Bush pleaded.

"It's just a tax cut for the rich!" Senator Tom Daschle responded. "It will only help the rich!"

"Liar! Liar! Liar!" Bush shouted back. "It will give money—"

Daschle covered his ears. "La la la! Not listening! Just a tax cut for the rich! La la la!"

"That's it!" Bush screamed. "I'm going to stab you with this letter opener!"

Daschle ran out of Bush's office, almost knocking over Condoleezza Rice on the way out. "Quick, Condi, hold him so I can stab him with my letter opener!" Bush called out.

"I'm not your secretary, Dubya," Condi answered angrily. "It's not my job to hold people while you stab them... and that's not a letter opener—it's a switchblade."

"A switchblade can open letters," Bush said, tossing the knife such that it stuck in the far wall. "I need your help, Condi; I have to get the economy improved to help me win reelection."

"I'm your National Security Advisor, idiot," Rice answered. "If it doesn't involve killing foreigners, it's not my problem."

"Hey, if the economy causes me to lose my reelection, then you're out of a job here and back to stripping at the Eager Beaver."

"I was never a stripper!" Rice exclaimed.

"Hmm... that must have just been a product of my overactive imagination. Anyway, do you have any ideas?"

"Don't you have an economic advisor?"

"Hell, I don't know. There are all sorts of people who come up to me and say stuff during the day. I don't understand what half of them are talking about."

"Well, I do have one idea," Rice told him. "You know how those Democrats fled Texas?"

"Yeah, what a bunch of wusses," Bush chuckled. "Wouldn't have happened during my term; I would have had Walker, Texas Ranger, kick them all in the heads."

"If you can get the Democrats in Congress to similarly flee to Canada, I can set up a task force to hunt them down and kill them."

"That's brilliant!" Bush exclaimed. "So all I have to do is scare them all into fleeing to Canada."

Laura Bush then entered the room. "You're not talking to that National Security Whore again, are you, George?"

"But she had a great idea to help with the economy."

"She was just trying to get you to drop your guard so she could trick you into nuking Finland again."

"No, I wasn't!" Rice protested as she hid an unsigned executive order behind her back.

"What do you have against Finland anyway?" Laura asked.

"That's between me and Finland," Rice said angrily as she left the room.

"Hey, honey, I've been wanting to talk to you," Bush said softly.

"What about?"

"Can I get a katana like Morpheus?"

"But you already have a katana like the guy from *Highlander*!" Laura said with exasperation. "How many katanas do you need?"

"Just one more, I swear! Oh, and I had another idea. You know how President Kennedy stopped wearing a hat and then set the style for everyone? I was thinking that to my next press conference I could wear a black trench coat and sunglasses, and maybe that would catch on."

"I knew letting you see *The Matrix Reloaded* was a bad idea. And it's not like letting you land on an aircraft carrier hasn't given you enough crazy ideas."

"What?" Bush smiled. "You saying you didn't like seeing me in that flight suit?"

"No, I didn't mean that," Laura answered, starting to giggle. "You think maybe you have time to put that back on and—"

"There is no time for that, woman," echoed a voice throughout the room. The shadows in the room slowly merged into the form of Karl Rove. "We have work to do."

"Hey, great you're here, Rover," Bush said. "I've been wanting to ask you a question: Who do you think will win American Idol? The big black dude or the little gay dude?"

"That's of no concern to me," Rove uttered darkly. "Now have your woman leave so we may talk business."

"I've never heard such condescension!" Laura exclaimed. "I'm going to give you such a talking to after I check if my brownies are done, by golly." She then stormed out of the room.

"You have plans to destroy the Democrats?" Rove asked hopefully. "Perhaps it is time for the prophecies to be fulfilled."

"Yeah, maybe that or something!" Bush said excitedly. "We're going to scare the Democrats into Canada." He then yelled, "Ari!"

"What?" Ari Fleischer asked as he arrived at the door.

"Hey! Were you eating my Cheetos?"

"No," Ari said, wiping an orange substance off his mouth. "What do you want?"

"We need to find something to scare the Democrats away. What are they scared of?"

"Well... they're scared of guns, cigarettes, loud noises, people spending their own money, certain spiders..."

"No, I mean, what really, like, frightens them and keeps them up at night?"

"The thought of blacks getting educations and good jobs and then voting Republican?" Ari ventured.

"Whatever it is, I need you to convince all the Democrats to flee to Canada."

"I'll try."

"And I'll use my dark powers to assist you," Rove said before fading back into the shadows.

"So is that guy part of your cabinet or something?" Ari asked. "I never really understood his function."

"I think he's my boss," Bush answered, looking around the room. "Where did I put my switchblade?"

* * * *

"So there is nothing that the Democrats can do to keep us from getting our tax cuts," Ari announced to the press. "Nothing can stop us."

"Nothing at all?" asked a reporter.

"Well, nothing... unless they fled to Canada," Ari said. "But that would be a bold move, and they would never do it. Instead, they'll stay here in DC, where there is soon going to be a big march of the AAGO, the Association of Angry Gun Owners."

"Isn't it illegal for people to march around DC carrying guns?"

"Bah! Laws are for those who don't have guns!"

"Is this all a trick so that you can slaughter the Democrats en masse after they have left US soil?" asked a reporter. Suddenly darkness surrounded him, and he burst into flames.

"New rule," Ari announced. "If you spontaneously combust, I don't have to answer your question."

"Why is it that when it seems a reporter is getting close to the truth," one reporter asked, "he then is killed by some demonic force and...?" A thought struck the reporter, and he suddenly became frightened. "Forget what I was just saying; I have a different question. Uh... does the president like kittens?"

"Yes, he finds them cute and easy to throw."

"Since the terrorists who committed the bombings in Saudi Arabia are probably from Saudi Arabia, why haven't we nuked the crap out of the area in retaliation?" asked a FOX News reporter.

"That wouldn't really be the diplomatic way to handle things."

"Then I have a follow-up question: why are you such a homo?"

"You think you can intimidate me with your pouty lips and your short skirt?" Ari shot back angrily. "We may not be as violent as you want, but we're plenty warmongering." Ari noticed protestors outside. "See, I'll go beat up a protestor with his own sign. I'll splatter some blood on a 'No Blood for Oil' sign; that would be ironic... or would it be ironic if I splattered oil on it?"

"Maybe you need to get both blood and oil on it for irony," suggested one reporter.

"You want a piece of me, too?!" Ari shouted back. He then stormed outside to meet the protestors. "Bush is Hitler... Bush is Hitler... Bush is Hitler..." Ari said, reading the signs, "...Bush is Stalin?!"

"Stalin was actually responsible for more deaths than Hitler," the protestor explained. "I thought it was a more powerful statement of Bush's evil."

"Are you belittling Communism?" shouted another protestor angrily. The "Bush is Stalin" protestor was then pummeled with a number of "Bush is Hitler" signs.

"Whoa, I'm staying out of this one," Ari said, backing up. He then looked at a nearby reporter. "You have any news feeds? Have the Democrats fled to Canada yet?"

"Only a few so far."

Ari sighed and started walking off. "Well, I got a bottle of Jack Daniels at home that isn't going to drink itself."

May 21, 2003

Orange Alert

Rumsfeld frowned at the crowd in front of him. "Why are there so many of you?"

"After the whole Jayson Blair incident, our editors are really cracking down on us about making up quotes or just stealing stories from the reporters nerdy enough to actually go to press conferences," explained one reporter. "So now we all had to come actually listen to you."

"I hate reporters," Rumsfeld muttered. "If you want a quote, here's one: When Jayson Blair's book comes out, I will personally beat him to death with it. Now get on with your inane questions."

"Why are we in orange alert now?"

"How the heck would I know?" Rumsfeld shot back angrily. "That's Homeland Security crap. My desire to kill foreigners is always at red alert."

"But do you know what the alert may be about?"

"No, all I know is it's some chatter about attacking a press conference."

"Infidels!" screamed four Muslim extremists who entered the room carrying AK-47s. "We are in charge now!"

"You know this pisses me off!" Rumsfeld growled.

"We do not care!" answered a terrorist. "We hate Jews, America, and all American officials—except for a few of the Democrats—for reasons of varying levels of coherency, and you reporters will broadcast our message, or we will kill you."

"Can't you do both?" Rumsfeld suggested.

"Laugh while you can, infidel!" shot back the terrorist. "We will execute you, the evil one who caused war against us Muslims and bombed our villages."

"Oh, and I'm really convinced that was a bad idea now," Rumsfeld chuckled. He then pulled out a tape recorder. "Note to self: bomb more villages."

* * * *

"Infidel!"

"No, my name is Buck, Buck the Marine," Buck corrected. "I'm waiting here to meet with Rumsfeld after his press conference. We are going to go to a bar, drink a moderate amount of alcohol, and discuss new wars where I would get to kill more for'ners. Hey, those are neat AK-47s you two have; looks just like the guns used by a lot of the for'ners I kill."

"You killed our Muslim brothers!" the terrorist exclaimed.

"You knew them?" Buck exclaimed. "What a small world. So what are you guys' names?"

"I am Mohammed."

"I am also Mohammed."

"That's funny; you're both named Mohammed. I was once in a platoon with two guys named John. We had to give them both crazy nicknames like 'Johnny' and 'Jonathan.'" Buck laughed. "So do you guys ever use nicknames like 'Mohammy' and 'Mohammathan'?"

"Do you insult our Muslim religion?"

"No, I don't mean to do that at all," Buck said sincerely. "My parents taught me to always be nice to people of other religions since they are destined for hell anyway because they haven't accepted Jesus into their lives." Buck nudged the terrorist's AK-47 away from him. "You really have to practice better gun safety and watch where you point those things. Never point a gun at anything you don't mean to shoot." A thought then struck him. "Hey, it's an orange alert right now, which means I'm being extra vigilant, and I'm starting to think you people are suspicious."

"We will kill you and this Rumsfeld!" shouted one of the terrorists. "Then we will spit on the American flag and burn it."

"You just made a big mistake," Buck said darkly. "You angered a Marine."

* * * *

"Try to negotiate with them," urged a reporter.

"No, we may end up with an outcome where they don't die," Rumsfeld answered. "That's unacceptable."

"Can you use your warmongering to save us?" asked another.

"Fine," Rumsfeld grumbled.

"Quiet, infidels! It is now time to execute Rumsfeld."

"Don't think that's going to happen, A-rab."

"Ha! How will you stop us, old man?"

"By drawing my guns and shooting you," Rumsfeld said, drawing his guns and shooting him. He then rolled across the ground and held out his

.45s in two different directions, quickly dispatching the other three terrorists in the room. “There may be more terrorists in the building,” Rumsfeld warned, “so everyone take out your guns.”

“We don’t have any guns,” a reporter said.

“No guns?!” Rumsfeld yelled. “You knew we were in orange alert and didn’t bring a gun?! Rarr!” He then grabbed the reporter and started shaking him.

Suddenly they heard more gunshots outside the room. They went on for a few seconds and then ceased. It was silent for a few moments, the silence finally broken by the shout of “Ooh-rah!”

Buck entered the room. “There was a bunch of evil for’ners outside,” he explained to Rumsfeld, “so I killed them good and then shouted, ‘Ooh-rah.’”

“We heard,” Rumsfeld answered. “Good job, Buck.”

Buck looked at the reporters as he carefully held an AK-47. “Are you sure none of them are terrorists?”

“Not that sure,” Rumsfeld replied. He then looked at his watch. “We still have time for one more question.”

“Do you think you used excessive force against the terrorists?”

“Hey, you all saw me,” Rumsfeld said. “I didn’t continue to shoot them after they were dead.” He looked at Buck. “I’ve decided that question was asinine; hand me something to break over his head.”

Buck handed him the AK-47. Rumsfeld smacked it over the reporter’s head, snapping off the wooden stock. “Time for drinks,” Rumsfeld announced to the reporters. “None of you are invited.”

“Do you think in the next war we could kill Commies?” Buck asked Rumsfeld as they headed out of the room. “I’m getting tired of killing these Muslim extremists; it’s too easy.”

“We’ll see, Buck; we’ll see.”

May 28, 2003

Black Project Insano Part I

Jacques Chirac sat in his office contemplating how superior he was to all other foreign leaders when suddenly the phone rang. "Hello?"

"Hey... uh... this is Pierre. You know... Pierre."

"Oh, hello, Pierre. How are you?"

"I'm great."

"You're not sounding very French today."

"I have a cold. Anyway, I was looking for Chezz. Do you know him?"

"No, I don't think so."

"Well, he should be with two other people somewhere near your office. The other two are Sue and Norm. If you could get them for me, I'd appreciate it."

"Certainly. Just to be clear, though, what are their last names?"

"Well, Chezz's last name is Eaton. Sue's last name is... uh... I can't remember. But I know Norm's; it's Unkies."

"Unkies?"

"Yeah, I don't what nationality that name is."

"Well, I'll go see if I can find them."

"Thanks Jacques-strap; you're a real help."

Chirac took his cordless phone with him as he headed out into the main lobby. "Are you Chezz Eaton, Sue, and Norm Unkies?" he asked the first group he saw. He then shouted out, "Are there Chezz Eaton, Sue, and Norm Unkies here? Someone check the nearby military base for Chezz Eaton, Sue, and Norm Unkies!"

Everyone started laughing.

"Oh, it's you again!" Chirac said angrily into the phone. "When I find out who this is, I'll impotently demand you to stop!"

The only response was more laughter.

* * * *

"Oh, that was classic," Bush chuckled as he hung up the phone. "Aren't you going to miss this when you leave, Ari?"

"Hey, man, I told you; I have to follow my heart," Ari Fleischer replied. "I just know my band 'American Hellbender' is going to take off big with its mix of reggae, techno, and country done to a new age beat."

"Can we get to the business at hand?" Condoleezza Rice demanded angrily. "There are lots of evil nations out there, and they aren't going to bomb themselves! Well, maybe North Korea is crazy enough to do that... but we can't count on it!"

"Fine. So who should we attack next, Rumsfeld?"

"See this map here?" Rumsfeld said, walking up to a large map on the wall. Suddenly he shouted "Rarr!" and started ripping away the map until finally nothing was left except for the US. He then stuffed the pieces of the map into a wastebasket and set them on fire.

"As your Secretary of State," Colin Powell began, "I'd like to point out that there might be some disadvantages to destroying all other countries."

"You weak-willed liberal!" Rumsfeld screamed. "You're on the terrorists' side!" He then tried to lunge at Powell, who ran out of the room while Rice and Ari tried to hold Rumsfeld back. Rumsfeld eventually calmed down and returned to his seat.

"So... have any smaller plans for who we fight next?" Bush asked.

"I do," Rice replied. "Ever heard of the small island country of Lintuvia?"

"No," Bush answered, "but yesterday was the first time I heard of Brazil."

"Well it's a small, isolated island dictatorship in the Indian Ocean," Rice continued, "and an easy target."

"What have they done to us?"

"What have they done *for* us?" Rice responded. "Anyway, it's great testing ground for our new military weapon: Black Project Insano!"

"Wow! That sounds cool!" Bush exclaimed. "What is it?"

"Well, I don't really know..." Rice admitted. "I just know it's our greatest project ever... but the exact details are beyond my security clearance."

"What about mine? I'm the president."

"Even beyond yours," Rice told him.

"What about you, Rumsfeld?"

"I just don't give a rat's ass."

"So who does know?" Bush asked.

"That's also classified beyond our level," Rice said.

"Wait," Bush suddenly exclaimed. "I think I do know who knows."

"Yes, you were fooled into knowing who knows," Rice explained. "That's part of Black Project Insano."

"Am I supposed to know that I was fooled?"

"Yes, you have the clearance to know that the one you think you know who knows doesn't actually know. That was a bit of an oversight."

"So who actually knows who knows what Black Project Insano is?"

"That is also too classified."

"So who knows who knows who knows what Black Project Insano is?"

"Dick Cheney."

"Ah, so we have to find Dick."

"This is idiotic," Rumsfeld commented. "Can't we just bomb countries and shoot people as normal?"

"Do not underestimate the power of Black Project Insano!" Rice shot back. "First we test it on Lintuvia, and then the world will be mine!" She started laughing evilly but then noticed everyone staring at her. "Uh... I mean, the world will be at peace and run by the US."

"I'm going to look for Dick Cheney," Bush said. He went to the door of the conference room and shouted out, "Laura! Is Dick in one of the cupboards in the kitchen?"

"Honey, I can't always be finding Cheney for you," Laura answered.

"Did you forget where you undisclosed him again?" Rice asked angrily.

"Uh... no."

"Remember, he was with us at the mall this afternoon," Ari said.

"Oh, then we just have to wait for him to drive back," Bush answered.

"But, dude, we drove him."

"Oh man!" Bush exclaimed. "I stranded Dick at the mall again. He's going to be all angry and having heart attacks."

"We'll send someone to get him," Rice stated. "Now we need to send a Special Forces group to clear Lintuvia of any resistance."

"I know who you should send," Rumsfeld said.

"Who?" Bush asked.

"Buck."

"Buck who?"

"Buck... the Marine!"

* * * *

"Hello, Buck here—Buck the Marine that is... This is the president? President of what? ...The United States of America?! That's the best thing to be president of. So what can I do for you, sir? ...You want me to do a mission in Lintuvia? Are there for'ners there? ...Then they're dead! Now I just need you to give me some supplies... What do you mean, I have to buy my own bullets? ...You can't afford bullets for me so you could have a tax cut for the rich?! That doesn't seem right... Well, yes, I guess rich people do deserve the money they earn, and they do contribute a lot to society through investments and creating new jobs... and it was selfish of me to think of myself when they were being overtaxed... Yes, I'll do that. I'll write an apology to the local Millionaires' Club before I head out... Yes, that too, I'll be more happy for what I have: my free room and board and my fifty dollars a month salary... What do you mean, you want me to pay rent now?! How much tax cuts do rich people need? ...That makes me so mad I could kill people! ...Yes, I guess that is good timing. I'll get ready for the mission."

* * * *

"Funny I have to leave now," Ari said at the press conference, "just as I've finally figured out how to handle Helen Thomas." He took out a laser pointer. "Get the red dot, Helen! Get it!"

Helen chased the laser point. "That red dot is mine!" She eventually followed it until it made her jump out the window.

"So, any questions?" Ari asked as he put away the laser pointer.

"What's this we hear about 'Black Project Insano'?"

Ari fiercely grabbed the reporter. "WHO TOLD YOU?" Ari screamed at the top of his lungs. He then noticed everyone was looking at him with fright. He gently set the reporter back down and patted him on the shoulder. "I mean, what a ridiculous thing. I've never heard of any... whatever it was you just said. That's just some crazy fiction you probably read about in the *Weekly World News* or the *New York Times*."

"I have a question," said the FOX News reporter. "Iran is reportedly harboring al Qaeda terrorists, so why haven't we marched in there and hung those supposedly responsible by their own entrails? Is it because the Bush administration sympathizes with terrorists, or is it because you're all a bunch of homos?"

"Well... uh... the diplomatic way to do this..."

"And my follow-up question," she continued, "is whether you think it's apt to describe your departure from the Bush administration by using the analogy of rats fleeing a sinking ship... with one of those rats being grotesque and balding."

"Now you're just being mean," Ari said angrily. "And... and... are you wearing a bikini?"

"Producer's idea; these press conferences don't get very good ratings." She then listened to something coming in from her earpiece. "No, I'm not going to jump up and down when I ask questions!"

"You know, at CNN we have higher journalistic integrity," proudly said a CNN reporter.

"You're only talking to me like that because you know I don't have anywhere to conceal a gun!" the FOX News reporter shot back angrily. "We're the number one news channel for a reason." She listened to a new message coming from her earpiece. "No, I won't take my top off!"

A Secret Service agent walked up to Ari. "It's time."

"Uh, I'm going to go hide out in a five-mile-deep, underground shelter for no particular reason," Ari announced, "so this press conference is over."

"Maybe I'll mud wrestle another reporter," the FOX News reporter said as she listened to her earpiece, "but we have to renegotiate my contract first."

TO BE CONTINUED...

June 02, 2003

Black Project Insano Part II

"Buck the Marine here. Can anyone hear me?"

"I hear ya, Buck. This is the President of the United States, George Dubya, but as long as we're using the radio, refer to me by my CB handle: Porn Star."

"Okay, Porn Star. I have set up base camp in Lintuvia."

"Did you experience much resistance?"

"Well, when I first arrived, the Lintuvians said, 'What are you doing here, for'ner?' and then I said, 'I'm not a for'ner. You're the for'ners, for'ners.' You get that? The stupid for'ners didn't even know they were foreign. Anyway, they're dead now."

"Good job, Buck. Be careful of those Lintuvians; they're extremists."

"Religious extremists?"

"Maybe, I'm not really sure. They may actually be extremists against people with religion, or maybe they just like extreme sports. But we are certain they are extremists, and you need to be careful."

"I can tell you they ain't Christian extremists; Christians shoot straighter."

"So what is your condition right now?"

"Well, I set down to make base camp, so I opened my cooler I brought and took out a good ol' American beer. Then snipers started shooting at me, so I shot back at them, rifle in my right hand while I continued to drink the beer in my left hand. Then I remembered I had to radio you guys, which meant I had to put down either the rifle or the beer. I think I made the right choice." Buck paused to take a sip of beer.

"Sounds like you got a handle on things. Soon people will be there to implement Black Project Insano. Whatever you do, do not look at what they have, as you do not have the proper clearance."

"To clarify, Porn Star, what am I supposed to not be looking at?"

"Uh... I'm not really sure. But if you see something that you think you shouldn't be seeing, stop seeing. Is that clear?"

Buck took another sip of beer.

"Good luck, Buck. We're counting on you. Porn Star is over and out."

A sniper shot hit near Buck, so he put down the radio and picked back up his M-16 and fired back while finishing off his beer. That seemed to be the last of them; there were no for'ners left to shoot. Suddenly Buck noticed a number of men in black suits and sunglasses approaching him.

"Are you for'ners?" Buck asked suspiciously.

"That's classified," answered one of the men.

"Hey, that thing you guys are carrying has some rust on it," Buck pointed out.

"He's seen too much!" one of the men said to another.

"What'd I do now?" Buck asked, confused.

"Put him in the target radius," one of the men in black said as they operated the device.

"Hey, that don't sound like a good thing..." Buck started to say but then saw a bright light followed by nothingness.

* * * *

"Wow, I've never seen this room before!" Bush exclaimed as he explored the underground war room. "What do these buttons do?" he asked as he reached for a control panel.

Condoleezza Rice slapped his hand. "That's why I haven't let you down here. Now go sit at the conference table."

"Hey, I'm the president," Bush said meekly. "I tell you what to do—"

"QUIET!" Rice screamed.

Bush took a seat at the conference table along with Donald Rumsfeld, Colin Powell, and Ari Fleischer, who was busy playing at a computer in front of him. "They let you down here, Colin?" Bush asked with surprise.

"He knows how to behave," Rice said.

"As long as I don't speak, they don't hurt me," Powell explained.

"I'll strangle you for speaking!" Rumsfeld shouted.

"There is no time for strangling," Rice said, sitting at the head of the table. "It is time to discuss Black Project Insano."

"First off, though," Bush interrupted, "who is that mysterious-looking guy standing in the shadows smoking a cigarette?"

"Ignore him," Condoleezza answered.

"But he's creeping me out."

"Then he is doing his job," Rice said irately. "As I was saying, more details of Black Project Insano are becoming known. Bush, remember when the aliens visited at the beginning of your term?"

"Sure do. They decided that since we no longer had a lecherous hillbilly as our leader, they were ready to meet with us. They said they would share technology that would end disease, famine, and ketchup stains. Then Rumsfeld strangled them all because they looked funny."

"And I'd do it again," Rumsfeld vowed.

"Well, the secret hidden government within the US government took possession of the alien technology," Rice explained, "and then began reverse-engineering it to see if it could be used for evil instead of good. Thus was born Black Project Insano, and we finally have seen its results in Lintuvia."

On a giant screen appeared an image of the island country of Lintuvia. There was a bright light, and most of the country disappeared.

"What happened?" Bush asked.

"Apparently we ripped apart the very fabric of time and space itself," Rice said with glee, "and transported the Lintuvians into an alternate dimension!"

"What about Buck?" Rumsfeld asked.

"He saw too much and was transported as well," Rice said dismissively.

"But he was my favorite drinking buddy!"

"You fool!" Rice exclaimed. "Do you not realize how much more important this is than one silly Marine? We now control the fabric of the universe. We'll be able to instantly transport people anywhere in the world for a surprise attack and escape just as easily. We can also disappear entire cities, such as transporting the entire population of Paris into an alternate dimension, where they will be eaten by the Velociwargs and the Jangowizers."

"What's a Velociwarg and a Jangowizer?" Bush asked.

"Those are the names I will give to the first two creatures that eat French people," Rice answered. "Now, not only will we be able to conquer this world, but we'll be able to travel to other worlds as well, conquering and uniting an uncountable number of planets into one nation ruled by one person alone." Rice rose to her feet. "Empress Condoleezza! All shall love me and despair!" She paused for a second. "I mean, all worlds will be united under the protection of the USA," she said meekly, sitting back down.

"I have just one question," Bush said, eyeing Rice with suspicion. "What about back in the fifties when everyone smoked? How would you be a mysterious guy who stood in the shadows? Would you *not* smoke a cigarette and be known as the 'Non-Smoking Man'?"

Rice shook her head with exasperation. "Why did I even involve you with this? This is all-important, highly classified material that must never leave this room. If even—"

"Sorry to interrupt," Laura Bush said, walking into the war room, "but I need to get the laundry."

"How did you get in here?" Rice demanded angrily. "You're not allowed through security!"

"Poppycock," Laura answered. "I always come down here to do the laundry." She opened a machine at the other end of the room and started pulling out pieces of clothing.

"Those aren't washing machines, you fool!" Rice screamed. "Those are matter destabilizers!"

"And they sure get the stains out," Laura commented.

"That's it!" Rice exclaimed. "Cyborg ninja monkey zombies, stop her! Yes... that's right, go toward her... now KILL! KILL! No... no... DON'T HELP HER FOLD!"

"I never heard anything about cyborg ninja monkey zombies," Bush said.

"It was a line item in the last budget I gave you," Rice said innocently.

"I've got my laundry, so I'm heading out," Laura announced. "The cookies I'm baking should be done soon; who wants some?"

"I do!" said the Cigarette-Smoking Man.

"You're not supposed to talk!" Rice exclaimed. "You're supposed to be mysterious!"

"But I want a cookie."

"Fools!" Rice screamed. "I'm surrounded by fools!"

"I know who is not getting a cookie," Laura said, giving a sharp glance to Rice before leaving the war room.

"This is so much crap," Rumsfeld finally commented. "All this inter-dimensional gobbledygook and whatnot is a fool's game. Give me a good old-fashioned war with shooting and stabbing."

"I wholeheartedly agree," Powell commented.

"You're not supposed to speak!" Rumsfeld shouted. "Rarr!"

Rice finally noticed Ari working busily at a computer. "What are you doing?"

"I always get bored by meetings," Ari said, "so I decided to play some Space Invaders."

"That's not a videogame!" Rice shouted. She then looked at his screen. "You've destroyed most of Luxembourg!"

"So?"

"So you have to go talk to the press and explain this," Rice told him.

"Yeah, stupid," Bush chided him.

"Whatever," Ari answered.

"And make sure they know nothing about our plotting!" Rice commanded him.

"Okie-dokie," Ari said as he left the room.

"Oh man; I'm outta smokes!" the Cigarette-Smoking Man exclaimed. "Can I bum one off someone?"

* * * *

"I see they let you wear clothes today," said the CNN reporter snidely.

"The producers and I came to an understanding," the FOX News reporter answered, fixing her blouse.

"If that skirt were any shorter, it would just be a frilly belt," the CNN reporter laughed.

"Oh, that's witty; you should share that with your *viewer*," the FOX News reporter shot back.

"People, can I have your attention," Ari Fleischer announced. "As you know, I am going to be leaving my post as White House Press Secretary soon, so I have two people here who will be trying out as my replacement."

"Yes, according to your press release, one had his former job as guard of a junkyard and has been diagnosed with severe anti-social personality disorder," pointed out one reporter.

"Yes," Ari answered, "you're referring to Chomps, rated by the Guinness Book of World Records as the world's angriest dog."

The Rottweiler Chomps simmered in his irrational fury, looking ready to explode at any moment into an orgy of violence.

"And you describe the other candidate as, quote, 'A fat load of crap who makes sham documentaries and, as hard as it is to believe, is actually uglier on the inside than on the outside.'"

"You're talking about Michael Moore," Ari said, pointing to Michael Moore himself, who stood near Chomps.

"And I'm going to tell the truth about the fiction that is the Bush administration," Moore blurted. "I'm going to... AHH!!! GET HIM OFF ME!!!"

Chomps attacked Michael Moore as if the devil himself was in him.

"AHH! THE PAIN!!!"

"Well, it's going to take Chomps a while to chew through that many layers of fat, so let's go on to questions," Ari said in a bored tone.

"OH!!! WHY WON'T HE STOP?!!"

"Did you just set this up so that Michael Moore could be attacked by the world's angriest dog?" asked a reporter suspiciously.

"Please stick to policy questions."

"I think... he stopped... AHH!!! HE GOT HIS SECOND WIND!!!"

"Michael Moore, what do you say to people who feel you deserve to be chewed on by the world's angriest dog?" the FOX News reporter asked Moore.

"PLEASE!!! SOMEONE HELP ME!!! DON'T JUST STAND THERE FILMING THIS!!!"

"Hey, questions go over here," Ari said angrily.

"Do you have any explanation for the sudden cruise missile attack on Luxembourg?"

"No. Not really."

The reporter thought about that for a moment. "Thank you for your candidness."

"What do you say to reports that you've sent a Marine to the small island country of Lintuvia in preparation for an experimental use of alien technology?"

Ari laughed unconvincingly for nearly a minute straight. "That... that is the craziest thing I've ever heard. Who, by the way, told you such a crazy thing? Because I would like to meet that person and say, 'Hey, you're one silly person.'"

"Well, I can't reveal my sources," the reporter answered.

"Even under threat of death?"

Two large men in black suits approached the reporter from both sides. "Well... uh..."

Suddenly there was a blinding flash of light. When it faded away, there was a ghostly image of a demonic face floating above Ari. "I am Lipitor!" it said in an earth-shaking voice. "Tyrant king of the multi-verse! You have disturbed my dimension, and now you will all pay dearly. I will destroy your world and make you all my slaves! There is nothing you can do to stop me! Muh ha ha ha ha!" The image then faded away.

"Dangit," Ari sighed. "You just know that right before I retire there is going to be an inter-dimensional incident."

"Will this conflict with Lipitor distract from Bush's war on terror?" asked one reporter.

"Has France the technology to appease evil dictators in alternate dimensions?" inquired another.

"Why haven't we collapsed threatening dimensions into a singularity?" demanded the FOX News reporter. "Is it because we lack the technology, or is it because the Bush administration is a bunch of momma's boys?"

"Where are my pills?" asked Helen Thomas.

"Everyone, let's calm down for a second," Ari told them. "Before we get on to answering more questions, let's first have a break for refreshments. Right now, a couple of men are handing out cherry-flavored beverages that may or may not erase your memories."

"Can I have one to forget this pain?" Moore asked meekly. "AHH! HOW LONG CAN HE KEEP BITING MY GROIN?!!"

"No, you can't have any," Ari answered.

"Mine has more of a raspberry taste," said one reporter.

"Just drink it!"

* * * *

"This is Buck the Marine," Buck said into his voice recorder. "The day is... Tuesday? I think Tuesday. The time is..." He looked at his wrist. "I cannot tell the time from the hairs on the back of my hand. Apparently I forgot my watch. Anyway, I have found myself on an alien landscape." He looked about him at the purple sky and yellow, rocky ground. Ominous mountains loomed in the distance, and strange creatures flew overhead. "Note to self: no longer accept missions where the objective is more complicated than 'Kill the foreign people.'"

"So, what are rules for engagement on an alien land?" Buck thought to himself as he put away his voice recorder. He then took out his *USMC Rules of Engagement* Manual. "'Rule one,'" he read aloud, "'Kill for'ners.' Hmm... I already knew that one. What about aliens?" He flipped through the small manual. "Here we go: 'When on an alien world, be extra careful. You cannot know how creatures may react, so it is best to try and avoid them. Only attack a creature if it appears it is about to attack you, or if it is just really, really freaky-looking.'"

Buck looked around. Overhead flew a creature resembling a manta ray. "That's not attacking me," he mused aloud, "and it's only somewhat freaky-looking, so I'll let it live."

A large lizard-like creature charged Buck, mouth agape and full of sharp teeth. "Now that's just mildly freaky-looking, but it appears to be attacking me... so it dies." Buck fired his M-16 at it, dropping it dead.

Near him he saw a giant animal, its body like that of a brontosaurus, but its head like that of a toucan. "Now that is pretty danged freaky-looking, but honestly not really, really freaky-looking, so I'll let it live."

Below him he saw a bug with three heads, each one with snapping pinchers. It also had bat-like wings and the tail of a mouse. "Now, that is not attacking me, but it is really, really freaky-looking." He crushed it with his rifle butt. "Now it's dead. Ooh-rah!"

"Greetings, outworlder," said a voice from behind Buck.

He turned to see three humanoid aliens, each with pale skin and large black eyes. "Greetings, alien creatures," Buck responded, "I am Buck the Marine from the planet America. I come in peace, but as you see, I am well-armed in case non-peace breaks out. In summary, I will talk to you, but if you make any sudden movements, I'll kill you all."

"We understand your terms, outworlder," answered one of the aliens. "We have come to warn you of a threat to your world."

"A threat to my world?!" Buck exclaimed. "That's bad!"

"Yes, it is," the alien continued. "The evil tyrant Lipitor wishes to destroy your world and put you all in slavery. It is up to you to stop him."

"Just tell ol' Buck what to do."

"You must travel the trail of despair to Lipitor's citadel, which rests on the edges of many dimensions. Inside you will find his trans-dimensional oscillator, and through its deactivation will Lipitor become vulnerable to the plasmic discharges within his inner sanctum. When he is weakened, then you can destroy his stronghold by overloading its stabilizers with positronic energy. Finally, you must escape to your dimension through a dimensional portal of your proper dimensional frequency."

Buck considered this for a moment and then took a sip of beer. "Why don't you break that down into pointing me in which direction I should walk and describing what thing I'm supposed to kill."

"You must head that way," one of the aliens said, pointing to a dark fortress in the distance. "Your enemy, Lipitor, is a trans-dimensional being, both massive and small, both there and not there. He is known by his presence, which disturbs the air with a—"

"On second thought," Buck interrupted, "why don't you just draw me a picture."

TO BE CONCLUDED...

June 04, 2003

Black Project Insano Part III

"Until this whole inter-dimensional mess is taken care of, you better lay low in your new undisclosed location," President Bush told Dick Cheney through their satellite uplink.

"It's not an undisclosed location!" Cheney said angrily. "You just stranded me on the median of some highway."

"Yeah, but do you know which highway?" Bush pointed out.

"No, I can't tell from here, but everyone driving by gawking at me probably knows."

"Well, stop looking so conspicuous. Dig a hole or something."

"But I'm in a three piece suit... and it's hot out!" Cheney yelled. "Ah! And someone just threw a beer bottle at me. And now I'm tasting copper..."

Bush cut the link. "Whine, whine, whine."

"Honey, there's an article in this month's issue of *Today's First Lady* I want you to see," Laura Bush said, entering the office and placing a magazine on Bush's desk.

Bush grimaced. "This isn't another article about drapes, is it?"

"No, just read it."

Bush picked up the magazine. "'Signs a coworker may be a supervillain,'" Bush read aloud. "'Sometimes a close associate may be plotting world conquest, and you may not even notice. Here are some signs to look for:

"'One. Maniacal Laughter.'" Bush looked at Laura. "So, what is that, exactly?"

"Well, if someone, instead of laughing at other people's jokes, laughs after bold statements of power or evil," Laura explained.

"Kinda like how Condi tends to laugh when she explains the destructive power of a new weapon," Bush said.

"Yeah, that might be an example," Laura answered innocently.

"So what's next?" Bush looked at the article again. "'Two. Lives at an odd, isolated location.'" He turned to Laura. "Speaking of odd, you should see Condi's place. I went to the address, and there was a hollowed-out volcano. When I tried to find the entrance, I was attacked by ninjas."

"Look at item three," Laura pointed out.

"'Three. Is protected by hired thugs or ninjas.'" Bush thought for a moment. "Wait! I know what this is about! You're trying to convince me that Condi is a supervillain!"

"I don't trust that woman, George," Laura said sternly. "Last time Barbara and Jenna visited, I swear I saw her trying to hire them to be twin assassins."

Bush chuckled. "That's silly; you want identical twins for that."

"I think you need to stop that Black Project Insano," Laura told him. "I think it's giving Dr. Rice too much opportunity for evil and world conquest."

"What? How do you know about that secret project?" Bush exclaimed.

"You're always leaving your papers scattered everywhere, making me clean up after you," Laura chided him. "I bought you folders—even labeled them for you—but still there's paper lying everywhere."

"I'll try to be more organized in the future," Bush moaned.

"That's not what this is about," Laura said sternly. "You need to pull the plug on that project and stop Dr. Rice from taking over this world and countless others... or before she gets us destroyed by some evil alien warlord."

"But... but if I make her mad, she may feed me to a Krackeldozer," Bush said timidly.

"What's a Krackeldozer?"

"That's the name she said she's going to give to the alien creature she'll feed me to if I bother her while she's plotting."

"It doesn't matter, George, you're the President of the United States, and you have to stand up to her," Laura told him firmly. "Didn't the American people elect a president with character who will stand up for what he believes?"

"I have plenty of character," Bush insisted. "Why, compared to the last president—"

"Oh, George," Laura interrupted angrily, "why don't you just say you're a champion runner by comparing yourself to a man without legs. Now you'd better go talk to Dr. Rice, or you're going to be spending a lot of time sleeping on the couch like that 'last president' you love to bring up."

Laura then left the room, leaving Bush to think by himself. "Aw, dangit," Bush grumbled, "better at least make sure my will is in order first."

* * * *

Laughter echoed throughout the room. "You're a clever adversary, Buck," the disembodied voice of Lipitor said. "You've broken into my fortress. Still, if you had any real intelligence, a mortal such as you would never dare to contend with a god such as me. Now that you are in my lair, you will find yourself in situations that will challenge your very understanding of physics itself."

"My understanding of what now?" Buck asked, taking another sip of beer.

"Do not mock me, Buck," Lipitor said angrily. "I will rip you apart, scattering your pieces among countless universes."

Buck stared a while at his can of beer and then looked quite displeased.

"Is that fear I see, Buck?"

"That was my last beer." He tossed it away and saw it torn asunder by an unseen force. Buck looked around with some confusion. There were glowing portals among doors and windows floating in nothingness. At times the room appeared quite small, and then he looked at it from another angle, and it seemed infinitely huge. He really wanted another beer.

"Better go to my all-purpose plan B," Buck announced. "Throw grenades everywhere and see what blows up."

* * * *

Bush knocked on the door of Condoleezza Rice's office. "Can we talk for a moment?"

"I'm busy with military matters," Rice answered with annoyance. "Why don't you go watch your *A-Team* reruns?"

"Uh... we really need to talk now."

"You're starting to bother me," Rice said, a bit of menace in her voice.

Bush took a deep breath then barged right into her office. Rice stared at him angrily as a map of the world with attack plans sat on her desk. Bush then glanced behind him to see the mysterious Cookie-Eating Man standing in the shadows. "Uh... I had a whole speech prepared about how we shouldn't fool around with the fabric of time and space," Bush said nervously, "but I was distracted by a squirrel on the way here and forgot it all. So I'll just cut to the chase: I'm going to shut down Black Project Insano."

"Why? Don't you see the power it gives us?"

"Well, that whole thing with that alien warlord appearing and threatening us..."

"Bah, Lipitor is a fool," Rice said dismissively. "I'll find a way to defeat him." She rose to her feet. "Then the multi-verse will be MINE!"

"See, there's the other thing," Bush said. "I think you're becoming too drunk with power and are not pursuing all this for the interests of the American people."

Rice laughed unconvincingly as she sat back down. "That's ridiculous."

"Well, my decision is final," Bush said, trying to look resolute. "Black Project Insano will be shut down."

Rice laughed again, this time more insidiously. "You don't even know which phony orphanage it's funded through to be able to shut it down."

"Well... well I'll... I'll de-fund *all* orphanages then, smarty-pants."

Rice shot to her feet again. "You can't do that!"

"Yes I can," Bush said firmly, "because I'm the President of the United States, the leader of the free world, and I can do anything."

"You fool! I'll destroy you!"

"Oh, and come to think of it," Bush added, "I'm taking your Snoopy mug as well." Bush snatched the mug from her desk.

"But... but... that's *my* Snoopy mug! You can't just take it!"

"Yes I can," Bush asserted, "because I'm the President of the United States, and I can do whatever I want. Good day, Dr. Rice." He then headed out of the office.

"Bring back Snoopy!" Rice shouted. She then became intensely angry. "You'll rue the day you ever heard the name Condoleezza!"

"Can I go now?" asked the Cookie-Eating Man.

"Yes, you're getting crumbs everywhere."

* * * *

The fortress crumbled as the demonic Lipitor stood there surrounded in flames. "I guess I underestimated you, Buck. First you broke into my fortress, solved the puzzles of the room of eternity, snuck into the kitchen and ate my lunch, and finally destroyed the stabilizers that kept my fortress existing between the universes."

"Yep, don't mess with a United States Marine," Buck answered, finishing off his four-dimensional sandwich.

"But the last laugh will be mine!" shouted Lipitor. "When my fortress is gone, you will be trapped with me forever in the void between dimensions. Muh ha ha ha!"

"You must flee to the portal to your world," said a voice in Buck's head.

"Is that Jesus?"

"No, it's one of us aliens talking to you telepathically."

"Doing what now?"

"Talking through your mind," the alien said with annoyance. "Now go through the inter-dimensional portal to your home world."

"Uh... and what's that exactly?"

"Go into the bright light to your right!"

"Okay, okay. You don't have to telo-mathematically yell," Buck said, heading out of the crumbling fortress.

"Your other right!" the voice shouted.

"Oh, whoops." Buck jumped into the glowing portal.

"I will have my revenge!" he heard Lipitor shout, just before the world around Buck disappeared.

* * * *

"Seventeen. Eighteen. Nineteen." Rumsfeld cocked his hand back really far for the last punch. "And twenty!" He dropped the reporter to the ground. "I hope that answered your question about whether the war in Iraq was started for false pretenses. If you didn't understand the answer, I could repeat."

The reporter just moaned in response.

Suddenly a bright light appeared in the air, and out of it fell Buck the Marine.

"Buck, you're back!" Rumsfeld exclaimed. "What happened?"

"Well, I was transported to an alien world where I killed me some freaky aliens, and then I went to the fortress of this evil warlord Lipitor who wanted to conquer Earth. I destroyed his fortress, casting him forever into the void, escaped back to my dimension, and then, having preserved American values and apple pie from the cold grip of alien forces, I shouted, 'Ooh-rah.'" Buck thought for a moment. "No, wait; I hadn't done that last part yet." He held his rifle over his head. "OOH-RAH!"

"Good job, Buck," Rumsfeld said. "And you're back just in time for happy hour. Now let's go get hammered and pick some country to invade through conventional means, forgetting forever this inter-dimensional crap."

"But we have more questions!" whined one of the reporters.

"Buck, fire your rifle into the air," Rumsfeld suggested. "That should scatter them."

Buck fired a three-round burst into the air, and the reporters fled in terror, except for one woman who held her ground. "Who's that?" Buck asked.

"That's the FOX News reporter," Rumsfeld explained. "She's a little harder to scare away." Rumsfeld then clapped his hands loudly in front of her face. "Now shoo! Scram!"

"But I have more questions about whom America will destroy next with its righteous power," she asserted.

"Hey, that's a nice dog you have with you," Buck commented.

"Oh, that's Chomps," she said. "He's been following me around since the last press conference. Problem is, I have too busy a schedule to take care of a dog."

"Well, I could see why he would want to follow around a pretty lady such as yourself," Buck said a bit shyly.

"That's so sweet," the FOX News reporter replied, blushing.

"Maybe we could go get some coffee, and I could tell you all about how I saved the world," Buck suggested.

"I think I'd like that."

The two of them walked off.

"What about alcohol?!" Rumsfeld called out. He then looked at the dog. "I guess it's just me and you, Chomps. Know what? I'm suddenly feeling angry for no particular reason. What about you?"

"Erg-err!" Chomps growled angrily and ripped a metal folding chair apart with his teeth.

"I guess you and I are a lot alike," Rumsfeld said, walking to the exit. Outside he saw a bunch of hippy protestors with anti-war signs. "Well, looky here. Maybe we should match their right to free speech with our initiative to inflict pain."

"Rah-grr!" Chomps said, not liking the sight of hippies.

"Hey, dog, no blood for oil!" one hippy yelled at Chomps.

Chomps's whole body started shaking with anger. Rumsfeld was almost afraid the dog was going to explode. Suddenly, with a loud yell, Chomps jumped into the crowd of hippies, flying forward with his mouth wide open and ready to bite.

"That's a good dog," Rumsfeld said with a smile and then ran into the fray. "Rarr!"

THE END

June 09, 2003

White House Press Secretary Had Built Up Many Sick Days

White House Press Secretary Ari Fleischer was less forthcoming than usual in his latest press conference.

"What is the White House's opinion on the Palestinian prime minister?"

"Wow, the Palestinians have a prime minister now?" Ari exclaimed.

"Yeah, don't you know that?"

"Know what, I think I remember Jon Stewart mentioning it on the *Daily Show*."

"Well, aren't you privy to special information in the White House meetings?"

"Yeah, but I haven't been to one in a while; I'm trying to use up all my sick days before I leave in July."

"So why are you holding this press conference?" demanded one reporter.

"I'm not holding a press conference," Ari said indignantly. "I just sat down to read the latest issue of *Maxim*, and then you guys gathered around me."

"Well, do you have any comment on how American forces have not found any WMDs?"

"We did find some!" Ari shot back, laying down his *Maxim* and standing up. He held out a vial of green liquid. "Here is the chemical agent XL-6 we just got back from Iraq. It quickly becomes airborne, causing a painful death by—" Ari accidentally dropped the vial, shattering it. "Oh my goodness!" he exclaimed, covering his mouth. "We're all going to die!"

The reporters looked terrified, but Ari started laughing. "It was filled with Mountain Dew. I've been playing that gag on people all day." He sat back down and started reading his magazine again.

"I have a question," said the FOX News reporter. "I just did an exposé on how many different countries there are and how the number of foreign nations is a threat to our national security. Is the White House doing anything to reduce the number of other countries?"

"Is this you?" Ari asked, holding open his magazine to a picture of a woman in lingerie.

"No!" the FOX News reporter answered angrily. She then looked more carefully at the picture. "Oh, wait, yes it is... but you still have to answer my question."

"I don't have to do anything," Ari answered.

"You said you had measles!" yelled one voice from the crowd. Ari turned to see it was President Bush.

"So I lied; what are you going to do about it?" Ari challenged.

"Uh..." Bush thought for a moment. "I'll have you executed for treason!"

"Whatever," Ari said dismissively as he went back to reading his magazine.

"Why do you want to kill Iraqi children?" Helen Thomas asked Bush.

"Because they smell!" Bush sprinkled salt on her. "Why won't you finish shriveling up?"

"Ahh! A voodoo hex!" Helen exclaimed, running away.

"Why haven't you found any WMDs?" one reporter asked Bush.

"We have plenty of WMDs," Bush answered. "Heck, we have enough nukes to kill everyone on earth."

"I meant found WMDs in Iraq," the reporter clarified.

"Oh... why would we need to find WMDs there?" Bush asked. "We just went there to steal their oil." He saw Ari shaking his head. "Uh... I got confused. We're currently preparing a military strike against North Korea for the oil stealing."

"You're going to attack North Korea?" one reporter said with surprise.

"Uh... why? Is that a good or a bad thing?" Bush asked, getting nervous. All the reporters now crowded around him and shouted questions at him. "Darn you, Ari!" Bush exclaimed. "That's why you're supposed to do all the talking!"

"Sick with measles," Ari answered, flipping through his magazine.

Bush spied a man jogging down the street near them. "Uh... that guy over there is the replacement," Bush said, pointing at him. "Ask him the questions."

The press swarmed the surprised man while Bush made a quick escape into a nearby manhole.

"Going to miss this job," Ari sighed.

June 11, 2003

Chomps, The World's Angriest Egg Timer

With North Korea theatening to get nukes for numerous crazy reasons and Islamic extremists continuing to threaten to kill Americans and Jews for far-from-coherent reasons, Secretary of Defense Donald Rumsfeld held a press conference to answer concerns.

"These press conferences are taking too long, and my doctor says I need to keep them short so that I don't have so much time to fester with rage," Rumsfeld explained. "Thus I have brought my friend Chomps, the world's angriest dog, and chained him to the wall."

At the front wall was a massive Rottweiler, furiously chewing away at the metal chain that bound him.

"That chain is made of reinforced steel," Rumsfeld continued, "so it will take him about ten minutes to chew through. I recommend you all have asked your questions and left by then if you don't wish to be eviscerated."

"I have a question about finding WMDs in Iraq," said a reporter as he stepped forward while cautiously eyeing Chomps.

"Let me help you save your breath," Rumsfeld answered. "I don't give a rat's ass."

"But people are concerned that this war was entered into for false reasons."

"What people? Bad people are dead, people are free from tyranny. No *American* would be concerned about the reasons for attacking. Sounds to me more like something Europeans would be worried about." Rumsfeld grinded his teeth. "I hate Europeans!"

"Grr-row!" Chomps growled at the mention of Europeans and then went back to chewing angrily at his chain.

"So you don't think people care whether a conflict was started for legitimate reasons?"

"Americans like killing bad people," Rumsfeld answered. "We're all for making up all sorts of excuses as long as bad people die in the end. If I claimed we were invading North Korea because they had imprisoned magical elves, and then we destroyed their evil regime and freed their starving, oppressed people, would you guys still whine about where the elves are afterwards while the Koreans celebrated in the streets?"

The reporter thought about that. "Yes, we would."

"Rarr!" Rumsfeld yelled, picking up the reporter and throwing him out the window. "Next question."

"What about those in the military who were sent overseas?" asked another reporter. "Don't they need to know the reasons they were sent to Iraq were legitimate?"

"As long as our troops get to kill bad people, they're happy," Rumsfeld replied. "It's not like anyone joined the military to not kill evil foreigners." Rumsfeld looked at Buck the Marine, who stood at the far end of the room. "Did you join the Marines to not kill evil foreigners?"

"Quite the opposite, sir."

"See?" Rumsfeld said smugly.

"North Korea says they need nuclear weapons so they can reduce the size of their military. What is your response to that?"

"I would like to remind North Korea that we also have a plan for reducing the size of their military that involves nukes. Next question."

"What would you say to those who characterize the Iraq mission as a failure since no WMDs were found and Saddam may still be alive?"

"Grr-row!" Chomps growled as he lunged at the reporter, the chain barely holding him back. His massive jaws snapped at empty air, making a hideous clicking sound. He then went back to the chain, chewing at it now with even more irrational fury.

"I don't have anything to add to Chomps's remarks," Rumsfeld stated.

"What is your reaction to Israel's botched assassination attempt on Hamas co-founder Abdel Aziz al-Rantisi?"

"Well, we've missed people in the past," Rumsfeld answered, "so I can't be too critical. Next time, if they think a terrorist is in a building, they should level the entire block. I demand more dead Palestinians!"

"Isn't the Bush administration against the attack?"

"I don't listen to those whiny pacifists," Rumsfeld said angrily. "They want pin-point accuracy destruction, while I support barely-focused carnage."

"What about—"

A loud metallic snap resonated throughout the room. There stood Chomps, a piece of chain now uselessly dangling from his collar. In his fevered dog brain, he could no longer recall exactly why he was angry, but he was quite certain that he was angry, and his eyes scanned the room for something to take vengeance upon. They soon settled on the horrified reporters, and the back of his lips curled to reveal jagged teeth. Drool dripped to the floor as he recalled the sweet taste of blood. A low growl emanated from his throat, in its own way resembling the hiss of a fuse to a powder keg that is about to explode.

"I'm sorry," Rumsfeld chuckled to the reporters, "but it looks like your time is up."

June 16, 2003

Nuke the Moon!

George and Laura Bush stood out on the balcony admiring the night sky. "It's a full moon," Laura said, cuddling close to Bush. "Isn't it beautiful?"

"Why?"

"What do you mean, 'Why?'"

"Well, it's just some big floating rock... that glows. Why's it glow? Is it radioactive?"

"That's just the sun reflecting off it, George," Laura explained.

"But sometimes it's dark over parts, like it's trying to hide something," Bush said, looking at the moon suspiciously. "And we always see the same face! What's it trying to hide on the other side?"

"George," Laura scolded, "the moon should make you feel romantic, not paranoid!"

"I saw something move!" Bush exclaimed. "I saw something move on the moon!"

Laura sighed. "No you didn't."

"I better alert everyone!" Bush said and then ran off.

"I'll leave a blanket and pillow for you on the couch!" Laura called out to him before storming back into the White House.

* * * *

"How certain are you that you saw something move on the moon?" Condoleezza Rice asked, pacing the floor of the war room.

Bush squinted his eyes and said in an ominous voice, "Not very."

"Then I recommend we immediately nuke the moon!" Rice responded.

"What do you think, Rumsfeld?" Bush inquired.

"I don't give a rat's ass!" he answered angrily. "I want to attack another Middle Eastern country! I hate this piddling crap!"

"Rumsfeld seems to be opposed," Bush said, thinking it over. "I better ask Cheney." He turned on the satellite hookup to Cheney. "How is your undisclosed location?"

"It's not an undisclosed location!" Cheney yelled angrily. "I'm dangling by a rope from the Brooklyn Bridge!"

"So what do you think about nuking the moon?"

"I can't hear you," Cheney answered. "Ahh! The wind's picking up." He blew off camera.

"No use talking to him," Bush said. "Where's Rover?"

"I'm here," Karl Rove said, emerging from the shadows. "A fire on the moon was prophesied by the elders. It will precede the fall of the Democrats."

"Coo'. But I better get another military opinion. General Tommy Franks, I understand you have some military experience."

"Yes, and I can also juggle. Watch." General Franks picked up three apples from a fruit basket on the conference table and started juggling.

Bush was still skeptical. "Hmm, but can you juggle four things at once?" He tossed an orange at Franks.

Franks caught it uneasily at first but was soon juggling all four items quite smoothly.

"Wow!" Bush exclaimed. "Everyone listen to what this man has to say!"

General Franks tossed all the items back into the basket. "I think there is a great tactical advantage to nuking the moon. It tells terrorists and other enemies that there is no hiding from us, even in the heavens."

"So, Condi, how many people do you think will be killed by this nuclear strike?" Bush inquired.

"I estimate zero casualties," Rice answered, "give or take two million."

Bush considered this carefully. "Sounds acceptable."

"I'd just like to point out," Colin Powell interrupted, "that the moon doesn't actually pose any threat, and the use of nuclear weapons could have high costs diplomatically."

"Thanks for the opinion," Bush said. He then looked at his Secret Service agents. "Take Powell away and zap him with tasers."

"Hey!" Powell exclaimed as the Secret Service dragged him away.

"That was very decisive of you," Rove commented.

"Thanks, but I'm still not sure about this whole nuking idea."

A man in a black suit with a black tie and black sunglasses approached. "I have some information that may help," he said.

"Who are you?"

"I'm Clancy, from one of the intelligence agencies."

"Which one?"

"You'd have never heard of it; it's too secret," Clancy answered and handed a folder to Bush. "This intelligence was gathered at great risk; many of our best agents got paper cuts compiling this report."

There were drawings of some astronaut uniforms. "What is this?"

"This is the conceptual design for the uniform the Chi-Coms will use to walk on the moon," Clancy answered.

"What's the weird thing at the mouth?"

"That's a special airlock that allows them to shoot saliva from their helmets while on the moon."

Bush thought about this for a moment, and then a terrible thought struck him. "They're planning to spit on the American flag we put on the moon!" Bush exclaimed.

"Precisely," Clancy answered.

"We can't let the Commies spit on our flag!" General Franks exclaimed. "We need to nuke the moon to keep them from ever thinking of landing on it."

Bush was silent in contemplation for a moment. "Do we dare to reach to the heavens and heavily radiate them?" he mused allowed. "Will we boldly blow up what no man has exploded-ed before?" He caught the eyes of everyone in the room with steely resolve. "I say it's time to be pioneers. Let's nuke the moon!"

A big portion of the table was ripped away from under Bush. It was Chomps, the world's angriest dog, who proceeded to bite the piece of table into smaller and smaller pieces.

"I told you not to bring your dog in here!" Bush shouted at Rumsfeld.

"I left him outside," Rumsfeld said. "He must have chewed through the steel door again."

"Have you at least been giving him his pills to control his severe paranoid schizophrenia?"

"I've tried," Rumsfeld said. "The vet told me it would be suicide to try and force the pills down his throat, but I think I found a good way to get him to take them. I give them to a hippy, telling him they're psychedelic drugs. Then when the hippy swallows them, I sic Chomps on him."

The phone rang in front of Bush, and he answered. "Who is it?"

"It is I, the evil Commie dictator of China," the evil Commie dictator of China answered, "and I warn you to drop your foolish plans to nuke the moon."

"What are you talking about?" Bush asked innocently.

"Don't lie to me, foolish American," answered the evil Commie Dictator of China. "If you try and stop us from going to the moon, there will be grave consequences!"

"Ha!" Bush answered. "You don't scare me. I don't care if you have brilliant tacticians like General Tso; we can kick your Commie butt any day. Now stay off our moon!" Bush hung up the phone. "Someone ratted us out to the Chinese!" he declared. He pointed a finger at Rumsfeld. "Was it you?"

"I'll murder you for accusing me! Rarr!" Rumsfeld shouted as he tried to leap across the table. The Secret Service stopped him.

"What about you, Buck the Marine?" Bush asked suspiciously.

"Only thing I have ever said to a for'ner is, 'You die now,'" Buck answered.

"How about you, Chinese guy with surveillance equipment hiding under the table?" Bush said, looking under the table. "You see anyone suspicious?"

He shrugged his shoulders innocently.

"Well, we better be prepared to take on the Chinese," Bush said. "General Franks, how many men do we have left to fight China?"

"I'm afraid all our forces are either in Afghanistan, in Iraq, or drunk off their asses," Franks answered.

"What about the gay guy who is always helping me out?" Bush asked. "Does he have any spare troops?"

"That's Tony Blair," Rice told him, "and he's not gay; he's British. And no, he has no spare forces."

"I guess it's up to you then, Buck," Bush told the Marine. "If things go sour, I want you to take out all the Chinese." He looked at Rice. "How many are there?"

"A billion."

Bush turned back to Buck. "Better take a billion rounds of ammunition with you, then... no, make that a billion and ten to be on the safe side."

"Uh... okay, sir," Buck answered dubiously and then looked at Rumsfeld.

"Just meet me at the bar after this meeting," Rumsfeld whispered to him. "He'll soon forget all about this."

Chomps jumped up on the table and began barking at the ceiling. He tried jumping toward it, his jaws snapping at the air.

"What's he doing?" Bush asked.

"I think he's trying to bite the ceiling," Rumsfeld said. "It must have made him angry somehow."

"Why?"

"I dunno," Rumsfeld answered, "but I tend to trust his judgment. Buck, eliminate the ceiling."

"Yes, sir." Buck emptied a thirty-round magazine into the ceiling. "Ooh-rah!"

Seeing that the ceiling was properly destroyed, Chomps lay down on the table and went to sleep.

"He can't sleep on the conference table!" Bush exclaimed.

"Well, don't try and wake him," Rumsfeld warned. "He'll rip off at least three of your limbs if you do."

"What's happening in here?" Senator Tom Daschle demanded.

"How'd you get in?" Bush asked.

"There was a big gaping hole chewed into the door," Daschle answered. "So what are you planning?"

"Important things like war," Bush answered. "That's why there is a 'No Democrats Allowed' sign out front. Don't you have some poor people to whine about or something?"

"I'm interested in war, too," Daschle replied. "I'm still waiting for your evidence of WMDs in Iraq."

"It's right here on the table," Bush said, walking over to Daschle.

"Where?" Daschle asked, looking closely at the table. "I don't see any."

"It's right... THERE!" Bush slammed Daschle's head into the table. The shaking of the table stirred Chomps, who looked at the two of them both groggily and angrily.

"Uh-oh."

* * * *

"The White House would like to wish Senator Daschle a speedy recovery from having both his legs and his left arm reattached," White House Press Secretary Ari Fleischer announced. "Also, we'd like to quash any rumors that we are about to nuke the moon."

"Uh... we haven't heard any rumors about your nuking the moon," said one reporter.

"Of course you haven't," Ari answered, "because that would just be silly."

"There are a number of places here on earth where people have said bad things about us," the FOX News reporter said. "Why haven't we nuked them?"

"I keep telling you there is a diplomatic process to things," Ari answered, "and... are you wearing a saucy french maid outfit?"

"The FOX News Channel refers to it as a saucy *freedom* maid outfit," she replied, shaking her feather duster at Ari. "My boss keeps pushing me to get better ratings for these boring press conferences."

"Oh, I thought you were just moonlighting at another job," Ari chuckled.

"I have a follow-up question," she said angrily. "What reflects more of the sun's light? The moon or your bald head?"

"Just ignore it, Ari; you're almost done with this job," Ari said to himself.

"Why does Bush want to kill the lunar children?" Helen Thomas asked. "What have the lunar children ever done to Bush?"

"There aren't any people on the moon, you crazy old woman," Ari shot back. "Then again, maybe you do have relatives up there since you were probably around when the moon first formed by splitting off from the earth."

"I believe in the condensation hypothesis about the moon's formation," Helen answered.

"You would believe that discredited theory, you old hag!" Ari looked at his watch. "Now excuse me while I shield my eyes from the moon for no real reason."

* * * *

George and Laura Bush stood out on the balcony admiring the night sky. A mushroom cloud was just visible rising from the top of the moon. "Isn't it beautiful?" Bush said.

"Why?"

"What do you mean, 'Why?'"

"You nuked the moon, George," Laura said irately. "Why is that beautiful?"

"It's the ultimate combination of the glory of nature and the ingenuity of man," Bush answered.

"How?"

"Uh... well, it's a big explosion on the moon, and it's romantic... just like the movie *The Matrix*."

"I didn't find the movie *The Matrix* romantic," Laura said angrily.

"But you were all over me while we were watching it."

"That's because I was bored and wanted something else to do."

"So is the nuclear explosion boring you, too?" Bush asked, winking at her slyly.

Laura rolled her eyes. “Put on your flight suit and meet me in the bedroom.”

“Woo-hoo!”

June 18, 2003

The Rumsfeld Strangler vs. Mayor Crackhead

Rumsfeld didn't know where Chomps got his copy of *Living History* by Hillary Rodham Clinton, but there appeared to be a couple of drops of blood on it. Chomps, being the world's angriest dog, could have easily shredded the book to pieces in seconds, but instead he destroyed it slowly and methodically, seemingly enjoying the careful destruction of each and every page. Every once in a while Chomps looked up from the book to view the sidewalk that raced by and get angry at whatever he saw, be it a man, a squirrel, or a mailbox, but then he would turn his attention back to the demolition of the book and calm down a bit. It looked as if he were saving the picture of Hillary on the cover for last.

"Doctor says I need to get more exercise to help control my rage," Rumsfeld told Chomps as he drove his Buick through the streets of DC. "So I was thinking, what better way to get some exercise than vigilante justice?" Rumsfeld petted Chomps on the head. "You up for killing some street punks?"

Chomps barked in approval. His happy expression was short-lived, though, because he soon saw a trashcan that completely enraged him. "Erg-row!"

"Save it for the street punks, Chomps," Rumsfeld told him. "We can take our anger out on inanimate objects any day." Rumsfeld stopped his car, pulled over to the curb, and started looking around. "Now all we need are some criminals. Wouldn't think they'd be hard to find in DC."

"Nice car, old man," said one carjacker, pointing a Glock at Rumsfeld.

"Here we go," Rumsfeld smiled.

Chomps immediately leapt over and snatched the gun with his mouth. He crushed it with his mighty jaws and swallowed the pieces.

"Now you did it!" Rumsfeld said angrily. "Chomps can't properly digest composites, so he's probably going to vomit all over the carpet when we get home." Rumsfeld's hand shot out, and he lifted the man up by the neck. "Rarr!"

* * * *

"For the third night in a row, the Rumsfeld Strangler has struck, killing multiple criminals in the DC inner city," Anchorwoman Jane Eyrehead announced. "We sent reporter Jack Assman to see if Secretary of Defense Donald Rumsfeld had any reaction to this killer who has been using his name. Rumsfeld gave the cryptic response, 'I'm the one who killed those people, you retard.' Assman was later found dead, having apparently been ripped apart by an extremely angry dog."

"He will be missed," Anchorman Ron Goodhair commented.

"Not really, Ron," Jane replied. "He was a bit of a jerk."

"That's true. Anyway, these killings of criminals are threatening to bring law and order to a city where it's unwanted. To address this issue, DC Mayor Xander Crackhead has called a press conference, which we now go to live."

"Citizens of DC," Mayor Crackhead announced, "this city has long been a safe haven for criminals, a place where they could mug and kill without worry of injury. We've kept law-abiding citizens from owning handguns and carrying cudgels, and we've limited them to the most innocuous pepper sprays. We've even banned Nuke the Moon t-shirts since they might intimidate criminals. We've had a near perfect utopia for criminals, but now this 'Rumsfeld Strangler' has upset that. Criminals are afraid to mug people and thus unable to bring home the money they need to feed their drug habits. Well, I assure you, this mayor won't stand idly by while people strangle our treasured street punks. From now on, shoelaces and piano wires are banned from DC. Plus, all citizens are required to wear mittens so they will be unable to use their hands for the purposes of strangling."

"This is Killer Charlie from the Muggers' Union," spoke up one man. "Will these new laws affect the criminal community in any way?"

"No," Mayor Crackhead answered firmly. "As always, criminals are not expected to follow any of these laws; only law-abiding citizens are expected to disarm. If any criminal finds himself being defended against by an otherwise law-abiding citizen, that criminal should immediately report such incident to the police. The District of Columbia will not tolerate people defending themselves. The police have been instructed to crack down on law-abiding citizens carrying anything that could be used as a weapon. If any criminal is stopped by police, though, he should immediately identify himself as a law-breaker so that police know he is supposed to have weaponry and to leave him alone."

"Will there be any extra effort to catch the Rumsfeld Strangler before he delivers street justice again?" a reporter asked.

"Yes there will be," Mayor Crackhead asserted. "I'll have my consultant, Drug Dealer Eddie, explain our strategy." The mayor looked around. "Where is Drug Dealer Eddie?"

"He's dead!" exclaimed one of the mayor's aides.

Everyone rushed over to the body of Drug Dealer Eddie, which lay still on the ground. On the body was a business card with the words, "Strangled by your friendly neighborhood Secretary of Defense, Donald Rumsfeld."

* * * *

"The criminal community is my main constituency!" Mayor Crackhead exclaimed. "If I can't keep them safe from justice, they'll find an even more incompetent crack junkie to elect as mayor!"

"Don't be so hard on yourself; not everyone can be Marion Barry," T-Bone, Mayor Crackhead's right-hand man, assured him.

"We need to find this 'Rumsfeld Strangler' and stop him! Muggings is one of the foundations of our city's economy; we can't have this vigilante justice destroying that."

"Maybe we could set a trap?" T-Bone suggested.

"Yes, a trap," Mayor Crackhead said, savoring the thought. "We will leave out some bait he can't resist, and then he will be ours. Muh ha ha ha ha!"

* * * *

Rumsfeld banged the teenager's head into the lamppost one last time. "So... has having your head repeatedly slammed into a metal lamppost taught you not to jaywalk anymore?" Rumsfeld asked.

"Yes, sir," the kid said before running off.

"Where are all the real criminals?" Rumsfeld complained to Chomps. "We didn't scare them all off, did we?"

"Grr-rah!" Chomps growled as he attacked a nearby building, ripping a brick out of its side.

"That building making you angry, boy?" Rumsfeld asked, going toward the front door for a look. Inside he spied two hippies.

"Let's smoke pot and protest the war!" suggested one.

"Yeah, that's a great idea!" said the other.

"I'm going to go in and strangle those two hippies," Rumsfeld told Chomps, who continued to attack the foundation of the building. "You stay here, since I'm the one who is supposed to be getting the exercise."

Rumsfeld approached the two hippies who stood at the center of a large room, his hands readying for a strangling. But as soon as he reached them, they both turned and produced shotguns. Rumsfeld looked around and found himself completely surrounded by hoodlums and thugs, all pointing their guns at him.

"Well, I should have known," laughed Mayor Xander Crackhead. "The Rumsfeld Strangler was Donald Rumsfeld himself all along. What made you think you could dispense justice in *my* city?"

"I have a doctor's note saying I need exercise," Rumsfeld answered, holding up a piece of paper. It was shot from his hand.

"You going to strangle us all, old man?" laughed one of the thugs.

"Only the lucky ones," Rumsfeld answered, the rage boiling inside.

"And don't expect your dog to help you," Mayor Crackhead said with faux sympathy. "I have one of my men putting that beast out of its misery right now."

There was the sound of a gunshot and a pain-filled yelp. Rumsfeld looked in the direction of the sound with intense worry.

"Does Rumsfeld miss his little friend?" Mayor Crackhead asked in a mocking tone.

"No," Rumsfeld answered. Suddenly the brick wall was knocked down, and there stood Chomps, a severed arm still clutching a Beretta hanging from his mouth. "It's just nothing pisses Chomps off like getting shot in the head with a 9mm."

"Stop them!" Mayor Xander yelled as he fled up some stairs.

Chomps immediately jumped at the nearest criminal and disappeared into a crimson mist. Rumsfeld used the distraction to spin around as he drew his twin .45s, shooting a number of punks as he ran for the stairs.

"I'll chase after Mayor Crackhead while you finish off everyone here," Rumsfeld called to Chomps as he headed up the stairs. He soon made it to the roof, where two thugs were waiting for him. He rolled away from their shots and then returned fire, the .45 slugs knocking them both backward off the building. Rumsfeld glanced up and saw Mayor Crackhead escaping in a helicopter.

"We'll meet again, Rumsfeld Strangler," Mayor Crackhead called out.

"You can bet on it," Rumsfeld swore as he reloaded his pistols.

Up behind him came Chomps, covered in blood. He started making some hacking noises, as if he were choking on something.

"What's the matter, boy?" Rumsfeld asked as he patted Chomps on the back.

Chomps coughed up a boot.

"That's my dog," Rumsfeld laughed, petting Chomps on the head.

Chomps panted happily, but then he saw a star in the sky that made him angry for some reason, so he tried to jump up and bite it. Rumsfeld wasn't sure which star it was that enraged Chomps so, but he vowed that one day future generations would destroy it.

* * * *

"A dozen criminals were found dead in an abandoned building this morning," anchorwoman Jane Eyrehead announced, "apparently killed by the Rumsfeld Strangler. He left new signatures this time, including bloody paw prints and large bites in the walls."

"That's right," anchorman Ron Goodhair added, "and now police have updated the profile of the Rumsfeld Strangler to a Latino woman with the ability to turn into a werewolf."

"A scary thought," Jane said. "Anyway, stay tuned after the break, when we will be joined by famous internet personality Glenn Reynolds, who will teach us how to turn a cute little puppy into a nutritious energy drink..."

June 23, 2003

Attack of the Belgians Part I

"There's nothing better than a game of golf, is there, Agent Smith?"

"I wouldn't know, President Bush," Secret Service Agent Smith answered. "I've never played. I just stand here in the sun and watch you. Rather asinine, if you ask me."

"Yep, nothing better than a good game of golf," Bush said as he adjusted his cowboy hat and then prepared for a swing.

"President Bush!" yelled out a voice.

Startled, Bush screwed up his swing, sending his ball into the brush. "Grrr!" Bush yelled. "Agent Smith, whoever just messed up my shot, I want you to inject him in the neck with that stuff that makes it look like he had a heart attack."

"That stuff ain't cheap, sir," Agent Smith reminded him.

"It was I who called out your name," said a sinister figure, "Chief Floopergibble of the Belgian International Police Force." More men in black uniforms emerged from the brush. "I, under the authority of Belgium, am placing you under arrest for lying about WMDs and having an illegal war with Iraq."

"Well, I guess we'll have to go peacefully," Bush said, dropping his golf club. "Wouldn't make much sense to... KILL THEM!" Bush drew his peacemaker while Agent Smith drew his Beretta, and they both started firing at the Belgians.

Nothing happened.

"What's the matter?" Bush asked desperately.

"Apparently they're too irrelevant," Agent Smith answered. "Our bullets are going right through them in search of more substantive targets."

"Darnit! This always happens when I'm finally making par!"

The Belgians closed in on them while laughing their evil Belgianian laughs.

* * * *

"The president has been captured by Belgians," Agent Smith announced.

"What?!" Condoleezza Rice exclaimed. "You lose him two more times, and you get a demerit!"

"Good," Rumsfeld said. "I think things will run smoother without him. There are a lot of terrorists out there who aren't getting any less terroristy..."

"We need to rescue the president," Rice insisted. She turned on the satellite connection to Dick Cheney. "The president has been captured by Belgians," Rice told him. "I think that means you're in charge."

"Good," Cheney answered, shivering. "Then I order all resources be used to find me. I'm on some mountain top and found shelter in a cave."

"Do you know which mountain?"

"No. But find me quickly," Cheney said desperately. "I think I saw a snowman. I didn't get a good enough look, but he may have been abominable. And I'm running out of ammo for my .357. So forget about the president and find me. I want—"

Chomps knocked the TV set down and tore it apart with his teeth. "He's never liked Cheney," Rumsfeld commented.

"He never likes anyone," Rice said.

"If you want my opinion," Rumsfeld said, "and you'll be getting it whether you do or not—this is all some plot from the Belgians to get nuked. And frankly, I think their plan is going to work." He looked at the map on the wall. "So where are they?"

"That's the problem," Rice said. "Belgium is so irrelevant that mapmakers stopped including it long ago."

Chomps jumped up and grabbed the map and tore it to pieces. "Yeah, destroy that useless map," Rumsfeld laughed.

"I have some intelligence that may help," Clancy told Rice. "We set up a number of surveillance devices on the Belgian embassy. At first, we thought they were speaking in some code language. Ended up, we were actually spying on the Swedes. That's when we went to Plan B. We spotted a Belgian diplomat visiting the UN and had one of our agents kick him the nuts, grab his briefcase, and run away. A simple but effective method." Clancy set a briefcase down on the table. "According to the documents inside, Bush is being held in the flying fortress of the tyrannical ruler of Belgium, Belgazor. They plan to put him on trial; they believe they have the authority to bring charges against anyone in the world."

"Those arrogant bastards!" Rumsfeld shouted. "Only America has that authority. We must kill them all!"

Chomps barked in approval and then tore out a section of a nearby wall.

"We'll need to send someone in to rescue the president," Rice said.

"I know who," Rumsfeld replied, picking up a phone. "Buck, do you want to kill some Belgians?"

There was a contemplative pause on the other end. "Sure," Buck the Marine finally answered. "They sound pretty foreign."

* * * *

"Captured by Belgians," Bush grumbled to himself. "This is almost as bad as when Carter was attacked by a rabbit."

"Things could be worse, chap," said a familiar voice. "At least we have plenty of chocolate and waffles to eat."

Bush looked into the other cell. "It's my gay friend Tony!" he exclaimed.

"Nice to see you, too," Tony Blair answered.

"So what did they arrest you for?"

"Said that I made a wide right turn," Blair answered, "so they kidnapped me and brought me here."

"Should have been more careful driving," said an ominous voice. There stood Belgazor, the evil, bloated ruler of Belgium, a giant crown upon his head. "Now we will dispense justice upon you."

Bush noticed that Belgazor had his cowboy hat in hand. "You give me my hat back, or I'll murder you dead!" Bush yelled as he tried to reach for Belgazor's throat through the bars.

"I'd worry more about your trial," Belgazor said. "First comes Tony Blair's trial for his reckless driving, then you for your illegal war, then me for my kidnapping of foreign leaders, and then all Israelis for the high crime of being Jews where they're not wanted. Muh ha ha ha!"

"We won't stand for this!" Bush shouted.

"I'm going to make sure we throw the book at you, President Bush," Belgazor said. "You'll be sentenced to a $150 fine plus time served. Muh ha ha ha!"

"You monster!"

"And as for you, Tony Blair, we don't look kindly on unsafe driving," Belgazor said, "so you will be thrown into the Pit of Eternal Horror. Muh ha ha ha!"

Belgazor walked off, continuing to laugh his evil Belgianian laugh.

"Well, chap, 'Pit of Eternal Horror' doesn't sound very good, does it?" Blair said nervously.

"It's not like I can't afford $150," Bush said, thinking aloud, "but it's the principle of the thing."

"Um, could we worry about this Pit thing?" Blair asked. "What do you think it is?"

"Probably some pit with horror in it," Bush answered. "Horror that's eternal. But don't worry, Tony, I'll think of something to get us out of here."

"That's very good and all," Blair answered, "but you aren't really known for thinking."

Bush didn't hear him, as he was deep in thought. "If only I had a gun and a blow torch, and we weren't in Belgium..."

TO BE CONTINUED...

June 25, 2003

Attack of the Belgians Part II

"I just want to assure everyone that the Belgians have not captured the president," White House Press Secretary Ari Fleischer announced.

"My question was about the tax cuts," said the befuddled reporter.

"Whatever." Ari took a big drink from his flask of whiskey. "Oh, and if anyone is mountain climbing and happens to see the vice president, please give us a call."

"You lost the vice president on some mountain top?" exclaimed one reporter.

"I did not say that," Ari answered. "Why do you people always have to read into everything I say?" Ari took another big drink of whiskey. "Man, how many more days do I have to do this?"

* * * *

The flying fortress of Belgium loomed in the distance as the helicopter continued its approach. "That's where the for'ners that need a killin' are, right?" Buck the Marine asked.

"That's what our intelligence says," Clancy answered. He was in his usual black suit with black sunglasses but was wearing a SpongeBob SquarePants tie.

"What happened to your black tie?" Buck asked.

"Oh... uh... this was a gift from my eight year-old for Father's Day. The wife said I had to wear it at least once."

Buck sharpened his KA-BAR. "So what do we know about the Belgians?"

"Unfortunately, we seem to have misfiled our data about Belgium," Clancy said, "or at least it wasn't under 'B.' Luckily, my six year-old niece had to write a short report on a country, and she was given Belgium. Here is what it says:

"Belgium is in Europe. Their money is called the Belgian Franc. They export machinery and chemicals. They speak Dutch and French. I like waffles."

"How sure are you of the accuracy of that report?" Buck asked as he checked his extra magazines.

"It got a B-minus. We also used an advanced search tool to glean information about Belgium from the internet."

"Google?" Buck inquired.

"Uh... I can't divulge my sources. Anyway, here is what we learned, most of it taken from blogs: The Belgians suck. The Belgians are possibly radioactive, so don't touch them. Everyone hates the Belgians. The Belgians have super strength and can fly. The Belgians are totally gay.

"I remind you that, as with anything found on the internet, there is a 12% chance of it being true. What we have determined for certain, though, is that the Belgians, so consumed by their irrelevance, have become wraith-like beings unable to be harmed by normal weapons. Perhaps, though, closer to their own land, they'll have more relevance and can be harmed."

"Don't worry," Buck assured him. "If there is one thing I know how to figure out how to do, it's kill for'ners."

"I think the acting President Dick Cheney would like to have some words with you," Clancy said as he turned on a monitor.

"I am very cold!" Cheney exclaimed. "Someone please come and get me. I can't hold out much longer. I think I hear something rattling around in my boot, and I'm afraid it's my toe."

"Don't worry, acting President Cheney," Buck said, "the Belgians will pay for their crime."

"Are you even listening to me? Please, just—"

Clancy switched the monitor so that now Laura Bush was on screen. "The First Lady also wanted to talk to you."

"Please bring my husband back home," she pleaded.

"I will not let you down, ma'am."

"And when you find him, ask him where the electric blanket is. I know he was the last one to have it, and I can't find it now."

"I will do that. Stay strong."

Clancy shut off the monitor. They were almost to the evil flying fortress of the Belgians. "It's time to get ready. All the American people—except for the most partisan Democrats—are counting on you, Buck."

"If it involves killin' for'ners, let them know that I always succeed." Buck chambered a round in his M-16 and prepared to disembark.

* * * *

"Almost got a brick out of the wall," Bush whispered as he pried at the wall with his waffle knife.

"You know the guards are watching you," Tony Blair whispered back.

"That's why I'm trying to be inconspicuous," Bush said as he frantically dug at the wall. "Why don't you tap dance to distract them?"

"Tap dance?"

"Just do it!"

Blair started tap dancing. "Stop that dancing!" ordered one of the guards.

"No, I'm British, and I need to dance!" Blair answered defiantly.

"Got the brick out," Bush whispered.

"I'll stop dancing now," Blair announced.

Bush curled up on the floor and started moaning. "Oh, I'm sick... much too sick to bash you two guards in the head if you come into this cell."

"We better help him," one guard said to the other. They opened the cell and entered.

"I'll bash your heads good!" Bush yelled as he jumped to his feet and knocked the two guards unconscious with his brick.

"Wow!" Blair exclaimed. "The Belgians are even dumber than you."

"Yeah, they're stupid," Bush laughed. "Uh... now what do I do?"

"You unlock my cell, and we get out of here."

Bush got the keys and let Blair out. "So, do you have any military experience?"

"Not really," Blair said. "What about you?"

"I flew some planes," Bush said. "Do you see any jet fighters around?"

"No, not in this cell block," Blair answered. "Why don't we look for a means to escape."

"First, I have to get my cowboy hat back," Bush declared.

"It's just a hat!" Blair exclaimed.

"Being gay, you probably wouldn't understand," Bush said, "but a Texan can't leave his hat behind."

"I'm not gay; I'm British."

"Well, whatever you want to call it; I don't mean to offend. I'm a uniter, not a divider."

They then sneaked through the fortress until they came to the hall of the minister of justice. Inside were numerous guards and a badger wearing a cowboy hat.

"Their minister of justice is a badger!" Blair exclaimed. "The Belgians are completely insane!"

"And he's got my hat!" Bush said angrily. "We need to distract the guards."

"But how?"

Bush pushed Tony Blair into the room. "Look, it's Tony Blair, and he's trying to escape!" Bush yelled.

"Oh, bugger!" Blair exclaimed before running off with the guards in pursuit; Bush hid behind a wall.

"Now to get my hat," Bush said as he approached the badger. "You give me my hat back, you stinky varmint!"

The badger leapt at Bush's leg and bit him.

"Ow! It hurts! Get him off!"

Bush then heard the evil laughter of Belgazor. "So you thought you could escape the arbitrary justice of the Belgians?"

"Well, yeah," Bush admitted. "Until the badger bit me."

"Guess what," Belgazor said with a smile. "You're just in time for your trial. Muh ha ha ha!"

Bush looked confused. "I don't get that joke."

"It's not a joke! It's evil laughter!" Belgazor explained with frustration.

"Oh," Bush answered with faux understanding before the minister of justice went for his groin.

TO BE CONCLUDED...

June 30, 2003

Attack of the Belgians Part III

Rumsfeld smashed the reporter's head into the podium. "That's your head being smashed against wood," he said. Rumsfeld then slammed the reporter's head through a window, breaking the glass. "And that's your head hitting against glass. Do you feel the difference?"

"Yes," the reporter said weakly.

"Let's continue to drive this point home," Rumsfeld said. He smacked the reporter into a brick wall. "That's your head against brick." He grabbed another reporter and slammed both their heads together. "That's skull against skull. Feel the difference?"

"I don't feel much of anything anymore."

Rumsfeld dropped his victim. "Then I think I've finished making my point. See, while all those things seemed similar in that your head was getting smashed against something, they were different, too. In the same way, Iraq is different from Vietnam, but it was an interesting analogy you tried to make. Any other questions?"

"Is it true the president and Tony Blair have been captured by the Belgians and are being put on trial?" asked one reporter.

"Why would I care?" Rumsfeld asked back angrily. "There are lots of people in the Middle East who are alive and shouldn't be, so I don't have time to worry about whether Bush or some pansy Brit has been taken prisoner by some idiotic European nation."

"But isn't he your boss?" exclaimed the reporter.

"Not so loud," Rumsfeld warned. "You'll wake Chomps." Chomps, the world's angriest dog, lay near the podium, chained to the wall, sleeping the world's angriest sleep. His legs started moving, and his jaws snapped at the air. "Aww, isn't that cute," Rumsfeld smiled. "He's dreaming of mauling someone."

Suddenly Chomps woke up and leapt to his feet. He started barking wildly and biting at the air. "Something making you angry, boy?" Rumsfeld asked, trying to understand.

Chomps's eyes stared distantly as he continued to snarl and bark.

"Something far away?" Rumsfeld asked. "You want me to unchain you?"

"No no no!" shouted all of the reporters.

Rumsfeld unhooked Chomps's chain, and the dog immediately leapt out the nearest window. "I hope you kill whatever made you angry, boy," Rumsfeld called out as he watched Chomps speed down the street.

* * * *

President Bush was chained to the wall while the evil Belgian minister of justice kept an eye on him. The savage little badger still had Bush's cowboy hat and seemed to want nothing more than to tear away at the hapless president.

Farther away, Tony Blair dangled in the air by some rope. "The first trial is of Tony Blair," the evil, bloated Belgazor announced. "If he is convicted of his war crime of making a wide right turn, he shall be dropped into the Pit of Eternal Horror."

The floor opened from beneath Blair to reveal a pit filled with angry, screeching monkeys. "Crikey!" Blair exclaimed.

"We poured eight barrels of monkeys into that pit," Belgazor laughed, "and we shook the barrels up good first to make sure the monkeys were extra angry."

"You madman!" Bush yelled. "If I had a baseball bat, I would beat you good! Oh... and if I weren't chained up, too. If I weren't chained up and I had a baseball bat, you would be so sorry."

"But you are chained up, and there are no baseball bats in Belgium," Belgazor said, "so instead you get to witness the perfection of our justice system. Instead of using biased humans to decide Tony Blair's fate, we use pigeons to determine justice." Belgazor pointed at the jury, which was a stand full of pigeons. "Before each one is two buttons: one for not guilty and one for guilty. If more hit guilty, then Blair falls into the Pit, and justice will be dispensed by the angry monkeys. Muh ha ha ha!" He looked at Blair. "You may now plead your case."

"To the pigeons?"

"Who else?" Belgazor asked angrily.

Blair looked at the many birds who stared right back at him. "Uh... I would like to say I've always liked birds, and England is a particularly good place for pigeons. I really didn't mean to drive unsafely, and if you find me not guilty, you're all invited to London, where you will be fed many bread crumbs."

"The jury does not respond well to bribery," Belgazor warned.

The pigeons started to peck at their buttons, and the tally could be seen on a large screen. The guilties began to grow in number much faster than the not guilties.

"Oh, bugger!" Blair exclaimed.

"Remember to tuck your head in and roll when you hit the ground," Bush told Blair. "That will help you with the fall. I don't have any advice, though, about how to not get torn apart by monkeys."

"That's quite alright, chap," Blair said in a depressed voice as he watched the results on screen while Belgazor laughed his evil Belgianian laugh.

* * * *

Buck slowly crept through the fortress, where he soon detected a scent. "Waffles," he muttered ominously.

Soon Belgian troops were all around him, so Buck made a run through the fortress as he fired back, all the while singing the ancient Marine killin' song:

Oh, God made for'ners for a killin',
Or so says my dear old pa.
So I shoot me some ugly for'ners
And then triumphantly shout, 'Ooh-rah!'

Yes, for'ners are for a killin'
So it's their blood I'm spillin'.
Once I kill me a million
I'll shout my last, 'Ooh-rah!'

If us Marines fire enough bullets,
The world will run out of lead.
Then we'll have to draw our KA-BARs
And stab them for'ners dead.

Yes, for'ners are for a killin'
So it's their blood I'm spillin'.
Once I kill me a million
I'll shout my last, 'Ooh-rah!'

Buck slapped another magazine into his rifle and looked for more Belgians to kill. He ran for what seemed to be the main room of the building. Knocking the door open, he saw Blair suspended in the air, Bush chained to the wall being guarded by a cowboy badger, and the giant Belgazor standing near a wall of pigeons. "Something weird and foreign is going on here," Buck announced, "and I don't like it much!"

"Another foolish American!" Belgazor shouted. He hit a button, and the stairs Buck was standing on turned into a slide. He slipped toward the pit of monkeys, but he quickly tossed his rifle aside and drew his KA-BAR, stabbing it into the ground to slow his descent. He ended up stopping right at the edge of the pit, the angry monkeys jumping up and clawing at his boots.

"My boots!" Buck shouted. "I need those for stomping on for'ners' necks."

Belgazor just laughed as both Buck and Blair dangled above their imminent doom. "I guess it's up to me," Bush uttered, "so there is only one thing left to do: a Presidential Power-Up!"

"US Presidents of old, hear me now!" Bush shouted into the air. "For I ask of your power! Give me the level-headed cunning of George Washington, the straight moralism of Abraham Lincoln, the mighty strength of Teddy Roosevelt, the alcohol tolerance of Ulysses S. Grant, and the don't-give-a-crap attitude of James Polk!"

A burst of light surrounded Bush, and he tore apart his chains as if they were papier-mâché. "Time for a ass-whoopin'... Texas style!" he announced.

"Stop him!" Belgazor screamed.

The minister of justice bared his sharp teeth.

"Uh-oh," Bush groaned, backing away.

The badger leapt at him, ready to bite, but he disappeared in a blur of black. The cowboy hat now floated to the ground while Chomps stood by, swallowing the badger in one big gulp.

"Chomps!" Bush exclaimed. "You saved me! And to think I had just signed an executive order to have you put down."

"I'll just have to stop you myself!" the giant Belgazor yelled, approaching Bush.

Chomps growled. "This one's mine," Bush told the dog. "You go help Buck and gay Tony." Chomps ran off while Bush bent down and picked up his hat. He firmly fixed it on his head and yelled, "You're going down, Belgazor!"

Belgazor growled and charged Bush, who fought back with a series of kicks and punches, sending Belgazor to the ground with a mighty crash. "You made the big mistake of messing with someone who has seen every episode of *Walker, Texas Ranger*," Bush laughed.

Chomps grabbed Buck with his Herculean jaw and helped him out of the pit. The tally board now announced Blair as guilty, so Chomps braced Buck as he leaned over, barely able to catch Blair as he dropped toward the pit. "Ooh-rah!"

"I will destroy you all!" Belgazor shouted as he got back to his feet. He then charged Bush again, but this time Bush flipped Belgazor, who couldn't stop himself before plunging into the Pit of Eternal Horror. His last scream of anger was drowned out by the screeching of monkeys.

The building started shaking. "It must have been Belgazor's evil power that kept this fortress afloat," Blair stated.

"So we done here?" Buck asked as he picked up his M-16.

"No, kill those pigeons," Bush said. "They're part of this!"

Buck launched a grenade into the jury stand, which disappeared into a mixture of fire and feathers.

"We better get out of here before it's too late," Blair said nervously.

"What's wrong with your voice?" Buck asked.

"He's just gay," Bush explained.

"I'm not gay!" Blair responded. "I'm British."

"British sounds foreign," Buck said, eyeing Blair suspiciously.

Blair took one good look at the intimidating Buck. "On second thought... yes, I'm gay. Very, very gay."

Buck thought this over for a second. "Well then, may Jesus's love lead you to the right path. Now let's get out of here."

"The exit was that way," Blair said, pointing at a wall. "I took a good look at a map of this place, so all we need to do is head down the opposite hallway, take a right, take a left..."

Buck launched a grenade at the wall, blowing it apart and giving them an exit to the outside.

"And that works, too," Blair said sheepishly.

They all fled outside, where a helicopter came to meet them. Standing at the doorway was Clancy. "Glad to see you all."

"Wow, SpongeBob!" Bush exclaimed. "Great tie!"

"Thanks, it was a Father's Day gift from my son."

"All my daughters gave me was a card," Bush complained. "I didn't even get the joke in it. Least they could have done was put a twenty dollar bill in there or something."

"May I remind you that the ground is crumbling beneath us?" Blair said impatiently.

"Oh yeah!" Bush exclaimed as they all rushed into the helicopter, rising into the air as the evil Belgian fortress plummeted to the ground. They each settled into a seat and breathed sighs of relief, except for Chomps, who eyed each of the individual seats until he found one that particularly enraged him. He then began to savagely tear it apart.

Bush looked back at Belgium. "Get me a line to the... uh... big military place."

"The Pentagon?" Clancy asked.

"Yeah, that place." Bush was given the phone. "This is the president! ...Yeah, the one of the United States. Nuke Belgium! Nuke it to hell!"

Bush looked out the window, waiting for a big explosion where the crumbled fortress lay, but instead he saw one far off in the distance. "I think you missed it," Bush said into the phone. "No, I don't know what country you nuked, but you better find out who and send them a fruit basket. Belgium is more to the right... no, my right... yeah, I guess you don't know what my right is." Bush looked at Clancy. "Which direction are we flying?"

"Southeast."

"So... if we are going southeast," Bush thought out loud, "then the explosion was to the... uh... and Belgium was to its... uh..." Bush picked up the phone again. "Forget nuking Belgium. It's too hard."

"Well, that was quite an experience," Blair exclaimed.

"You can say that again," Bush responded. "This has to be my biggest misadventure since the time I got my head stuck in the banister. I did learn a lesson, though: it's insane for any one country—other than the US—to try and have jurisdiction over the entire world."

"I learned that one should turn into the nearest lane and properly signal before going into a farther lane, or one may be kidnapped by Belgians," Blair said.

"I learned something too," Clancy added, "but it's classified."

"And I learned that I like killin' for'ners," Buck said with a wide smile. He thought for a moment. "Wait; I already knew that. Guess I didn't learn anything. Ooh-rah!"

THE END

July 02, 2003

Reading to Underprivileged Kids

"I got some questions about my book," Buck the Marine said.

"What?" Laura Bush asked with annoyance.

"Is it just the eggs that are green, or both the eggs *and* the ham?"

"Well, according to the picture, it's both."

Buck thought about this. "I have a moral objection to reading this story."

"You have a moral objection to reading *Green Eggs and Ham*?" Laura asked with exasperation.

"Well, I read this story to some children, and then one may see some spoiled meat that is green in color and go eat it. Then, someone would ask him, 'Well why would you do such a thing?' And he would reply, 'Because Buck the Marine told me it was alright, and I trusted him.' And then people would say, 'I guess you shouldn't trust Buck the Marine.' And I wouldn't want people saying that."

Laura rolled her eyes. "Fine. Read this one instead."

Buck accepted the book. "*Hop on Pop*?!" he exclaimed. "The Bible says to respect your parents."

Laura groaned and then handed him another book. "How about this one?"

Buck looked through the pages and laughed a bit. "Heh heh; the stupid bird can't find his mother."

Condoleezza Rice approached Laura while dragging Chomps on a leash.

"What are you doing here?" Laura exclaimed. "And why do you have that horrible creature with you?"

"Your husband bailed, because the kids laughed at him last time when he read them *Hello Moon* and stumbled on a sentence," Rice explained, "so he sent me in his place. It was Rumsfeld's idea to bring the dog. He said Chomps likes children."

"To play with, or to eat?" Laura asked skeptically.

"He wasn't specific on that," Rice admitted.

"Can you control him at least?"

"I do have a choke collar on him," Rice said, "but all that seems to do is make him really angry at whoever has the leash."

Chomps saw two water fountains on the wall, and he looked between the two trying to decide which one made him angrier. He finally decided on the left one and ripped it out of the wall.

"No, Chomps! Bad dog!" Laura yelled and then struck Chomps on his snout. Chomps dropped the fountain and started barking and snarling ferociously at Laura. She cocked back her hand for another strike while she kept staring at Chomps sternly. Chomps quieted down quickly but stared back just as intensely. They locked eyes for quite some time, but finally Chomps just snorted and turned away.

"That's what I thought," Laura said triumphantly. "Had to do the same thing when Putin came to the visit the White House."

"Heh heh; stupid bird," Buck laughed, reading his book. "That's a steam shovel, not your mother."

"I have what I'm going to read," Rice said, holding up a magazine. "It's an article about radar from *Jane's Defense Weekly*. I hadn't had a chance to read it yet, so it will be a learning experience for both the kids and me."

"You read one of the books I brought," Laura said.

Rice looked at them. "Anything by Tom Clancy?"

"No, but there are a lot from Dr. Seuss."

"His books are coded Commie propaganda."

"Where did you hear that?" Laura asked in surprise.

"I just made it up," Rice admitted, "but it sounds like it could be true."

"The stupid bird finds his mother in the end," Buck said, disappointed. "I thought there would be some sort of twist."

"We were also supposed to have a Democrat here to make this bipartisan," Laura stated. "Where is that nice Zell Miller?"

"He had to cancel," Rice answered, "but a replacement is coming."

All of a sudden Laura started shivering. "Why does it suddenly feel so cold in here?"

"Hello," said Hillary Clinton, walking down the school hallway.

"Hillary Rodham Clinton!" Laura exclaimed.

"That's Senator Clinton to you!" she shot back.

"I'm still trying to undo all the damage you did to the position of First Lady," Laura said. "Plus replace the furniture!"

Chomps started snarling and barking wildly at Hillary, but she hissed and bared her teeth at him. Chomps whimpered and hid behind Rice.

"Hello, Condoleezza Rice," Hillary said slyly. "So, what are your plans for 2008?"

"Wouldn't you like to know," Rice answered back with a smile.

"Anyway, Laura dear, I'm going to read to the kids from my new book *Living History*," Hillary said.

"Yes, I've heard about that book," Laura answered. "If you read it backward, it summons Satan."

"Much like if you read it forward," Rice added.

"You have to read one of the books I brought," Laura told Hillary.

"But the kids may be interested in history," Hillary said.

"Then they would have no interest in your book!" Laura shot back.

Hillary became enraged. "Do not cross me, librarian; I will destroy you!"

Laura thought of a number of things she wanted to say in response but instead simply stated, "*One Fish, Two Fish, Red Fish, Blue Fish*," as she shoved a book at Hillary.

"I thought of a better ending for mine," Buck said. "It has a shootout and everything. Can I read the kids the new ending?"

"No," Laura told him sharply. She saw more people coming down the hallway. "The press is coming, so everyone be on your best behavior."

"I can't believe I was assigned to this," complained the FOX News reporter as she was followed by her camerawoman.

"Even your cameraperson is a leggy blonde?" Laura exclaimed. "Does FOX News do all of its recruiting at Hooters?"

"Sometimes strip clubs," the FOX News reporter responded. She then spotted Buck. "Why haven't you called me?"

"I was on a secret mission," he answered. "I didn't even know what kind of for'ners I was killin'."

"So what's this all about?"

"We're reading to underprivileged kids too dumb to read themselves," Buck explained.

"Is reading important to a Marine?"

"Not really; most of the places we go, all the writing is in crazy for'ner gibberish that one can't be expected to read anyway."

"Hey, where is Chomps?" Rice asked, noticing she had an empty leash.

"I want my mommy!" cried a child whom Chomps was holding up in the air by his collar.

Both Rice and Buck slowly approached Chomps. "Drop the kid, and you get a treat," Rice said softly.

Chomps turned and ran off down the hallway, still holding the kid. Rice and Buck chased after him with the FOX News reporter and her camerawoman following the action.

"I guess your reading to kids is a disaster," Hillary cackled. "The office of First Lady must be too much for a po' wittle wibrarian like you."

Laura steamed. "You, me. Outside. Now!"

* * * *

"Laura Bush's program to help get underprivileged children to read ended up being a disaster when Chomps, rated by the *Guinness Book of World Records* to be the world's angriest dog, ran off holding five year-old Billy Johnson in his mouth. He eventually dropped the kid unharmed when the dog found some history books that particularly enraged him. Most of the books were damaged, primarily the section in each that had to do with the sixties. Hillary Clinton also sustained injuries, a black-eye and a swollen lip she reportedly received from a fall.

"In other news, North Korea is now actually launching nuclear missiles at us, and we still don't give a rat's ass. We now turn to our expert..."

July 07, 2003

I Am Ah-Nuld!

"The economy is still not improving," President Bush announced. "I need new ideas."

"How about more tax cuts?" offered one of the president's advisors.

"I don't know if that will work," Bush said dubiously.

"I got it!" exclaimed another advisor. "Even *more* tax cuts!"

"I like that!" Bush responded. "Let's go with it."

Suddenly the doors to the conference room burst open as two Secret Service agents were thrown to the floor. Then a large man walked in. "Your puny Secret Service agents tried to stop me," the man announced. "But I will see the president whenever I please. I am Ah-nuld!"

"And who are you?" the president asked.

"I am Ah-nuld!"

"Oh, Arnold Schwa... uh..." Bush paused for a moment. "Well, we all know your last name. What do you want?"

"I wish to become governor of California, and I demand your support, or I will crush you!"

"No *problemo*," Bush said. "I fully support your efforts with the recall."

"I have no time to wait for recall," Arnold shouted. "The voters are puny; they reelected Gray Davis. I will crush them! I take governorship now! I am Ah-nuld!"

"So what are you planning?"

"You will fly me down to California now, and I will crush Gray Davis, for he is puny. Then I am governor. I am Ah-nuld!"

Bush thought about this for a moment. "I like your moxie; let's do it." He called up his staff. "Get Air Force One ready; it's time for a road trip!"

"Just one more question," Arnold said. "What is this dog that is biting my leg?"

"Oh, that's just Chomps, the world's angriest dog. Gnawing on your leg is just his way of saying he likes you... Or is it his way of trying to sever a major artery and kill you? I forget; to be honest, I try to stay as far away as I can from that horrible thing."

"Ha! His bite is puny; he will never gnaw through my leg! I am Ah-nuld!"

* * * *

“Governor Davis, you were supposed to get those bills signed,” the governor’s aide reminded him.

“I was going to,” Governor Gray Davis said, “but I broke my pen and forgot where my other pens are.”

“You are so incompetent!” the aide exclaimed. “You have to get things together before your disapproval rating gets any higher. People are actually moving here from other states just to hate you.”

“Is it really that bad?”

“Haven’t you been watching the news?”

“I was going to,” Davis said, “but I accidentally took the batteries out of the TV remote and couldn’t figure out how to put them back in.”

“Ah!” the aide exclaimed. “You are so incompetent!”

Suddenly they heard a loud crash. “What happened?” Davis cried.

The aide looked out the window. “Apparently a Humvee has crashed through the front of the mansion.”

The doors to Gray Davis’s office were kicked opened. “I am Ah-nuld! I am governor now!”

“Now just wait one moment,” a befuddled Gray Davis responded. “You can’t just barge in here and—”

“You are puny! I will crush you!” Arnold yelled and then picked up Gray Davis and threw him out the window. “Now I am governor! I am Ah-nuld!”

“You can’t just become governor by throwing the current governor out the window,” the governor’s aide protested.

“You are puny, too!” Arnold shouted and then picked up the aide and tossed him out the window.

“Wow, democracy in action,” Bush said, having followed Arnold into the office. “It’s a beautiful thing to behold.”

Soon the press had swarmed into the office as well. “I am Ah-nuld!” Arnold announced. “I am governor now!”

“Do you really think you can take the governorship by—” one reporter started to say, but Arnold then grabbed him.

“Do you question me? I am Ah-nuld! You are puny; I will crush you!”

“No, I’m not questioning you, Mr. Governor,” the reporter said meekly.

“How about you, President Bush?” said another reporter. “Do you support this violent coup?”

"I wouldn't call it a violent coup," Bush answered. "If you look at California law, storming into the governor's mansion and throwing the current governor out the window is a perfectly legit method for succession of power."

"What part of California law says that?"

Bush started laughing. "Come on; what's the chance I know anything about California law? I was just bluffing."

"So, Arnold, why is there a very angry dog chewing on your leg?"

"I do not know, and I do not care. His bite is puny; I am Ah-nuld!"

* * * *

"Former Governor Gray Davis was critically injured by being thrown out the window of his office, that critical wounding getting 62% approval from California voters. Arnold Schwarzenegger has announced his plan for California, saying quote, 'The deficits are puny. I will crush them. I am Arnold.' Still, the courts are disputing the fact that he is now governor simply by inflicting grave injury on Gray Davis."

"Just when you thought California couldn't get any screwier," quipped the anchorwoman. "How long until it breaks off the continent and floats into the sea?"

"That's at least two earthquakes away."

July 09, 2003

The Hunt for the Rumsfeld Strangler

"It's been months, and still no leads on the Rumsfeld Strangler," the police chief chided his officers. "So I've decided to bring in some outside help. Straight from San Francisco Homicide Division, meet Detective Callahan."

"Just to get things straight," Callahan announced, "I do things my way, and no one messes with me."

"I just want to say that—" the police chief started to say, but Callahan grabbed him by his collar and pointed his .44 magnum at the chief's head.

"Are you talking back to me?" Callahan demanded angrily.

"This isn't going to go well on your review," the chief answered.

"I don't care about my review," Callahan answered, putting away his gun, "I only care about catching my man. So what evidence do we have on this so-called 'Rumsfeld Strangler'?"

"We accidentally burned it all," answered one of the detectives.

"Why?"

"We were cold and wanted a fire."

Callahan looked at the chief. "Are all your people this incompetent?"

"Pretty much. O'Brien is going to be your partner, by the way."

"And it's a great honor to be working with you," O'Brien said. "I hope that we can—"

Suddenly a sniper bullet came through the window and killed O'Brien. Everyone was shocked except for Callahan. "Don't mind that," he said. "Always happens to my partners. I'm better off working alone."

"So what's the plan?" the chief asked.

"I cruise the streets looking for evidence and end up in some blood bath, you take away my badge, and then I finally get the perp in a violent conclusion."

The chief thought about this. "Could I just take away your badge now to speed things up?"

"Don't mess with me!" Callahan warned and then stormed out of the police station.

* * * *

The Rumsfeld Strangler's most recent victim had been a mugger in the inner city. It was a dangerous neighborhood, but it was strangely quiet now that hoodlums had been turning up dead. Detective Callahan inspected the chalk outline and then looked at a nearby dumpster that looked like its sides had been torn apart by large teeth.

"What are you doing here, pig?" demanded a voice behind Callahan. He turned to see five thugs standing behind him.

"I'm looking for the Rumsfeld Strangler," Callahan answered. "What do you know about him?"

"I know that *we're* going to handle him and his dog," the leader answered. "Not some stupid cop."

"A dog?"

"Yeah, he is known as '*El Perro Loco Diablo*,' but we'll kill the beast just the same as we'll kill you if you don't get out of here, pig." The thug pulled away his jacket, revealing a handgun, as the rest began to ready their weapons.

Callahan just smiled. He then drew his .44 magnum, quickly shooting the five before they could retaliate. The leader lay on the ground with a wound in his shoulder, eyeing his handgun that lay nearby.

Callahan pointed his gun at the thug's head. "I know what you're thinking, punk. Did I fire six shots or only five? To tell you the truth, in the heat of the moment, I lost track myself. But, being that this a Desert Eagle, which holds eight rounds in a magazine, with possibly a ninth chambered, the question is quite moot. So, you gotta ask yourself, do you know what 'moot' means? Well do ya, punk?"

The thug looked between the barrel of Callahan's gun and his own gun and finally raised his hands. Callahan then used his foot to kick the other gun out of the way.

"I gots to know," pleaded the thug.

Callahan smiled. "The main definition of moot is 'debatable,' but I was using the secondary meaning of 'of no practical importance; irrelevant.'" He then turned to leave. "I got all I need here. Now get off the street before I fine you for littering for getting your blood and your friends all over the street."

* * * *

"We here at Animal Control would sure love to help you, Detective Callahan."

"You better," Callahan shouted, grabbing the man by his collar and pointing his gun at the man's head, "because I have a short fuse!"

"Apparently," the man said meekly. "Anyway, we've heard about the dog you're looking for. Loves to chase cars and tends to rip them to shreds if he catches them. Especially hates any that are fuel-efficient. I can tell you where he tends to chase cars the most."

"Then maybe I'll let you live," Callahan said, putting away his gun.

"So is this how they do things in San Francisco?" the man asked nervously.

"You don't want to know how they do things in San Francisco."

"Alrighty... So do you want to adopt a puppy before you go? Any that are still here at the end of the week go to Glenn Reynolds... and we all know what he does with them."

"Well I'd just use them for target practice," Callahan responded. "Just like I'm going to do with you if you don't give me the info I need."

"Whoa," the man exclaimed, handing Callahan a map. "There is this little word we call 'please.'"

* * * *

Another bad neighborhood filled with even worse people. As soon as Detective Callahan entered the area, he was greeted with a number of smiles that didn't look at all friendly. He picked out a large group of tough-looking punks to question. "I'm looking for a savage dog and the man who owns him."

"We ain't talking to you, copper!" shouted one of the thugs.

Callahan pulled out his gun and shot the man. "Anyone else not want to talk to me?"

"You can't just shoot people!" protested another.

Callahan shot him. "Anyone else want to tell me what I can and can't do?"

"Hey man, I don't want any trouble," said one thug, raising his hands.

Callahan grabbed him and pushed the barrel of his gun against his head. "Well maybe I do. Now you're going to tell me what I want to know, or I'm going to pull the trigger. I used to think a .44 magnum could take a man's head clean off with a single shot, but it actually penetrates right through it and then through the building behind it and then maybe hits a little girl playing hopscotch outside. So, do you want a little girl being shot on your conscience, or, more precisely, do you want me shooting your conscience all over that little girl?"

"Just calm down!" the thug shouted. "We saw that dog and the crazy man just yesterday. He tried to strangle Chico!"

"Yeah," Chico responded. "I thought I was done for, but then he saw this French diplomat drive by, and apparently there is nothing he hates more than French diplomats. I think the guy's name is Pierre Rudepierson, and he's going to appear tomorrow on *Meet the Press* after the interview with Senate Majority Leader Bill Frist to talk about what he feels is wrong with American foreign policy."

Everyone stared at Chico.

"So what? I like watching the Sunday morning talk shows. Can't a murderous thug keep up on current events?"

They kept staring at him.

"Aw, people and their stereotypes."

Callahan let go of the man he was holding. "I might be back later for more questions... or just to kill you all."

"Okay, but you should really think about taking some anger management classes."

"I shot the last man who suggested I need anger management!" Callahan said angrily. He thought for a moment and then shot the thug. "Now I've shot the last man who suggested I need anger management."

* * * *

"You're out of control, Callahan!" the chief shouted.

"I'm just getting my job done," Callahan shot back.

"The rest of our Homicide Division is tied up investigating the homicides you've committed during your homicide investigation. Pretty soon, you'll have killed more people than the Rumsfeld Strangler."

"And I've almost cracked the case," Callahan answered, "so why don't you shut up before I shut you up."

"I think it's time I take your badge."

Callahan flung his badge at the chief's face. "It never suited me anyway."

"And your gun."

Callahan grabbed the chief and pressed his gun to the chief's head. "The only way you are getting my gun is bullets first."

"Then eject the magazine, and remove the round in the chamber," said the chief.

"No, I mean I'm going to shoot you."

"Oh, I get it," the chief chuckled, rolling his eyes. "Duh, that was a threat. Keep your gun then."

* * * *

Chomps carefully inspected the pictures on the wall. When he found one that particularly enraged him, he ripped it down and tore it apart with his teeth.

"Nice dog you have there," Callahan commented.

"What's so nice about him?" Rumsfeld answered.

"Didn't think you were booked on *Meet the Press* today, Defense Secretary Donald Rumsfeld," Callahan said. "So what are you doing here?"

"I'm waiting here to strangle Pierre Rudepierson... and maybe Tim Russert if my arthritis doesn't act up."

"Kind of coy about this, aren't we?" Callahan asked.

"Can we talk about this later? I have someone to strangle."

"We talk about this now," Callahan demanded.

Rumsfeld saw Pierre coming by. "Fine, we'll talk as I strangle." He grabbed Pierre by the neck and started choking him.

"I know you're the Rumsfeld Strangler," Callahan said.

"So? I leave notes saying as much. Don't want other people taking credit for my strangling."

"Well, it has to end."

Rumsfeld dropped Pierre dead to the ground. "You're that cop they brought in from San Francisco," Rumsfeld declared. "You're the one shooting all those street punks. Those are *my* street punks to kill. Why don't you go back to San Francisco and march in a gay pride parade or something."

"First I have to take you in."

"For what? Strangling some thugs and some French people? Is that the kind of future you want for the next generation? One where French people walk around unstrangled? Don't you have real criminals to take care of? Or at least some pot-smoking hippies to hassle?"

"It ain't my choice. I'm just enforcing the law," Callahan answered, his hand near his gun.

All the while, Chomps ignored the scene, jumping up onto a table so he could bite a light fixture that was really, really pissing him off. "Well, I guess you gotta do what you gotta do," Rumsfeld said, parting his coat to reveal his handguns. "It's your call."

* * * *

"I've got the Rumsfeld Strangler," Callahan announced to the police chief as he stood next to the body bag that was about to be carted off to the morgue.

The chief unzipped the bag. "It's Pierre Rudepierson."

"Yes, he's been behind the stranglings all along," Callahan explained, "and when I confronted him, he strangled himself."

"Just like you'd expect a Frenchman to do," the chief said. "Still, one thing doesn't seem quite right..."

Callahan grabbed the chief and put his gun to the chief's head. "Are you questioning me, punk?"

"I haven't looked it up yet, but I'm pretty sure there's a rule against pointing a gun at your boss."

"I only know my own rules," Callahan said, putting back his gun.

"Anyway, your expense report is too much for us," the chief said. "Either you have to shoot less people or get a cheaper brand of bullet. I think it's time for you to head back to San Francisco."

"Fine with me," Callahan answered.

"Just one more question, Callahan."

"What?"

"Do you know anything about that dog outside who's ripping apart my Hyundai with his teeth?"

"Yeah," Callahan answered, checking the bandages on his left hand. "If you're giving him a dog biscuit, throw it; don't hand it to him."

July 14, 2003

Blood is Also Symbolic of Blood

"Know what superhero I'd like to be?" Bush asked. "The Hulk. Then I'd get to just smash everything I don't like... but it wouldn't be my fault, because I'm the Hulk. It would be other people's fault for making me mad."

"I'm mad, too," Cheney answered.

"I hope you at least like your new undisclosed location."

"I'm sitting right next to you," Cheney said with annoyance.

Bush covered his ears. "Well don't tell me!"

"Idiot," Cheney uttered.

"I heard that!"

"Then you need to learn to cover your ears better!"

"I'm not mad at you," Bush said. "I'm mad at all those people out there who are saying I'm a liar for saying Iraq was trying to get uranium from Africa. I was just reading the teleprompter! Instead of getting credit for good reading, they call me a liar! It makes me so mad I want to grow big and green and smash them all!"

"And some are saying I knew it was untrue ahead of time!" Cheney stated irately. "I didn't even know what undisclosed location I was in when your speech was made!"

"It was the crawl space of my friend Ralph's house," Bush said, "but that's neither here nor there. We need to get these people and tell them to stop saying lies about me lying!"

"What's your plan?" Cheney asked.

"I'm going to invite Daschle over for a meeting and then hit him in the knee caps with my six iron!" Bush exclaimed, holding up his golf club.

Cheney thought about that. "This is the part where I leave."

"Where to?"

"Undisclosed," Cheney said, exiting the room.

"A bar," Bush muttered. He then heard Senator Tom Daschle coming, so he hid his club behind his back.

"I heard you're ready to compromise on that bill," Daschle said, entering the room, "but you just didn't say which bill."

"Uh... the one all you Democrats are whining about," Bush answered.

"You have to be more specific."

"Anyhoo, there is another initiative I decided to veto."

"Which one?"

"The 'Not hitting you in the kneecaps' initiative!" Bush yelled, hitting Daschle in the kneecaps with his club. Daschle screamed like a girl and went straight to the ground. "That's for saying I lied in my State of the Union address and putting out those commercials."

"It wasn't me, I swear!" Daschle yelled. "It's Moveon.org; they're putting out those commercials."

"Well then, get out of here," Bush commanded.

"I can't! You broke my kneecaps!"

"Fine," Bush said as he went to the phone. "Secret Service, please come and drag Daschle somewhere he can get medical attention."

Two men came in and started dragging Daschle away. "I am saddened by this assault on me," Daschle said as he went out the door.

"Yeah yeah yeah," Bush answered.

Laura Bush then came in the room, looking quite shocked. "Did you just hit Daschle with your six iron?"

"Maybe," Bush said, putting down his golf club.

"What have I told you?" Laura scolded. "If you are going to cudgel someone, you go and buy a cudgel. We use things for what they're intended for in this house. If you break all your irons on people's knees, I'm not going to let you buy any new ones. And then won't you look stupid playing golf with no irons?"

"I'm sorry, dear," Bush said, looking at his feet. "It's just everybody is saying I lied in the State of the Union about Iraq trying to get uranium. I don't even know what their point is! Do they want me to pull out of Iraq and let Saddam go back to torturing everyone?" Bush then thought about that. "Hmm... there's an idea. I pretend to apologize for the invasion, and when Saddam goes back to Baghdad to retake power, we snipe him good!"

"Uh... you run that idea by your advisors, George," Laura told him. "So who is calling you a liar?"

"Lots of people," Bush answered, "and then there are these commercials by Moveon.org that says I'm a '*Mis*leader'." Bush then started to laugh. "Hey, I finally just got that; that's clever. Before I thought they were insinuating I'm a woman."

"So, George, have you thought of talking to these people and explaining your side?"

"No, but I've thought of bombing them followed by the deployment of ground troops; that always seems to clear up misunderstandings."

Laura rolled her eyes. "Well, if you're not going to talk to them, I will. It's time for someone to be an adult."

"I dunno know about this..."

"It's a little thing called 'diplomacy'," Laura said. "If you plan on being president for another four years, one of these days you should learn it."

* * * *

"Hello, is this the headquarters for Moveon.org?" Laura asked with a pleasant smile.

"Yeah," answered an unshaven hippy man in a tie dye t-shirt, "this is where we fight Bush and his lying and his killing."

"Well, that's what I wanted to talk to you about," Laura said softly. "You see, President Bush is my husband, and I know he is an honest person. The mention of Iraq trying to obtain uranium in his State of the Union speech was an honest mistake, and it seems silly to condemn everything the Iraq war has accomplished by focusing on that one thing. Maybe you people should 'move on.'"

The hippy looked confused.

"You know; the name of your organization..." Laura prompted.

"Bush lied; people died!" the hippy responded.

"I think that oversimplifies things," Laura said, struggling a bit to keep her pleasant demeanor. "The war in Iraq was fought for many reasons, and you have to admit the people in Iraq are better off now that the murderous Saddam is out of power."

"He had his illegal war for oil!" the hippy shouted.

"I'm not quite following you now."

"He lied; people died."

"Uh... you said that already," Laura responded, getting frustrated. "Now, I want you to think really hard. Do a few words in the State of the Union address invalidate that a horrible, evil regime is gone and that a once oppressed people now has a chance at freedom?"

The hippy seemed to try to think, but it looked painful. Finally, he just grabbed a canister next to him and threw it at Laura, splattering her with red paint. "That's symbolic of the blood of the dead Iraqis! Blood you helped enable!"

Laura was in complete and utter shock. "You... just... threw... red paint... on me."

"That will teach you to support a war with oil involved and things!" the hippy yelled.

Laura was still shocked beyond sense. "My favorite blouse... covered in paint..."

"Bush is a misleader!" the hippy continued. "He is a misleader! Bush lied; people were killed... I mean... died."

"You threw red paint on me!"

"That's to protest warmongering and all those countries being so unilateral together and... uh... uh-oh!"

* * * *

"Clancy, you're my intelligence guy, right?" Bush asked.

Clancy fixed his black tie and sunglasses. "I can neither confirm nor deny that."

"That's what I wanted to hear. So do you have some intelligence about terrorism I can include in this speech I'm about to give?"

"Yes, we have just learned that Syria is working with the Umbrella Corporation to develop something called the 't-virus', a biological weapon that turns people into killer zombies."

Bush started to write that down but then paused. "Hey, I just got burned for using bad intelligence recently. I want to be sure about this before I include it. What are your sources?"

"I can't tell you that; it's classified."

"But I'm the president!" Bush exclaimed. "I get to know everything!"

Clancy chuckled. "Yeah, like we're going to tell all our secrets to just *any* American president. If we did that with Bill Clinton, every whore in the tri-state area would know where the aliens are buried. You first have to be cleared by the secret, hidden government before you can hear about our sources, and that won't happen until that measure is cleared by the doubly-secret government that actually runs the secret government, unbeknownst to the secret government."

"But I want to know now!" Bush whined. "Where did you hear that intelligence from?"

"Fine," Clancy answered. "We were tipped off by British intelligence, which had intercepted it from Polish intelligence which had heard two Swedes talking about it, who had read it from an independent Danish newspaper which was quoting a Japanese kid what he heard from another kid during recess."

"So how certain are you of the zombie story, then?"

"We give it a certainty ranking of 3L."

"And what does that mean?"

"While you are cleared to hear our rankings of intelligence certainty, you aren't cleared enough to be told what those rankings mean."

"Dangit!" Bush exclaimed. "Hell, I'm going to include it in the speech. Everyone will support me if they think the terrorists have zombies."

Laura now entered the room, covered from head to toe in red.

"Uh... how'd it go, dear?" Bush asked, a bit confused.

"They aren't going to say mean things about you anymore," Laura answered firmly.

"Then why are you... uh... covered in red paint?" Bush inquired, handing her a handkerchief.

Laura wiped her face with the handkerchief. "It's not all paint."

July 16, 2003

That'll Teach Mr. Squawkers to Think He's 'All That'

"You don't have a better picture of him?" Condoleezza Rice asked as she looked at the photo of Chomps's open maw.

"Cameras make him intensely angry," Rumsfeld answered. "Anyway, this is the view most people get of him." Rumsfeld hung up another poster reading, "LOST DOG: Responds to the name Chomps—or any other name—with extreme anger."

"I'm sure you'll find him," Rice told him.

"I'm just worried he's all alone in the middle of nowhere with nothing to take his anger out upon."

"He always finds something to take his anger out on," Rice assured him.

"Well, better get back to work," Rumsfeld sighed.

* * * *

"I lost my dog and am extra angry today, so don't piss me off," Rumsfeld warned.

"I have a question—"

"Rarr!" Rumsfeld yelled, jumping onto the reporter and pummeling him. "I don't like the tone of your voice."

"Uh, how do you respond to people who describe the current situation in Iraq as a 'quagmire'?" asked another reporter.

"With murderous rage!" Rumsfeld shouted, charging that reporter.

"Someone distract him with another question!" the reporter pleaded.

"What are your plans for those currently attacking US troops?"

Rumsfeld stopped to think about the question. "We will paint murals on the walls in Iraq depicting a glorious future free of tyranny. And the paint we will use will be... THE BLOOD OF OUR ENEMIES! Rarr!"

"What about North Korea and their nuclear weapons?"

"They will die for their insolence!" Rumsfeld declared. "I will have the poofy-haired head of Kim Jong-Il on a pike!"

"I thought Bush wanted a diplomatic solution?"

"Bush is a pansy! I will beat him with Kim Jong-Il's head! Rarr!"

Rumsfeld was getting so worked up that he looked ready to kill all the reporters in attendance, but then a familiar face came through the doorway.

"Chomps!" Rumsfeld exclaimed and rushed over to Chomps to give him a hug. Chomps licked Rumsfeld on the face.

"Aww, isn't that nice," said a reporter as he got a cameraman to move closer to the scene.

Chomps saw the camera, and it made him angry. Very angry.

* * * *

President Bush relaxed on a couch watching a nature show. "The penguin, while awkward on land, swims gracefully in the water," the narrator said.

"Ha, stupid penguins," Bush laughed. "If they can't even fly, why do they bother being birds? They might as well be fish."

"Don't you have work to do?" Laura called out to him. "Like sign some bills or take out the trash?"

"No one is ever so busy they don't have enough time to watch a documentary on penguins," Bush answered.

"Down in Antarctica, there are very few predators on land," the narrator continued, "but now approaches a very angry-looking dog that seems intent on ripping all the penguins to pieces. Actually, no, it appears there is just one penguin he doesn't like. And the dog has caught him and is shaking the penguin vigorously. The penguin is now injured, dazed, and confused, and the dog seems satisfied that the penguin has paid for its crimes and begins to leave. No, wait, he stops to attack a snowdrift. And now he leaves."

"Wow, nature is beautiful," Bush exclaimed. "I didn't like that penguin either. In fact... ack... ech... erk..."

Laura rushed behind Bush to give him the Heimlich maneuver. "For pete's sake, I told you not to buy pretzels anymore."

July 21, 2003

First Day

"Hey Ari, you grew fatter and got some hair. Not sure if I like it."

"Actually, Ari Fleischer left, Mr. President," Scott McClellan told Bush. "I'm your new White House Press Secretary, Scott McClellan."

"Oh yeah," Bush said, slapping his forehead. "Anyway, I'm going to give you a nickname so we'll all feel like friends. Your nickname will be... uh... Ari."

"Uh, okay," Scott answered dubiously.

"Anyway, Ari, I don't know if you've heard about it yet, but apparently my two daughters have run off with their cousin Noelle—always told them to stay away from her—and, fueled by crack, they're driving across the country robbing every liquor store they see."

Scott looked concerned. "No, I hadn't heard that."

"Yeah, well, you'll have to come up with some good spin for that that makes me look good."

"A good spin on drug use and robbery?"

Bush patted him on the back. "You're a professional; you'll think of something. I bet those cops had it coming."

"Cops?"

"Anyway, on to Iraq."

"Yeah, I know the administration's position on that," Scott said confidently. "We'll be able to help them get on their feet with their oil reserves—"

"Hold on a bit there," Bush interrupted. "You know how all those stupid hippy protestors were saying all we wanted to do was steal Iraq's oil? Well, we never had any such intention, but once we actually got in Iraq, we thought about it and was like, hey, why not? So play down the whole 'Iraq has oil' angle, because we don't want people to be too surprised when it ends up there is none."

"You're stealing their oil?!" Scott exclaimed.

Bush rolled his eyes. "And that's how you don't want to put it."

"I don't know if stealing Iraq's oil is such a good idea," Scott said. "We already avoided disaster when we found out the Iraqi museums weren't actually looted."

"We were glad to hear that, too," Bush answered, "because we always planned to steal those artifacts for ourselves."

"You're taking Iraq's treasures?" Scott exclaimed.

"And their women... the young attractive ones, at least," Bush chuckled. "Anyway, maybe you can relate *our* stealing to Jenna's, Barbara's, and Noelle's robberies—except ours will involve less gunplay. Just a suggestion. Now go out to the press and put a good spin on everything while I go play some Xbox."

Scott stood there speechless as the president walked off.

* * * *

"Hello, everyone, I'm Scott McClellan, the new White House Press Secretary. It's my first day, so go easy on me." He chuckled a bit, trying to hide his nervousness.

"Why does Bush want to kill the Freedonian children?" Helen Thomas asked. "What did the Freedonian children ever do to Bush?"

Scott looked confused. "I don't think there are such things as Freedonian children."

"That's because Bush killed them all!"

Scott looked around at the reporters. "Is someone supposed to be watching this woman?"

"Hello, I'm Melinda Hawkish from FOX News Channel, the foxiest news around—"

"I'm sorry, what?" Scott interrupted.

Melinda looked a bit peeved. "It's the new tagline; the producers made me say it. Anyway, my question is about North Korea and Iran: when will we annihilate them?"

"We don't plan to annihilate anyone," Scott laughed. "There is a diplomatic solution—"

"There is a diplomatic solution," Melinda repeated in a mocking tone. "Doesn't the president know we pay tax money and want more dead foreigners as a result?"

"Now that's just being childish," Scott said, taken aback.

"Are you going to cry, Tubby?" Melinda asked patronizingly.

"Someone else have a question?" Scott demanded angrily.

"I do," said another reporter. "I heard that just this morning a soldier in Iraq fell off a tank and broke his leg. Will the Bush administration finally admit the situation has turned into a Vietnam-like quagmire?"

Scott looked befuddled, but then he started laughing. "Oh, I get it now," he announced. "This is some big joke they play on the new guy."

The reporter appeared confused.

"Oh my; you're serious," Scott sighed.

"I've heard reports that the Bush daughters are on a drug-fueled spree of liquor store robberies," said yet another reporter. "Do you have any comments on that?"

"Yes," Scott answered. "The White House applauds Jenna's, Barbara's, and Noelle's striking out against liquor stores in an attempt to curb underage drinking. Any other questions?"

"How can you say that with a straight face?"

"I practiced for a while in front of the mirror. Next question."

Suddenly a Mercedes crashed through the pressroom wall. Looking out the car window was President Bush, wearing a racing helmet. "Hey Ari, I just stole Tom Daschle's car and am going to go enter in a demolition derby," Bush told Scott. "Try to put a good spin on that." He then backed the car through the hole in the wall and drove off.

Scott stood at the podium in stunned silence.

Finally a reporter broke the quiet. "So why *did* Bush kill the Freedonians?"

July 23, 2003

Buck Goes to Liberia Part I

"Good news, Buck; you're going to Liberia," Rumsfeld announced.

"Time for for'ner killin'! Ooh-rah!" Buck exclaimed. "So I'm one of the thousands of Marines going over there."

"Yeah, about that," Rumsfeld said, his expression getting serious. "We told the UN we were going to send thousands, but we're too busy in the Middle East to dedicate that many Marines there. So we're just sending you. I'm sure you can handle it."

"Well, who am I supposed to kill?"

"I dunno; I honestly haven't been following the news about Liberia. Mad Arab, you know who Buck is supposed to kill."

"Yeah, it's simple," General John Abizaid said. "Just find any crowded area, stand up on a platform where everyone can see you, and yell, 'Hey! Look at me! I'm an American!' while waving your arms in the air. Whoever shoots at you, they're the bad foreigners. Kill them."

Buck thought about that. "Sounds simple."

"And if you see President Charles Taylor," General Abizaid continued, "tell him he's a jackass, and he should get out of office."

"I think I can remember that."

"There's also the UN there."

"Should I kill them too?"

Rumsfeld and General Abizaid thought about this for a while. "Nah, they might be useful," Rumsfeld finally said. "Just kill any foreigners that look evil. And you can take Chomps with you; he could use the exercise." Rumsfeld looked at Chomps, who was lying on the ground asleep. "Hey Chomps, what do you think of foreigners?"

Chomps sprung to his feet, growling and randomly snapping at the air. Chomps didn't like foreigners.

"That's my boy."

* * * *

Chomps kept violently attacking the dirt, clawing at it with his feet and biting it while growling. He hated foreign soil.

"I know how you feel, Chomps, but we have to keep our minds on the mission. There are lots of foreign people out there who need a killin', and it ain't goin' to happen without our help."

Buck ventured into the nearby town, and many citizens stopped to stare. "Hello, I'm Buck the Marine, from America. I've come to help some of you for'ners and kill others. If you are a for'ner I'm supposed to kill, please signal by attacking me violently."

Most of the people just stared at them, but soon gunfire erupted, and everyone fled the streets. Buck rolled for cover and returned fire at the building the gunfire was coming from. Chomps ran toward the building and attacked its foundation. Soon the whole building collapsed.

"We're supposed to be avoiding collateral damage, Chomps," Buck scolded him.

Chomps spat out a piece of cement.

Walking a little further into town, Buck caught a glimpse of a tank. He knocked on its side. "Hello! Anybody in there?"

"Yes," answered a voice. "We're the UN. We're observing."

"But there's people gettin' killed out there," Buck protested. "Shouldn't you help them?"

"No," answered the voice. "It's nice and safe inside this tank. If we were to come out and help people or do anything useful, we'd be going against everything the UN stands for."

"Crazy for'ners," Buck muttered. "How can you watch evil happening and not want to kill bad people? I just don'ts understand it, right, Chomps?" Buck looked to his side and saw that Chomps wasn't there. Instead, Chomps was on top of the tank, tearing off the hatch with his teeth. He jumped down into the tank, and there was a lot of screaming. Soon Chomps emerged again, sporting a big, slobbery smile and a blue helmet.

"Silly dog," Buck laughed. "Now take off that helmet." Buck reached for it, but Chomps started growling. "Fine, keep it. You can be the UN representative. Now where do we go next?"

Buck surveyed the area and noticed a dark street from which a chilled wind of foreignness blew. He readied his rifle and prepared to embark. "Now let's start killin' for'ners until the for'ners we haven't killed look happy. Ooh-rah!"

TO BE CONCLUDED...

July 25, 2003

Buck Goes to Liberia Part II

"You gotta see this!" Rumsfeld exclaimed with a smile.

"What?" President Bush asked.

"Instead of just showing the dead bodies of Uday and Qusay, we came up with something more creative," Condoleezza Rice said, turning on a TV and playing a tape.

"We strung those two bastards up like marionettes and made them dance!" Rumsfeld laughed.

On screen were the two bullet-riddled bodies of Uday and Qusay Hussein dancing. Bush began to shield his eyes. "This is the most disgusting, grotesque, vile thing I've ever..." He then started laughing. "Hey, Uday just hit Qusay!" he said excitedly. "Hit him again! Uh-oh; Qusay is fighting back!" He turned to Rice and Rumsfeld. "This is great. We should make a series."

"Dancing dead Iraqis aside," White House Press Secretary Scott McClellan said, "what am I supposed to tell the press when they find out we only sent one Marine to Liberia?"

"I dunno, Ari; we didn't want to send more until that goof Charles Taylor steps down," Bush said. "Why are we even concerned about Liberia anyway? They don't have oil."

"I don't think we want to say that," Scott answered.

"Ari, you've really become more of a worry-wart since you grew hair," Bush told him. "Why don't you make up some other excuse for why we aren't sending more troops, such as that we hate black people."

"I don't know if that's a good idea," Rice said.

"That's for Ari to decide," Bush assured her. "He's the professional." Bush then started laughing hysterically. "Hit him again, Uday! Hit him!"

* * * *

Buck hid behind cover as Chomps stood nearby, still wearing his blue helmet (which made him the world's angriest UN peacekeeper). They were being fired upon by some people on the top story of a building. Buck and Chomps were pinned down tight.

"I'm almost out of ammo!" Buck exclaimed. "I may have to use one of these AK-47s from the for'ners I killed, and I hate AK-47s."

Chomps took an AK-47 in his mouth and snapped it in two. He also hated AK-47s.

"I have an idea," Buck told Chomps. "Maybe if you're smart like Lassie, you could take a grenade and run it into the building where all the for'ners are. Then you could pull out the pin and run away." He held out a grenade to Chomps. "Can you do that, boy?"

Chomps took the grenade and swallowed it.

"Oh, that ain't good."

Chomps started hacking and coughing.

"You better not explode on me," Buck said, shielding his face.

Chomps walked out of cover and hacked out the grenade with such force that it flew through the air and into the window of the building where their attackers hid. The grenade exploded, taking out the top floor. Chomps walked over to Buck and dropped a grenade pin into his hand.

"Wow!" Buck exclaimed. "That's quite a trick. When we get back to the States, we're going to have to have you do that on Letterman."

Buck readied his weapon and continued through the streets with Chomps following close behind. He soon spotted a woman ahead of him.

"Hmm, she don't look so foreign," Buck said, approaching cautiously.

It was FOX News reporter Melinda Hawkish, standing outside a building. "What are you doing here?" Buck asked.

"Trying to scoop Jennifer 'look at me I'm so pretty and in dangerous places' Eccleston by interviewing President Charles Taylor."

"Won't you need a cameraman?" Buck asked.

"Mine got kidnapped, and they're asking for a ransom," Melinda said with frustration. "All I really want to do is get a nice anchorwoman job. They once let me co-host on FOX & Friends, but get in one fist fight with Susan Estrich, and suddenly you're banned for life." She fixed her blouse. "So do you think this is an appropriate amount of cleavage for a serious newswoman to show?"

"Uh... I guess," Buck answered. "So is Charles Taylor in that building? I have a message for him."

"Yeah, he's locked in there."

Buck walked over to the building. "President Charles Taylor, I have a message for you!" Buck called out. "It's from General Abizaid."

"What is it?" Taylor asked, peeking out a window.

"You're a jackass, and you should get out of office!"

"I won't leave until the Americans commit troops!" Taylor responded.

"Uh... well, I'm an American Marine."

"Where are the rest of you?"

"Uh... I'm a fast runner... they're just behind me."

Taylor though about this. "Okay, I'll leave office, but I first need to talk to a UN representative."

Buck looked at Chomps and patted him on his blue helmet. "I guess that means you."

Chomps ran forward and busted through the front door. Soon Buck and Melinda could hear screaming, and then Taylor jumped out the window and ran off down the street. Now looking out the same window was Chomps with a big slobbery smile.

"Good negotiating, Chomps," Buck called out. "Ooh-rah!"

Melinda watched Taylor run like hell down the street. "There goes my interview," she sighed.

* * * *

Bush ran into Rumsfeld's office. "UPN just offered to pay for thirteen episodes of *The Uday & Qusay Show*."

"Okay," Rumsfeld said, "but I need to keep creative control."

A phone started ringing, and Rumsfeld picked it up. "Who is this? ...Buck? Buck who? ...Oh, Buck the Marine. How are things going?"

"We got President Charles Taylor to resign, so I'm taking a break to enjoy some Liberian liquors with Melinda Hawkish," Buck said.

"Okay, have a nice rest; you deserve it. Then I want you to head out to the Congo and fix whatever is wrong there."

"But I'm almost out of ammo and—"

"So how is Chomps?" Rumsfeld interrupted.

"He took a flight back to the States with some other people... I think to New York."

"What? He's all alone with strangers?"

"He seemed to know what he was doing."

* * * *

Chomps stood at the front of the auditorium of the main UN headquarters, wearing his blue helmet and looking at all the UN representatives with confusion. Kofi Annan stood next to him.

"For negotiating the peaceful resignation of President Charles Taylor, we would like to award UN peacekeeper Chomps this medal," Kofi Annan said and then moved toward Chomps with the medal in his hand.

Chomps took that as a threatening motion. And it made him angry. Now that he thought of it, all the people in this building made him angry for some reason. His eyes opened wide and became bloodshot. His lips curled up, revealing his jagged teeth. A growl started emanating from him, first low, then building in volume. Yes, the UN representatives made him angry. Very angry.

"Oh dear."

THE END

July 28, 2003

~~Rabbit~~ ~~Duck~~ Saddam Season

Co-Written by Mike the Marine

"We need to get Saddam Hussein!" Bush shouted, pounding the table with his fist. "NBC is willing to commit to thirteen episodes of the *Uday and Qusay Dead Body Puppet Hour*, but only if I can add Saddam to the cast."

"Most people think showing the dead bodies of Uday and Qusay was appropriate for the circumstances in Iraq," Scott McClellan said. "But don't you think dancing the dead bodies of our enemies around like puppets is going a little too far?"

"Hey, we're talking a series on a major network," Bush shot back. "And who the heck are you?"

"I'm Scott McClellan," Scott answered. "I've been the White House Press Secretary for two weeks now."

Bush thought about this. "Sounds right, but to be on the safe side, I'm going to have the Secret Service beat you up while I check on that."

"Hey!" Scott protested as the Secret Service dragged him away.

"New guys are so stupid," Bush chuckled once Scott was out of the room. "After they've roughed him up for five minutes, I'll tell him it was a joke. Now, back to business: how is our progress toward finding Saddam?"

"No new information," Cheney said, "but we do have a twenty-five million dollar bounty on his head."

Bush jumped to his feet. "Twenty-five million dollars! Hot damn! I'm gonna find him myself!" He paused to think for a moment. "He's probably not somewhere in the White House, is he?"

"Nope," Cheney answered.

"Then we'll need a plane, I guess. Who wants to go Saddam hunting with me?"

"Lord knows I'm always ready for killing anything!" Rumsfeld answered.

"My doctor tells me such activity could be bad for my heart," Cheney said, "but what the hell does he know? He's never had one heart attack! I think I'm the expert on the subject. Count me in."

"I'll come too," Condoleezza Rice said.

"No girls," Bush answered. "Hunting is a guy thing. Why don't you go knit a sweater or devise some war plans, Condi."

"Fine!" Rice said angrily as she stormed out of the room. "I'll just stay here and work on my planned military coup."

"You do that," Bush responded. "Now let's get what we need to bring on the trip."

Out of the shadows emerged the hooded figure of Karl Rove. "Don't forget to bring a camera. If people can witness you, the president, killing Saddam Hussein by yourself, it will show such strength that surely the Democrats will collapse, as prophesied by the ancients in the *Book of Shadows and Punditry*."

"Forget about the Democrats, Karly," Bush responded. "We're talking about twenty-five million dollars. With that kind of money, I could buy all the Democrats gold-plated baby bottles to go along with their whining."

"Or have them killed," Rumsfeld said. "At least at my going rate."

* * * *

"Hey, Laura, look; I got my hunting cap with the earflaps and everything," Bush exclaimed.

"What are you doing?"

"I'm going Saddam hunting with Cheney and Rumsfeld and Chomps," he told her. "I'm going to get that twenty-five million for myself."

"Don't you think it will look bad if the president takes the reward the government is offering?"

"I think I've made it pretty clear throughout my administration that I don't think at all," Bush responded indignantly. "That's why I got a group of smart people in my cabinet."

"I'll bring the beer," Cheney announced, holding his hunting rifle.

"I'm bringing the whiskey," Rumsfeld said.

"Well, don't shoot each other," Laura said with concern.

"That won't happen unless we get so drunk we mistake each other for Baathists," Bush assured her.

"I'm not promising anything," Rumsfeld said, loading his hunting rifle.

* * * *

Bush, Cheney, Rumsfeld, and Chomps waited in the Iraqi desert, hiding behind cover. "This is what I love about being an American," Bush said, loading his gun. "We can go into any country we choose and do whatever the hell we want. And who is going to stop us? No one, because we're too big and powerful."

"Other countries are stupid," Rumsfeld responded, taking a drink of whiskey. "Now, let's shoot people."

"By the way," Cheney said, "did you ever tell the Secret Service to stop beating up Scott?"

Bush thought about that for a moment. "Eh, I'm sure they tired out eventually."

Chomps, the world's angriest hunting dog, fiercely attacked the desert sand. Sand made him angry. Then the sun got in his eyes. He really hated the sun and dreamed of ripping it apart with his teeth. For now, he just barked at it.

"Quiet, Chomps," Bush scolded him. "We have to be silent when hunting for Baathists. Cheney, use the terrorist call."

Cheney blew into a whistle, and out came a loud ululation. From behind Bush came a terrorist who exclaimed, "Death to America!" Bush shot him.

"Go fetch him, Chomps," Rumsfeld commanded. Chomps ran out and dragged back the terrorist.

"Now to check him against my deck of cards of the Iraqi Most Wanted," Bush said, pulling out his cards. "Sure are a lot of fugitive naked women."

"I think that's the wrong deck of cards," Cheney said.

"Oh yeah," Bush answered and then pulled out another deck of cards. "He doesn't match any. Must just be some random Baathist. Toss him back, Chomps."

"I'm very hurt, and your dog swallowed my boot," the terrorist pleaded.

"Hey, we all got problems," Bush answered.

With a quick shake of his head, Chomps tossed the terrorist back out into the field.

"Hey, I see another one!" Bush exclaimed and took a shot.

Chomps dragged back the body.

"You killed a monkey!" Cheney exclaimed.

"A terrorist monkey," Bush said.

"I think he's just a regular monkey."

"Something is dead; let's be happy," Rumsfeld declared.

"Let's just keep an eye out for a man in a yellow hat seeking vengeance, to be on the safe side," Bush said. "Now we have to find a better way to draw Saddam out." He looked at Cheney. "Go out in the field and pretend to be a Kurd. Then I'll shoot Saddam when he comes out to gas you."

"No," Cheney answered. "Every time I pretend to be a Kurd, it always ends in trouble."

"Well, we have to find Saddam somehow," Bush declared. "I want that twenty-five million to make me extra richer!"

Suddenly, bullets came whizzing by their ears. Sand kicked up at their feet as metric ammo went flying by all around them. Loud ululations echoed around them, and the very ground shook beneath their feet. Over a sand dune in the distance came... Helen Thomas.

"Why are you trying to steal twenty-five million dollars from Iraqi children?" screeched the Wicked Witch of the West Wing.

Bush looked at her with a mix of contempt and confusion. Mostly it was exasperation, though. "Holy snikeys! What are you doing here, you old bat? Didn't the doctors tell you not to leave your house? And where'd you get the AK-47 from?"

"Those doctors were fakes, and the AK-47 was given to me by Peter Arnette. It's one he picked up during the first Gulf war. Of course, he was too much of a wuss to ever shoot it."

"Well, no argument on the Arnette thing," Bush said, smiling at her. Out of the corner of his mouth, he whispered to Rumsfeld. "Fire those danged 'doctors' and get somebody more believable next time."

"Done," said Rummy, the satellite phone already to his ear.

"Why are you illegally here in Iraq stealing millions of dollars?" she heckled Bush again.

"Listen, you mindless old crone, I can't be stealing it from them—it's already ours. What's that shadow?" Bush looked up.

FOX News reporter Melinda Hawkish landed squarely on Helen's head. Her parachute was immediately consumed by Chomps before it even had a chance to hit the ground. Parachutes made Chomps angry, for reasons even the world's angriest dog didn't really understand.

"What did I land on?" asked Melinda.

"A desert rat," Bush said coldly. "A big, fat desert rat."

"What are *you* doing here?" Cheney gasped. He was still using up heartbeats after diving away from Helen Thomas's wildly erratic gunfire.

"Buck the Marine called me and said that he'd gotten some intel about you guys going on a Saddam hunt. I want Saddam's last interview before you turn him into a marionette."

"Hey, that TV deal's supposed to be hush-hush!" Bush cried. "I don't want anybody stealing my idea."

"How is ol' Buck?" Rummy asked. "He's a good man, holding down the fort in Liberia for us."

"He said the weapons drop wasn't nearly large enough," Melinda said. "He needs another pallet of ammo and some MREs, too."

"Didn't we send him 150,000 rounds of .223 and a whole box of chicken tortellini meals?" Bush asked.

"He's a Marine. They want two things: food and ammo," Melinda said matter-of-factly. Chomps yelped in agreement. Buck was one of the precious few people that made him less angry. Not happy, mind you—just less angry.

"Well, nobody ever killed Saddam by sitting in one place and waiting for him to ditty-bop on by. Let's roll," said Rumsfeld.

"I can't move too fast in this heat," Cheney said.

"Awww, woook... Widdle baby is gonna have another coronary. Boo freakin' hoo," Rumsfeld chided him. "Get to steppin'. In thirty miles you can have a nitro pill."

"Owned!!" Bush laughed at Cheney. "Hey Rummy, you gonna share that water?"

"What water?" Rumsfeld asked as he screwed the cap back on his canteen. "I think there's a watering hole aboouuuuttttt... thirty miles from here."

"I miss being undisclosed," Cheney said as he shuffled off behind the others.

July 30, 2003

The Saudis Are Great People... for Me to Strangle!

"I'm strangling you because you're a Saudi!" Rumsfeld shouted, strangling the Saudi prince.

"Let's not be so quick to strangle each other," Colin Powell urged.

"Rarr!"

* * * *

"So which is closer to Bush's position," asked a reporter, "Rumsfeld's 'Strangle the Saudis' stance, or Powell's 'Please don't beat me with that Saudi' stance?"

"Bush likes to hold the middle ground," White House Press Secretary Scott McClellan answered.

"What about this new report out?" said another reporter. "Some people find it alarming."

"What's so alarming?" Scott asked.

"Well, it starts with, 'US intelligence has determined' and then there are twenty-seven pages blanked out, followed by the word 'the' and then fourteen pages missing until the phrase 'brain-eating zombies' then thirty-two pages missing until the phrase 'nuclear deaths for everyone' then eight pages missing, followed by 'the Saudis are planning to stab us in the back and' then eighty-three pages missing until the report ends with the word 'happy.'"

Scott chuckled nervously as he adjusted his collar. "How can anything be 'alarming' if it ends with the word 'happy'?"

"According to our poll, 68% of American people are for military action against the Saudis, and 32% against," said Melinda Hawkish of FOX News. When are we going to use military action against those 32% who are terrorist sympathizers?"

"Hey," Scott cautioned, "the Saudis are not necessarily terrorists and, in the least, are much better at pretending to be our allies than the French."

"Then why is Rumsfeld strangling them?"

"Well, Rumsfeld comes from a different time, when it was normal that if you saw a fat man with a devil beard wearing sheets, you strangled him."

Scott started laughing. "Why, he was even joking with me earlier about how he was going to kill all of you."

Suddenly a Buick crashed through the wall. Out jumped Rumsfeld. "Rarr!"

* * * *

"I can't be giving these press conferences if Rumsfeld is trying to strangle everyone," Scott complained.

"If they're that important to you," Bush said, "then tell Rumsfeld to stop strangling people."

Scott looked at Rumsfeld. He sat in a chair, calmly petting Chomps, who was drinking water from his UN helmet.

"Uh, Rumsfeld," Scott said, "could you please cut back the strangling just a little bit?"

Rumsfeld considered this for a moment. He then shouted, "Rarr!"

Scott cowered, covering his face defensively, but Rumsfeld and Chomps ran out of the room. Scott looked out into the hallway. "Hey! They're trashing my office!"

"That's Rumsfeld's way of saying 'No,'" Bush explained. "Anyway, I found this old Atari. Want to play *Combat*?"

"*Combat*?"

"It's a game where you shoot each other with tanks and planes, idiot," Bush said, turning on the Atari.

"Shouldn't you be involved in policy talks or something?" Scott asked.

"No, my staff says things go much smoother if I'm not there," Bush said and then started the tank game. "Ha! I'm whooping your butt!" Bush laughed as he shot Scott's tank.

"I'm getting used to the controls!" Scott said defensively.

"It's just a button and a joystick, stupid."

"I would like to talk more about policy," said a Saudi prince, appearing at the doorway. He was then knocked down as a desk crashed into him.

"Your desk killed a Saudi," Bush told Scott. "You're going to be in trouble for that."

"Hey, I got you!" Scott exclaimed, having shot Bush's tank.

"No fair; I wasn't paying attention," Bush yelled angrily. "Secret Service, take Scott away and beat him!"

"Hey!" Scott exclaimed as the Secret Service grabbed him and dragged him away.

The Saudi crawled out from under the desk. "You're not dead," Bush said. "Want to play Atari?"

"Sure," the Saudi said, taking the other controller.

He started hitting Bush's tank repeatedly. "Ha! Allah be praised! I destroy your imperialist tank!"

"What?!" Bush yelled. "I can't move." He then looked at the console. "You unplugged my controller, you backstabbing Saudi! This means war!"

August 04, 2003

The Duke Versus Stalin

Based on a true story.

Moscow, Soviet Union, 1949

Stalin's mustache brimmed with Commie fury. "This John Wayne, he is an enemy to our people. His cowboy mentality, his knowledge of right and wrong... it goes against everything Communism stands for. He must die!"

"You want us to kill the Duke?!" exclaimed one of Stalin's advisors.

"You question me?!" Stalin shouted. "Off to Gulag!"

Stalin's secret police grabbed the man and dragged him away.

"Our intelligence says that John Wayne is currently in a bar with another actor named Ronald Reagan," said another advisor.

"Send our agents to kill him now!" Stalin ordered.

"What about Ronald Reagan?"

"He is just a B-movie actor; he is no threat to the Soviet Union," Stalin said dismissively. "We kill John Wayne, and Communism will live forever!" Stalin stood up and lifted his arms high into the air. "I am Stalin! Fear my mustache!"

* * * *

"My agent says I should do some movies with monkeys in them," Reagan said. "Comedies might be good for my career."

"Only thing a monkey is good for is target practice," the Duke answered and took a drink of whiskey.

"Ever thought of doing a comedy?" Reagan asked.

"Nothing funny these days with Reds about."

"Anyway, this is a nice bar."

"It's outta the way," the Duke answered. "Keeps me from getting bothered."

"Jeepers! It's John Wayne!" exclaimed a kid, running up to the table.

"Dangit," the Duke uttered.

"And I'm Ronald Reagan," Reagan told the kid with a smile.

"Who?"

"Never mind," Reagan answered, turning back to his drink.

"Golly gosh, Mr. Wayne," the kid said excitedly, "I'm your bestest fan. I want to be a cowboy just like you."

"Well, it will never happen, so scram, kid," the Duke answered.

"Aww, Mister, why'd you have to crush my dreams like that?" the kid said mournfully.

"You could be a little nicer," Reagan told the Duke.

"You're starting to annoy me, too," the Duke growled.

"I'm sorry, but—"

"Quiet," the Duke ordered and observed the air carefully. "I smell Reds," he whispered.

Two men in suits approached. "I am FBI agent Yuri, and this is FBI agent Ivan," said one in a thick Russky accent. "You must come with us, Mr. Wayne."

"Sure," the Duke said, standing up slowly. He then whipped out his peacemaker and shot them both.

"Holy moly!" the kid exclaimed. "You killed them!"

"Commies," Wayne answered. "And it ain't over." The Duke knocked over the table for cover, and more gunfire came their way. The Duke fired back until his gun was empty. He tossed it to the kid, along with some ammo. "Make yourself useful, and reload that for me."

"Golly! But I don't know anything about guns, mister."

"Well, figure it out," the Duke demanded. He looked at Reagan, who huddled behind the table. "Dutch, you have a gun?"

"I am an American," Reagan said as he took out a 1911.

"Cover me as I kill these Reds," the Duke said as he emerged from behind the table. He saw four evil Commies, and he and Reagan shot them dead as the Duke kept moving, finally taking new cover behind the bar.

"That was six shots, Yankee scum," said an evil Commie the Duke hadn't seen, who now stood over him.

"Here you go," the kid yelled, tossing a gun to the Duke. He caught it and rolled out of the way of the Commie's shots, finally returning fire with one bullet through the man's evil Commie brain.

The Duke stood and observed the room. "That's all of them."

"Should we call the police?" Reagan asked.

"Nothing left to do here except clean up," the Duke answered.

"Gosh, I thought you were done for, Mr. Wayne," the kid said.

"Thanks for your help," the Duke answered and then handed the kid the peacemaker. "Here, keep this gun."

"Wow! Thanks!"

"So what's your name, kid?"

"Clinton Eastwood, sir."

"That's the gayest name I've ever heard," the Duke said. "I'll call you Clint."

"Clint it is," the kid answered. "Thanks again, Mister. You're the bestest!"

Reagan looked at the dead Commies. "One day I'll see the Soviet Union destroyed," Reagan vowed, "but first I need to do that comedy with a monkey in it."

"I have some business to finish myself," the Duke said, reloading a gun.

* * * *

Moscow, Soviet Union, 1953

"Time to retire to bed so I can plot more Commie evil in the morning," Stalin said, brushing his mustache with his fingers. He looked around and noticed he couldn't see any guards in his country home. "Guards!" he called out. "Where are you?"

He made his way to his bedroom. Inside, he noticed a cowboy hat sitting on his nightstand. As he slowly approached it, he heard the bedroom door close behind him. He turned to see the Duke standing there, a peacemaker pointed right at him.

"Say hi to Lenin for me in Commie hell, Joe," the Duke said and unloaded his gun into Stalin's chest. The Duke then slowly walked over and picked up his hat, put it back on, and strolled out of the room.

Soon guards arrived and found Stalin lying on the ground bleeding. "Oh no!" exclaimed one of them. "We let John Wayne kill Stalin. We'll be in big trouble for this. We better think of some other story to explain his death."

"I'm not dead," Stalin muttered weakly.

"First let's drink some vodka," said the other guard. "Vodka helps us think."

"Great, comrade," said the other guard. "We'll drink vodka and then come up with a story for Stalin's death."

"I'm not dead," Stalin pleaded, "and can I have some vodka, too?"

"Here, have a pillow," the guard said and took a pillow off of Stalin's bed and pressed it over Stalin's face.

Another guard entered the room. "Hey! You guys are killing Stalin!" he exclaimed. "I don't think you're supposed to do that!"

"John Wayne shot him," another guard answered. "We're just helping Stalin along."

"He's taking forever to smother," said the guard with the pillow. "Let's go raid the liquor cabinet."

"Hey, after we get the vodka, we can go watch the movie *Bedtime for Bonzo* in Stalin's private screening room," said one of the guards. "It's supposed to be funny!"

August 06, 2003

Condi's Coup Part I

"Man, I was going to get in trouble for my Secret Service not being diverse enough," President Bush told Donald Rumsfeld. "I was told I need to hire either a woman or someone with a handicap."

"So did you hire a woman?" Condoleezza Rice asked, listening in.

Bush started laughing. "Yeah, I hired a woman," he said mockingly. "She'll be sitting there filing her nails while I get mowed down by machine gun fire. Don't you have some dishes to clean, Condi?"

"I was working on threat assessments for Middle Eastern countries," Rice answered furiously.

"That's cute, Condi; you keep doing that."

Rice gave him an angry look and stormed out of the office.

"I heard that, George!" Laura Bush exclaimed. "That was mean and sexist, and I think you should go apologize to her."

"Bah, women and their feelings," Bush answered. "They should be like us men and not have any."

Laura just shook her head and walked away.

"So who did you hire?" Rumsfeld asked.

"Kôtôichi, the blind samurai!" Bush answered.

Slowly into the room walked Ichi, tapping ahead of himself with his cane. Chomps walked up to him, watching with reserved anger. "Nice doggie," Ichi said, blindly reaching out to pet Chomps. Chomps snapped at him, but he had quickly retracted his hand.

"Wow! What reflexes!" Bush exclaimed. "And there's a sword in his cane he can pull out and cut people with. He's so cool."

"Giving sharp objects to blind people seems like a bad idea to me," Rumsfeld said.

"You should see him, though!" Bush answered. "A hippy bothered us on the way here, and with one swing of his sword, Ichi cut the tie-dye shirt right off the hippy without touching his unwashed skin."

"So he completely missed the hippy," Rumsfeld scoffed. "Sounds like a piss-poor samurai to me. And how well is a sword going to help you nowadays? What happens if he comes up against a blind rifleman? He's dead, that's what."

"Don't listen to him, Ichi," Bush said. "I know you'll make a great Secret Service agent." He turned to Rumsfeld. "And he only cost fifty bu to hire."

"What's a bu?"

"I don't know; I'm having an intern look into it. Anyway, I have to get going and give some speeches and stuff. Come on, Ichi."

* * * *

"Man, I don't like talking to people," Bush sulked. "They always laugh at me when I mess up my speakering. But I guess you don't have to worry about things like that, Ichi, since you can't hear them laughing."

"You're thinking of deaf," Ichi said, following Bush.

"Whatever. Anyway, I just had this last addition added to my schedule. I'm supposed to meet some school children in this scary alleyway."

As they walked further into the alleyway, Ichi grabbed Bush by the arm and carefully listened around him. "I sense danger."

"Oh no! Danger is bad!" Bush exclaimed.

"Stay close to me," Ichi said, now holding his staff with both hands.

Five terrorists emerged holding scimitars. "We kill you, President Bush, because of our extreme Islamic view which dictates we want to destroy America or something," said one of them.

"Oh no! Islamic extremists!" Bush exclaimed. "Be careful, Ichi; they're extreme!"

The terrorists charged Bush, but with lightning speed, Ichi drew his sword and cut all five down, returning the sword to its sheath with a click.

"That was so cool!" Bush said. "I need to get attacked by terrorists more often. That will learn them for sure! If they want to destroy America, they should do it through non-violent means, such as helping the Howard Dean campaign."

"I think this was a trap," Ichi said.

"But who could have set it up?" Bush asked. "This was a last minute addition to my schedule added by Condoleezza Rice, who currently has a grudge against me." Bush thought for a moment. "It must be the Syrians!"

"Maybe it was this Condi in vengeance for those mean things you said," Ichi suggested.

"You think?" Bush asked dubiously. "If that's true, she's going to get a talking to. Nobody tries to kill this president and gets spared a talking to!"

* * * *

Chomps stared at a control panel. It made him angry. "Grrrow!" he growled as he attacked it.

"Self-destruct in ten... nine... eight..." said a pleasant computerized voice.

Rice ran over to the controls. "Self-destruct deactivated," said the computer.

"You have to control your dog," Rice said to Rumsfeld irately. "That's the third time today he's done that!"

"Hey, he doesn't like buttons and switches," Rumsfeld answered. "What am I supposed to do?"

"Hello, Condi," Bush said angrily as he entered the war room, Ichi following close behind him.

"Oh, you're alive," Rice said with disappointment.

"That's right; it takes more than a couple terrorists to stop ol' Dubya. Now why did you try to kill me?" he asked. "Is it like your time of the month or something?"

"Rarr!" Rice exclaimed and hit a button on a controller. A door opened, and in came a number of giant robots. "These are my military death machines," Rice explained. "With them I will achieve military victories you only dreamed of. Then I, Condoleezza Rice, will be known as the savior of America! All shall bow before me!"

Bush looked at the robots warily. "We got trouble, Ichi."

"Describe them to me."

"They're eight feet tall, have glowing red eyes, and have Gatling guns for arms. Now pull out your sword, and cut them up good. Chop chop, Ichi. Ichi?" He looked around and couldn't see Kôtôichi anywhere. "For a blind man, he sure can run fast."

The robots approached Bush. "Rumsfeld, do something!" Bush pleaded.

"Hey, I stay out of this politics stuff; this is between you and Dr. Rice."

Bush noticed Chomps nearby, chewing apart a folding metal chair. "Hey Chomps, go bite these robots. Do it now! As your president, I command you!"

"Ordering Chomps around really makes him angry," Rumsfeld warned.

Chomps started growling at Bush. "Uh-oh."

* * * *

"In other news today, President Bush has been declared incapacitated, as he is currently trapped in a tree on the White House lawn by Chomps, holder of the title of the world's angriest dog, according to the *Guinness Book of World Records*." A file photo of Chomps tearing the treads off a Russian tank appeared on screen. "Next in line for the presidency would be Dick Cheney, but his location is undisclosed, so no one can find him to swear him in. Instead, National Security Advisor Condoleezza Rice has declared herself Empress. This is an unprecedented move and highly unconstitutional..."

A large robot appeared behind the anchorman and pressed a Gatling gun to his head. "...but you have to praise Empress Rice for her initiative. All hail Empress Rice! By the way, war has been declared on all countries that begin with the letter 's.' So if your country begins with the letter 's,' remember: resistance is futile. Now let's all join in singing our new national anthem in praise of Empress Rice."

TO BE CONTINUED...

August 08, 2003

Condi's Coup Part II

"What's this place?" Rumsfeld asked, looking around.

"It's my secret fortress inside a hollowed-out volcano," Condoleezza Rice answered, sitting at her throne. "I decided to move my operations here to keep a lower profile."

"I don't know if I like it," Rumsfeld said. Chomps added a growl for good measure.

"You don't need to," Rice said sternly.

"And what's with the mask?" Rumsfeld asked. "Everyone knows who you are."

"It goes with the cape," Rice answered tersely.

Jenna Bush walked into the room. "France is calling. They're trying to surrender again."

"But I haven't even threatened them yet!" Rice fumed. "Tell them they can't surrender until I at least threaten them with war. If they call again, just hang up on them."

Jenna left the room. "Was that one of Bush's daughters?" Rumsfeld inquired.

"She and Barbara needed summer jobs for beer money, so I hired them as evil minions," Rice answered.

"I don't know if I like all this hollowed-out volcano and evil minion crap," Rumsfeld growled.

"Just keep to your warring," Rice ordered. "I now have even more military death machines to help you." The giant robots marched into the room, looking ready to kill. "They are in every way superior to human soldiers. They are tireless, strong, and... is one missing a head?" She spotted Chomps chewing on a robot head. "That dog is an annoyance!" She thought for a moment. "But maybe I have a use for him..."

"North Korea called," Jenna called out. "They say they won't have multilateral talks and will only talk with the United States."

"I'll tell them who they will talk to!" Rice shouted. "I know who to send to handle this. Ha. All these international problems are so easy to deal with now that Bush is out of the way. Soon I will be known as the most effective leader of the US ever. Muh ha ha ha!"

"I'll be at a bar," Rumsfeld grumbled as he walked away.

* * * *

"Ha ha ha! Pretty colors!" Kim Jong-Il laughed as he played with his kaleidoscope.

"We're here to talk to you about your nuclear weapons," said a fierce voice behind him.

"What?!" Kim exclaimed. "I only talk to US."

"Well the US don't want to talk to you," said the thug. "Instead, you're talking to me."

"And who are you?"

"Vinnie, from Jersey," the man answered. He moticned to the muscle-bound man next to him. "And this here is Rocko."

"I don't know you! I don't talk to you! Only to US!" Kim exclaimed.

"Oh, I think you'll talk to us," Vinnie threatened. "And guess what; we'll give you a free hair cut as part of the deal." Vinnie snapped his fingers. Rocko pulled out an electric clipper and approached Kim Jong-Il.

"No!" Kim exclaimed. "Not my poofy hair! Noooooo!!"

* * * *

"What are you doing up in that tree?" Laura demanded. "Were you drinking again?"

"No," Bush answered. "Chomps chased me up here. Is he gone now?"

"I think so," Laura said, looking at the tree. "Nearly chewed the tree down, though."

Bush climbed down. "Is that Kôtôichi behind you?" he asked angrily. "That coward ran away!"

"You said nothing about large robots," Ichi answered sternly. "You want me fight robots: 100 bu."

"That's double your fee!" Bush yelled angrily. "There's no way in hell I'm going to pay that—"

The click of the sword returning to its sheath was the only evidence Bush had that Ichi's sword was drawn. Bush's tie fell off his neck to the ground.

"Okay, you drive a hard bargain, Ichi," Bush said more calmly. "100 bu it is."

"Have you heard what happened while you were up in that tree?" Laura asked. "Dr. Rice has taken over America and turned it into a police state.

You need to talk to her and apologize for your sexist remarks so you can end this madness."

"Laura, Laura, Laura," Bush chuckled, shaking his head. "Politics isn't about talking and apologies; it's about blind samurai and robots with Gatling-gun arms. Now come on, Ichi, we have work to do."

* * * *

"Okay, everyone, I know this is new for all of us," White House Press Secretary Scott McClellan announced. "This is the first time the US has had a military coup, and this is also the first time I have given a press conference with a robot pointing a gun at my head in case I misspeak." He glanced warily at the large robot behind him. "So, any questions?"

FOX News reporter Melinda Hawkish stepped forward.

"I would think you'd be happy with all this," Scott said. "We are at war with just about every country out there. What are you concerned about?"

"I'm just wondering, as I assume most of our viewers are, what caliber bullet will be shot through your head if you misspeak?" Melinda asked.

"I don't know," Scott answered with annoyance. "Any other questions?"

"Why does Bush want to kill Iraqi children?" Helen Thomas asked. "What did Iraqi children ever do to him?"

"Are you even paying attention?" Scott exclaimed with exasperation. "That question has nothing to do with anything!"

"Where are my pills? Who took my pills?" Helen responded.

"For the last time, Ari Fleischer stole them before he left," Scott answered. "Go talk to him."

"Is it true that mafia thugs shaved the head of Kim Jong-Il at Empress Rice's command?" asked another reporter. "Is it really wise to be associated with organized crime?"

"Empress Rice is trying to come up with creative solutions to problems," Scott said, "and she thinks her new strategies are much more effective than Bush's, whom she terms a 'goober.'"

"Many Democrats are complaining about being hunted down by robots when they oppose Empress Rice's policies," said a reporter. "They are then hunted down by robots after that complaining. How do you respond to that?"

"That's just politics," Scott said. "Sometimes it's rough, but if all the Democrats can do is whine about it, that just shows how bereft of ideas they are. Any other questions?"

"Is that samurai who is approaching you blind?"

"Huh?" Scott exclaimed, looking behind him. With a swish of a blade, the Gatling-gun arm of the robot was severed off. With another slice, the head fell to the ground.

"Come on, Scott," Bush said, running in front of the reporters. "We're taking America back."

"Uh, okay," Scott said dubiously.

"Is it true, ousted President Bush, that you said mean, sexist things to Empress Rice?" asked a reporter.

"I was just joking," Bush responded. "She shouldn't be so sensitive. And I want to assure the American people that Condi's reign of terror will soon end. I will get back in power, stop her mindless hawkishness, and get the economy on track."

"Actually, the stock market shot up when people found out you were pinned up in a tree by an angry dog," Melinda told him.

"What?!" Bush exclaimed furiously and looked right into the cameras. "You guys suck! I'm going to be president again anyway, though."

* * * *

"Where's Chomps?" Rumsfeld inquired.

"Right where he won't give me any trouble," Rice said, walking over to a metal cage. Inside was Chomps, who was extremely angry. Condi made faces at him, and he snarled and growled but couldn't bite through the metal bars.

"That's cruel!" Rumsfeld exclaimed. "He should be running free, exacting his mindless anger on whatever he sees."

"I have better plans for him," Rice answered.

"And what's this about laying off the troops?" Rumsfeld asked.

"Now that I have my robots, I have no need for them. Come to think of it, I have no need for you."

A robot walked up from behind Rumsfeld and grabbed him. "Rarr!" Rumsfeld shouted, but he couldn't break the robot's grip.

"'Rarr' all you want," Rice said. "These robots are too strong for you." Rice thought evilly for a while. "Actually, save your rage; I have use for it. Muh ha ha ha!"

"Jenna and I are going for a lunch run," Barbara interrupted. "What kind of sandwich do you want from Subway?"

"Turkey with light mayo," Rice answered, "and they'd better get it right, or they will be destroyed!"

* * * *

Bush, Kôtôichi, and Scott barged into Buck the Marine's house. "Buck, we need your help!" Bush exclaimed.

Buck was sitting in a chair, looking sullen.

"What's the matter, Buck?" Bush asked with concern.

"I got dismissed from the Marines," Buck said mournfully. "They think robots can replace us Marines, but a robot can't understand the intricacies of killin' a for'ner no more than it can paint art or write poetry."

"I'm sorry, Buck," Bush answered. "Can't you get a job as a mercenary?"

"But I only liked killin' for'ners for America," Buck said. "That's my favorite thing of all to kill people for."

"Well, we're going to overthrow Condi," Bush told him. "Then you can be back in the Marines. Want to help us?"

"Sure," Buck answered, cheering up a bit, "but won't we be killin' robots? I only know about killin' for'ners. It's not like you can stick robots with a KA-BAR."

"If it helps," Bush said, "I think a lot of their parts are made in China."

"Foreign robots!" Buck exclaimed. "I'm in!"

"So, do you have weaponry?"

"Some." Buck opened the door to a room filled with all kinds of guns.

"Holy!" Bush exclaimed and then picked up a machine gun. "Condi will be sorry she usurped me, that's for sure. You want a gun, Ichi?"

"I prefer sword," he answered curtly.

"You pick something out, Scott."

"Uh, I'm not really a gun person," he said uneasily. "I don't think I'll be much use during a siege or anything."

Bush rolled his eyes. "What a diverse staff I got now. I have women, minorities, a blind guy, and now a homosexual."

"Hey!" Scott exclaimed. "That's not called for!"

Bush tossed him a shotgun. "Be a man!"

Senator Tom Daschle walked into the room. "I've been looking for you," he said. "The current government is a disaster."

"And we're handling it, Daschle," Bush answered with annoyance. "And we don't need any whiny Democrats to help us."

"I think this just proves what a poor leader you are," Daschle said. "I am saddened that you couldn't keep control of your own administration, your sexist remarks leading to—"

"Hey Daschle," Bush interrupted. "There's something on your nose."

"What?"

"My forehead." Bush grabbed Daschle by the shoulders and head-butted him.

"You broke my nose!"

"Then I did it right."

Daschle ran out of the room.

"Now are we going to blow up some foreign robots?" Buck asked, loading some magazines.

"Damn straight," Bush answered. He then put on his cowboy hat and chambered a round into his rifle. "Time for some politics of massive destruction!"

TO BE CONCLUDED...

August 11, 2003

Condi's Coup Part III

"Place could be booby-trapped," Bush declared. "Scott, open the door."

"Why do I—"

"Stop being such a pansy!"

"Okay." Scott carefully opened the door to the White House while Bush, Buck, and Kôtôichi watched. "Man, looks like the place was trashed!" he exclaimed.

Garbage littered the floors. Most of the furniture was overturned. "Terrorist attack," Bush ventured.

Ichi sniffed around. "Smells like... kegger party."

Bush spotted his two daughters. "Jenna and Barbara, did you throw an all-night kegger party at the White House?"

"I'm Barbara, and she's Jenna," Barbara said angrily.

"Whatever. You two are twins; how am I supposed to tell you apart?"

"We're not identical twins!" Jenna exclaimed. "We don't even look alike in the least."

"Fine. Now stop avoiding the question. Did you trash my White House?"

"It's not *your* White House, Mr. Not-President," Barbara answered. "Dr. Rice said we could use it for our parties."

"You don't listen to Condi; you listen to your father!" Bush demanded.

"Hey, at least she gives us money," Jenna responded.

"I stopped giving you money at college, because I know all you do is spend it on booze. What is she giving you money for?"

"She's paying us ten bucks an hour to help her take over the world," Barbara explained.

"You shouldn't help her!" Bush exclaimed. "She's evil!"

His daughters both rolled their eyes. "Yeah, she's the one who is evil," Jenna laughed. "I heard about the mean, sexist things you said to her."

"You really should apologize," Barbara added.

"She's just being too sensitive," Bush insisted. "Now where is her secret fortress?"

"We're not telling you," Jenna said. She turned to Barbara. "Let's get going. Dr. Rice said we can pick the next country to bomb."

"Why don't you and your friends go back to your ranch in Texas and play war there?" Barbara commented derisively as she followed Jenna.

"You should discipline your daughters better," Ichi stated.

Bush scoffed. "Why does every blind samurai without children think he knows better how to raise *my* daughters?"

"What mean, sexist things did you say?" Buck asked.

"Forget it, Buck," Bush commanded. "The important thing is I get back my presidency without apologizing."

Just then Laura Bush walked into the White House. "Oh dear!" she exclaimed, looking at the mess in complete and utter horror. "White House tours start in an hour. They'll think I'm the worst First Lady ever!"

"It was all Barbara's and Jenna's doing, now that they're working for Condi," Bush told her. "Or was it Jenna and Barbara? Which one has red hair?"

"Neither," Laura answered angrily. "And I can see why they would act like this when their father sets such a bad example. If you had just apologized to Dr. Rice for being so sexist, we would never have had this mess."

Bush groaned. "It's like people think I'm supposed to apologize every time I do something wrong; it's ridiculous." He turned to Scott, Buck, and Ichi. "Let's try and find that secret fortress."

"We could follow your daughters," Ichi suggested.

"Good thinking, Ichi," Bush responded. "I'll drive, and you keep an eye on them."

Ichi shook his head. "You're an idiot."

Bush fixed his cowboy hat. "An idiot who's getting his presidency back."

* * * *

Bush, Scott, Buck, and Kôtôichi slowly approached Condoleezza Rice's secret fortress. "I always knew there was something suspicious about this hollowed-out volcano just outside of DC," Bush remarked.

Suddenly a gunshot hit near them, and they all ran for cover behind a large rock. "Is that Barbara shooting at us?" Bush asked, peeking out from behind the rock.

"It's Jenna!" she answered angrily as another shot flew just past Bush's head.

"Barbara is watching us from the other sniper tower," Buck commented. "I think we're pinned down."

"You can get past them," Bush told Ichi. "They can't see you."

"That's invisible!" Ichi exclaimed with annoyance. "Blind means I can't see them!"

"Good grief; calm down, Ichi."

"We need a diversion," Buck said, "someone to draw their fire."

All eyes went to Scott. "What?"

"Run out there, Scott, and distract them," Bush commanded.

"But... uh... I don't want to get shot."

"Don't be such a baby," Bush said. "They're just firing paintballs."

"You sure about that?"

"Yeah," Bush answered, shoving Scott out from cover. Scott started running.

"Man, is that guy gullible," Bush chuckled. "Now let's get going!"

Bush, Buck, and Ichi ran for the fortress's entrance, with Bush guiding Ichi along by holding on to his cane. Once they got to the entrance, they heard Scott yell, "Ahh! My leg!"

"Should we go help him?" Buck asked.

"That's what they want us to do," Bush answered. "She wounds someone so she can pick the rest off as we try and help him. I've seen Jenna do this before, and I ain't falling for it again."

"It was Barbara who shot him," Ichi remarked.

"Who can tell them apart?" Bush exclaimed.

There was another gunshot. "Ahh! My other leg!" Scott yelled.

"You're doing great, Scott!" Bush called out to him. "Way to take one for the team!" Bush then prepared to open the door to the fortress. "Everyone get ready."

Inside were six military death machines. Bush and Buck charged, firing their machine guns, while Kôtôichi drew his sword and came in swinging. "Who's the leader of the Executive Branch?" Bush yelled as he blew up the last of the death machines.

"Blowing up robots is kinda fun," Buck declared with a smile. "If I can't become a Marine again, I think I'll get a job as a robot exterminator."

"You'll get your job back," Bush declared as he charged forward. They soon came to a large room where Condi sat on a throne at the far end.

"Ha!" Bush laughed. "Your military death machines fight like they were made by a girl!"

"I'll make you eat your words!" Condi shouted as she stood up. She wore a costume of green with a purple cape and mask.

"Wow!" Bush exclaimed. "You have a villainess costume and everything!"

"I take my job seriously," Condi said, "unlike some people." She then pressed a button on a remote control, and even larger robots came after Bush and his company. "Let's see how you do against my new and improved models! Muh ha ha ha!"

Bush and Buck fired their guns, but their bullets bounced off the robots' metal hides. Ichi's sword clanged uselessly against them. The three then cowered in the center of the room while the robots surrounded them.

"I think we might be done for, Chief," Buck declared.

"Ichi, use your ninja magic or something," Bush said.

"I'm a samurai!" Ichi yelled with annoyance and then swung his cane, hitting Buck in the head. "Sorry; I'm not so magically attuned to my other senses when I'm mad."

"It's alright," Buck said as he looked at the deadly robots and tried to contemplate what to do.

"There's an extra secret ingredient to these robots," Condi said. A wall opened up, and there was Chomps in a cage and Rumsfeld chained to the wall. "I've collected the combined anger of Chomps and Rumsfeld and imbued the robots with it. To stimulate that anger, I have a hippy reading political opinion pieces by Noam Chomsky to them.

There sat a hippy, gleefully reading a book by Noam Chomsky as Chomps and Rumsfeld struggled with all their might to break free from their constraints and kill the hippy.

"Oh my!" Bush exclaimed. "That's so diabolical it's kinda funny!"

"With my robots, I'll destroy all of America's enemies, foreign and domestic," Condi declared. "Then all shall worship me and declare you a worthless idiot."

"So are you going to kill us with your robots?" Bush asked.

"That is the plan," Condi said.

"Just like a woman to have robots do her killing," Bush laughed.

Condi looked steamed. "Fine! I'll kill you myself!" She walked up to Bush and dropped into a martial arts stance.

Bush rolled up his sleeves. "Now, I don't want to hit a gir—"

Condi kicked Bush in the stomach and elbowed him in the chin, knocking him to the ground.

"Help!" Bush exclaimed. "Condi is beating me up!"

Laura stormed into the room, dragging Barbara and Jenna by their ears. Scott crawled in behind her. "Do you know what your daughters were doing?" Laura asked angrily. "Trying to snipe their own mother, that's what!"

"Why are they always *my* daughters when they're trying to kill us?" Bush groaned as he got himself off the ground.

"Dr. Rice, what are you doing in that silly outfit?" Laura asked.

"Killing your husband and then taking over the world," Condi said defensively.

Laura rolled her eyes. "Okay, I cleaned up the White House and made enough punch and pie for everyone... but you only get it if you all make up. Now, George, why don't you finally apologize to Dr. Rice for the mean things you said, and set a good example for your daughters."

"Apologize?" Bush said distastefully.

"Come on," Ichi urged. "We want punch and pie!"

"Fine," Bush said, first looking at the ground for a moment, then finally facing Condi eye to eye. "I'm sorry I said those mean, sexist things. You can be just as mindlessly hawkish as any man around... if not more so."

"And do you have something to say to George, Dr. Rice?" Laura urged.

"I guess I overreacted a bit when I tried to have you killed by Islamic extremists, became a supervillain, and turned America into a police state," Condi told Bush. "I'm sorry."

"Happens to the best of us," Bush said, patting her on the shoulder. He looked at Laura. "So do we get punch and pie now?"

"First you have to apologize to Tom Daschle for breaking his nose for no good reason," Laura said as Daschle walked into the room with bandages on his nose.

"But I had a good reason!" Bush insisted. "I don't like him!"

"George!" Laura shouted sternly.

"I'm sorry, Daschle," Bush said. "It's not your fault you're a slimy weasel; that's just the way God made you."

"I'm saddened by—"

"Hey," Bush interrupted, "you're not going to help by talking!"

"Guess I better let Chomps and Rumsfeld go," Condi said as she hit a button on her remote. The constraints fell off of Rumsfeld, and the cage door opened for Chomps.

"Rarr!" Rumsfeld shouted.

"Grrraw!" Chomps growled.

"Uh-oh!" exclaimed the hippy, holding the Noam Chomsky book in front of him as a shield.

"That's one dead hippy," Bush remarked, quickly looking for a place to shield himself from the splash damage.

* * * *

The entire group sat around a picnic table on the White House lawn, enjoying punch and pie. "I've learned something today," Bush said. "Anyone can be whatever they set their heart on. A woman can be just as good a cabinet member as a man, a blind man can be a samurai, and a dog with a severe anti-social personality disorder can be an award-winning UN peacekeeper."

"I learned something, too," Condi said. "That if what someone says offends me, I should confront the person directly instead of secretly trying to have him killed and then turning the US into a police state."

"That last part is Ashcroft's job," Bush chuckled.

"And I learned that while blowing up robots is fun, nothing beats stabbing a for'ner with my KA-BAR while the Old Glory flies on a pole behind me," Buck stated.

"And I learned to never trust President Bush," Scott said angrily. "He even signed my cast with the name 'I. P. Freely.'"

"Yeah, that was pretty funny," Bush chuckled.

"Sorry about shooting you in the leg," Barbara said. "I didn't mean to. But that's what I learned: when sniping, you have to adjust for the gravitational arc of the bullet."

"And don't forget windage," Jenna added.

"I didn't learn anything," Rumsfeld grumbled. "I'm too old."

"I learned that Bush's ineffectual leadership can cause tragedy in both the foreign and domestic arenas," Daschle commented, "and it saddens me."

"That reminds me of another thing I learned," Bush said. "The capital of Thailand."

"The capital of Thailand?" Daschle said with confusion.

"Yeah: Punchyouintheballs!" Bush exclaimed and then punched Daschle in the groin.

"I learn I charge 150 bu for this job," Kôtôichi said.

Bush rose to his feet as Daschle fell out of his chair. "150 bu?! That's outrageous!"

Ichi's hand moved toward his cane.

"Okay! Okay! 150 bu it is!" Bush said, sitting back down and covering his neck. "These ties are expensive."

"Well I'm glad most everyone learned something today," Laura said, serving more pie.

"I bet Chomps didn't learn anything," Bush chuckled. "He's just a stupid dog. Look at him sitting there on the lawn chewing on a car bumper—hey! That's my car bumper!"

Bush rolled up a newspaper and ran over to Chomps. He struck the dog on the head while yelling, "Bad dog!"

Very slowly, Chomps stopped chewing on the car bumper and turned his head to look at Bush. "I don't think he liked that," Rumsfeld said. "What paper was it?"

Bush unrolled it. "It was the *New York Times*."

"Then you just added insult to injury," Rumsfeld stated gravely.

Chomps brimmed with fury. His bloodshot eyes bulged as he growled and bared his jagged teeth.

Bush backed away slowly as he prepared to run. "If anyone needs me, I'll be up in a tree."

THE END

August 13, 2003

Ride of the Warmongerers

"What are you guys doing?" White House Press Secretary Scott McClellan asked as he approached President Bush, Dick Cheney, and Donald Rumsfeld, who were all wearing black leather jackets and wielding switchblades, bats, and chains.

"We're starting a biker gang called the Warmongerers," Bush answered.

"Is that a good idea?" Scott inquired dubiously.

"All the cool presidents were in biker gangs in their spare time," Bush explained. "Reagan cracked skulls every weekend, Nixon stabbed more people than you can count, Eisenhower was wanted by the law in most states, Teddy Roosevelt used to exercise his big stick while speeding on his hog, and Lincoln used to jump school buses on his Harley."

"Enough talking," Rumsfeld said. "I want to smash something!"

"You coming?" Cheney asked Scott.

"I don't know if this is smart," Scott said.

"The guy is a dweeb," Bush remarked. "Let's ditch him."

"I'm not a dweeb!" Scott protested.

"Uh-oh; my old lady is coming!" Bush exclaimed. "Everyone act cool."

Laura Bush walked by and looked at the four of them. "This looks suspiciously like a biker gang," she commented.

"No, we're just getting ready for Bible study, ain't we guys?" Bush said. Rumsfeld and Cheney nodded in agreement.

"Mr. McClellan, is this true?" Laura asked Scott.

Bush pointed a switchblade at Scott and gave him a stern look. "Uh... yeah... Bible study," Scott answered.

"Alright," Laura said, not looking quite convinced, "but I'd better not hear otherwise later."

She walked off, all the while keeping an eye on the four men until she was out of sight.

"Thanks for covering for us, Scott," Bush told him. "You can be part of the gang now. We all have cool biker names." He pointed at Rumsfeld. "He's Mad Dog." Then at Cheney. "He's Chainman Charlie... and I'm Tex. Your biker name will be 'Skippy.'"

"Skippy?"

Condoleezza Rice walked by. “Hey, Condi,” Bush called out, “do you want to be a biker slut?”

“Someone has to stay here and keep watch of the country,” she answered.

“But it’s the weekend!” Bush exclaimed. “International incidents never happen on the weekend.”

“Hey, do you want Colin Powell trying to make peace with everyone while we’re all gone?” Condi asked.

“Okay, stay,” Bush grumbled. He then turned to his gang. “Let’s get rolling!”

“Yeah!” Rumsfeld and Cheney shouted, while Scott looked warily at one of the motorcycles.

“I’ve never driven one of these before,” Scott said. “Do you at least have some helmets?”

“Of course not,” Cheney answered. “If I wreck my hog, I don’t want to live!”

“Just get rolling, Skippy,” Bush commanded. “Time to show everyone who owns this town!”

* * * *

“Yee-haw!” Bush shouted as he rode his Harley over the top of the French ambassador’s limousine.

“I surrender!” squealed the ambassador.

“Not accepted, Pierre!” Cheney answered, smashing one of the limo’s windows with his chain as he rode by.

“Rarr!” Rumsfeld shouted, smashing the windshield with his bat.

“Now hit him with the Molotov cocktail, Skippy!” Bush called out to Scott.

Scott threw a bottle at the limo. The bottle shattered and splashed liquid everywhere, to no effect.

“You’re supposed to light it, moron!” Cheney yelled.

“I’m sorry, but I’m not very experienced with this sort of thing,” Scott said.

The limo drove off. “Aww, he got away!” Bush whined. “You have to shape up, Skippy.”

“I’m trying,” Scott said, “but did I really have to get a green Mohawk?”

"Hey, we decided one of us needed to have a Mohawk, and it was a three to one vote that it should be you," Bush said.

"I want some drinking!" Cheney yelled.

"And I want some fighting!" Rumsfeld shouted.

"Off to the biker bar!" Bush yelled as he drove off, Rumsfeld and Cheney following, with Scott wobbling far behind.

Soon they arrived at a shady-looking bar and parked their motorcycles. "We need to find the toughest guy in there and beat him up," Bush told his gang. "That will show everyone we're boss."

"I don't know if this is all legal," Scott stated uneasily.

"We're above the law!" Rumsfeld shouted.

They entered the bar, and Bush walked over to the bartender. "Who is the toughest guy here?"

"That would be Murderin' Carl," the bartender said, pointing out a massive man who looked quite unstable. "He just got out of jail... for murder!"

"Thinks he's so tough because he's ripped people apart with his bare hands," Bush scoffed. "Go beat the crap out of him, Skippy."

"What?"

"Hey, Murderin' Carl!" Bush yelled. "Skippy says the reason they let you out of prison is because you cried like a little girl!"

"Then Skippy is dead!" Murderin' Carl yelled, grabbing Scott and lifting him into the air.

"Eep." Scott uttered as his life passed before his eyes.

"Hey, look over there, Tex," Cheney told Bush.

At a nearby table sat the Warmongerers' rivals. "Hey, Scott," Bush called out, "stop getting beaten up by the murderer for a second and get over here."

Dizzy and in pain, Scott stumbled over to Bush. "What?"

"See over there?" Bush said, pointing at the table. "There's our rival gang, the Hell's Democrats."

"That's Governor Howard Dean, Representative Richard Gephardt, Senator Ted Kennedy, and Senator John Kerry," Scott stated, a bit surprised.

"Yeah, but in the biker world, they are known respectively as The Dean, Dick the Knife, Big Fat Teddy K, and By the Way I Served in Vietnam."

"Let's kill 'em!" Rumsfeld shouted.

"Be cool, Mad Dog," Bush said and then slowly walked over to the Hell's Democrats. "So," he chuckled, "if it isn't Deany Weenie, John *Fairy*,

Big Fat Teddy *Gay*, and Dick... uh..." He thought for a moment. "Gephardt... Gephardt... What sounds like Gephardt?" He looked back at the Hell's Democrats. "....and Dick Dumbfart." Bush turned to his own gang. "Best I could come up with on short notice."

The Hell's Democrats all stood up. "We're going to rule this town!" Kerry shouted. "Just like I ruled when I was in Vietnam!"

"Yeah, you ain't so tough!" Dean said.

Big Fat Teddy K just chewed on a shank of ham.

"You guys think you can beat us," Bush laughed, "but you're just a bunch of jokers. By this time next year, the economy will have improved, and we will have found WMDs in Iraq... and then we'll make you eat them!"

Big Fat Teddy K just laughed.

"Hey, Chainman Charlie," Gephardt said snidely, "I see you ain't in hiding no more."

"Keep it up, and the undisclosed location of my foot will be in your ass!" Cheney threatened.

"You guys are all talk, and I know talk, having been in Vietnam," Kerry said.

"You're soon going to be known as the haughty, French-looking Massachusetts Democrat who by the way served in Vietnam and got ripped a new one by Rumsfeld!" Rumsfeld shouted.

Senator Joe Lieberman then showed up. "Hey! There is no need for violence," he said. "I think we can settle this in a bipartisan—"

"Quiet, Jew-boy!" Big Fat Teddy K shouted as he broke a pool cue over Lieberman's head.

"I'm gonna cut me a 'publican!" Gephardt yelled, pulling out a knife.

"Now why don't you guys back off before you get hurt?" Dean said with a smirk.

"Know what?" Bush said. "I think it's time for a preëmptive strike... AGAINST YOUR FACE!" Bush punched Howard Dean. Cheney whipped out his chain and knocked down Dick Gephardt.

"Rarr!" Rumsfeld shouted as he picked up John Kerry and tossed him across the room.

"Grerawerr!" Big Fat Teddy K snarled as he charged Scott, who quickly tried to hide under a table.

"Eep."

* * * *

"I keep telling you," Condi said with frustration into the phone, "I had the nuclear launch codes, but I misplaced them. Now, I wouldn't want to be in your shoes if Finland isn't nuked by the time the president gets back... Yeah, that's right; he explicitly ordered Finland to be nuked while he was away... Hey, I'm not the one who is going to lose his job if Finland exists an hour from now... Yes, and he approved me to get that pizza on his credit card... President Bush is going to be so mad if he hears you denied me that pizza!"

"You in here, Dr. Rice?" Colin Powell called out from the hallway.

"Don't come into the war room!" Condi shouted, quickly trying to hide her map of the world that had marks on it such as "Bomb here," "Invade here," and "Genocide here." "I'm not decent!"

* * * *

"You were supposed to have the pardons on you!" Cheney said angrily to Bush.

Rumsfeld snarled and held onto the prison bars.

"I'm sorry!" Bush exclaimed. "I left them in my other biker jacket!"

"I can't believe it!" Scott cried. "I'm actually in prison!"

"Keep coo', yo," Bush told him. "Keep coo'."

"Okay, you troublemakers," the police chief said, "I'm letting you guys out for one press conference."

"Put a good spin on all this," Bush ordered Scott as they walked out to the prison steps where the press was waiting.

"Is it true that Bush and his administration are involved in a violent biker gang called the 'Warmongerers'?" asked one reporter.

"Now that's just silly," Scott said with a forced laugh.

"The French ambassador has told the police you harassed him," said another reporter.

"I'll murder him dead!" Bush shouted.

Scott raised his hand to silence Bush. "As we all know, the French are a race of liars," Scott told the press. "Only a fool would believe anything they say. Any other questions?"

Melinda Hawkish from FOX News stepped forward. "That green Mohawk you have is so gay."

"That's not a question," Scott answered with annoyance.

"Uh-oh; my old lady is coming!" Bush shouted. "Everyone hide your microphones and cameras."

"What's happening here?" Laura Bush demanded.

"We're just having a Bible study, dear," Bush answered innocently.

"On the steps of the police station?" Laura asked with suspicion.

"Yes; Police Chief O'Malley was nice enough to let us have our study here."

"Is that true, Chief O'Malley?"

He looked into the air. "Uh... sure, it's true."

"And why does Mr. McClellan have a Mohawk?" Laura asked.

"You know Scott," Bush said with a laugh. "He's an idiot; doesn't know how to present himself for Bible study."

"It's true; I am an idiot, ma'am," Scott stated.

Laura kept looking at them all with suspicion. "From the clueless expressions of these people here, they look a lot like reporters," Laura said. "Reporters assembled to hear a story about some lawlessness related to a biker gang."

"It's nothing like that, honey," Bush said. "We're just studying our Bible stories."

"Which story are you studying, then?" Laura inquired.

"Uh... the one where Jesus... uh... fights the lions and... uh... blows up the Death Star."

"That doesn't sound like a real Bible story!" Laura exclaimed.

"Uh, Mrs. Bush," Scott interjected, "you see, being a bunch of dufuses, we forgot our Bibles and had to try and draw the stories from memory... and... well, we're all really dumb."

"It's true," Bush said, and everyone nodded in agreement.

"Alright then," Laura said, beginning to walk away as she kept a stern gaze on Bush. "I'm heading to the store and am going to pick up your diarrhea medicine."

"Thanks, dear," Bush said with a smile while everyone snickered.

Once Laura was out of view, everyone let out a sigh of relief. "That was a close one," Bush said and patted Scott on the back. "Quick thinking there, Skippy. You'll make a great member of our violent biker gang yet." He then remembered the press was still there. "Which does not actually exist and did not smash up the German ambassador's limo."

"It was the French ambassador's limo we didn't smash up," Cheney reminded him.

"Oh yeah," Bush laughed, smacking himself in the forehead.

"Grerawerr!" came a snarl from nearby.

"It's Big Fat Teddy K looking for revenge!" Bush exclaimed, pushing Scott into the charging beast's path.

"Eep."

August 18, 2003

Vice President Day

Bush sat in the Oval Office playing Nerf basketball until Attorney General John Ashcroft walked in. "Hey, it's little Johnny Ashcroft!" Bush exclaimed. "How are you doing?"

"Not so good, by golly," Ashcroft said. "Everybody says mean and untrue things about me, like that I want to take away their rights and everything, and it makes me feel bad."

"I know how you feel," Bush replied. He then started laughing. "Can you believe that some people say I'm dumb?"

Ashcroft just stared at him. "Anyway, I don't want to take any nice people's rights away. I was just trying to fight terrorists, by golly, like by passing the Patriot Act, the Victory Act, and the Question This Act and I'll Put You in Jail Act."

"That's the first bill I've seen with the word 'bitch slap' in it," Bush remarked.

"Well, the bitch slap is needed in the fight against terrorism," Ashcroft said, "but I can only use it after getting a court order, you betcha. To speed things up, of course, I have a whole court follow me around in a bus."

"So what's been happening lately on the terrorist front?"

"Golly, we found this guy who looked pretty darn suspicious, so we questioned him about terrorism," Ashcroft answered. "He wouldn't tell us nuttin', don't you know. So we put some electrodes to his gonads, and he started singing a different tune, you better believe it."

"So what did we find out?"

"There's a terrorist hideout here in DC full of illegal arms, wouldn't you know."

"We better go take 'em out!" Bush exclaimed.

"That's what we're going to do, by golly."

"And I'll go with you."

"This is not a good idea," Kôtôichi told Bush. "It safer here in the Oval Office."

"Who is that?" Ashcroft asked.

"That's a blind samurai I hired as a Secret Service agent under the People with Disabilities Act."

"And you need to listen to me and stay safe," Ichi told him.

"Bah!" Bush answered. "Safety is for cowards and smart people! Let's roll!"

* * * *

"We're pretty sure the terrorists are in that building, I tells ya," Ashcroft said, pointing to the building ahead of them. The ATF agents gathered around, getting ready for the assault. "By the way, Bush, I want you to meet our head ATF agent, Psycho Stan. He used to be a psychotic, remorseless killer."

"And then you reformed him and made him an ATF agent?" Bush asked.

"Well, we made him an ATF agent," Ashcroft answered.

"I wants me to kill someone," Psycho Stan said, twitching.

"When you raid that building, Psycho Stan, we need you to take some people alive so we can question them," Ashcroft ordered.

"A... live...?" Psycho Stan said, confused.

"That's when you don't kill someone," Ashcroft explained.

"What bullets and explosives do you use to not kill someone?"

"Well you don't use any bullets or explosives at all," Ashcroft answered, chuckling. "If someone drops his weapon and raises his hands, don't shoot him."

Psycho Stan still looked confused, but then he started laughing. "Oh, now I get it. I always wondered why people would drop their weapons and raise their hands, because that seemed a funny way to attack me. I guess they were actually trying to get me to *not* shoot them."

"See, you learn something new every day, by golly."

Psycho Stan and the rest of the ATF agents prepared for the raid. Bush nudged Kôtôichi while laughing. "That guy was dumb."

Ichi just grunted.

There was a lot of shooting and exploding, but then Psycho Stan emerged, bringing out a terrorist at gunpoint. "I got me one," Psycho Stan said, "and I got him... uh... not dead... uh... what did you call it?"

"Alive."

"Yeah, he's alive."

"And I tell nothing to you infidels!" the terrorist shouted.

"Golly gosh, I think I'll need to use a bitch slap here," Ashcroft said and then turned to the judges behind him. "Court order, please."

They handed him one. Ashcroft then cocked back his hand like a pimp and slapped the terrorist.

"Okay, I talk!" screamed the terrorist. "We are plotting to kill the vice president today!"

"Oh no!" Bush exclaimed. "It's Vice President day! That's when the vice president emerges from his undisclosed location. If he stays out, it will mean economic recovery is on its way. But if he's scared back in by a terrorist attack, that means six more weeks of recession! It's covered by all the press."

"We better call his Secret Service agents and tell them to expect an attack," Ichi suggested.

"That's too simple," Bush said. "We need to race over there and stop it ourselves!"

"Okay," Aschroft answered. "And I'll take care of things here, you betcha." He turned to the ATF agents. "Secure the building."

The building exploded.

"Jeepers," Ashcroft exclaimed. "We need to work on our communication here."

"I need your car," Bush said, pulling open the door to a Corvette and yanking the driver out. "Wow! This is just like Grand Theft Auto!" he remarked as he sat in the driver's seat. "Now get in, Ichi."

Ichi felt around for the passenger-side door.

"Just get in!" Bush urged. "What are you? Blind?"

Ichi simply grunted as he finally got into the car.

* * * *

"You're holding the camera backwards again!" Melinda Hawkish of FOX News yelled at her camerawoman. "It's important we get good coverage of the vice president."

"Having trouble again?" asked her arch nemesis Lefty Stevens of CNN. "Too bad you're not professionals like us." He then thought out loud, "Now how am I going to work into this story that Arnold Schwarzenegger's father is a Nazi?"

Melinda just gave him a stern look. She then noticed some odd reporters beside her. "That's a weird-looking camera you have," she told them. "Almost looks like a bazooka with a lens cap on the end."

"Quiet, infidel woman!" shouted one of the men. "Your unconcealed face and body both disgust and intrigue me!"

"How rude," Melinda remarked. She then saw someone start to emerge from the cave in front of them. "The vice president is emerging!"

Suddenly a Corvette sped onto the scene. Out leaped Kôtôichi, who cut down three men.

"Those were MSNBC reporters," Bush told him.

"I hate MSNBC," Ichi answered.

"But we need to find the terrorists!"

Ichi listened carefully. He could then hear the sound of tension upon a trigger. He quickly tossed his sheath which hit the terrorist's bazooka so that, instead of firing at the vice president, it was knocked off-target to fire into a group of reporters. Ichi then ran forward and cut down the terrorists.

Having successfully emerged from his undisclosed location, Dick Cheney now danced a jig.

"Hooray!" Bush exclaimed. "Now we'll soon have economic prosperity! And all who were killed were a bunch of stupid reporters who can easily be replaced."

"I save vice president," Ichi stated. "You pay me ten ryo."

"What?!" Bush yelled. "That's the most ridiculous thing—"

With a quick swipe, Ichi cut off Bush's tie.

"Ah, fine, you blind bastard," Bush grumbled. "Let me get my bag of ryo."

August 22, 2003

The Rumsfeld Strangler vs. Cyber-Lenin Part I

Ernst Stavro Blofeld sat at the head of the table, stroking his cat as he scanned the other faces in the room. "The Legion of Doom is failing," he said. "We have yet to bring about the destruction of America. Why is that?"

"We need more bombing in the name of Allah!" yelled the Mad Mullah.

"Bombings have gotten us nowhere," Blofeld answered. "We need fresh ideas. What have you been up to, Dr. Doom?"

"I'm a little caught up right now in keeping up my home practice," Dr. Doom answered.

"We are trying to take over the world!" Blofeld yelled. "Why must you keep up your medical practice?"

"Hey! I spent all those years in medical school, and Dr. Doom will have a family medical practice that delivers quality care to its patients, and no one can stop me. Muh ha ha ha!"

"I can defeat America!" Kim Jong-Il vowed. "I have nukes; I am very scary."

"You couldn't scare anyone!" Blofeld responded.

"Maybe if we sold more of my books," Hillary Clinton suggested. "I think if more people came to like me, then America could be destroyed."

"True, but your book is boring and insipid," Blofeld answered.

"Well, we could try and get my universal healthcare plan passed," Hillary said. "It would so cripple the American healthcare system that it would kill millions! Heh ha ha ha!"

"The only way to defeat America is to first destroy Aquaman!" Black Manta exclaimed.

"I thought we threw you out of the Legion of Doom," Blofeld grumbled.

Black Manta looked down at his feet. "But I don't have anywhere else to go."

"Birds and umbrellas! That's the way to attack America!" the Penguin exclaimed.

Blofeld looked at Chirac. "Do you have any *new* ideas?"

"Well, I'm not here as part of the Legion of Doom," Chirac explained. "I'm just here to keep a dialogue open. Also, I would like to note that France's surrender is on the table for whatever plan you eventually decide upon."

"More explosions!" demanded the Mad Mullah. "Allah will see to it that we destroy America through irrational bombing!"

"Fools!" yelled a voice in the shadows. "The more you attack America on the outside, the more determined and powerful it becomes. The only way to destroy America is to corrode it from the inside."

"How dare you contradict my wacky, extremist Islamic beliefs!" shouted the Mad Mullah. "Suicide bombers, kill him!"

Two suicide bombers ran at the figure in the shadows, but a red shield formed around him protecting him from the blasts. "Regular weapons are no match for me."

"Who are you?" Blofeld demanded.

As he stepped out of the shadows, the legion saw a large, robotic figure. Through the glass around his head, though, they saw a recognizable face accented by a red beard. "I am Cyber-Lenin. I am kept alive by a robotic body and powered by the most powerful force known to mankind—Pure Commie Evil! Witness its power!"

Two red beams shot forth from Cyber-Lenin's hands and hit the Mad Mullah, quickly disintegrating him into nothing but a skeleton.

"Wow! Pure Commie Evil is very powerful! Very scary!" Kim Jong-Il exclaimed, jumping up and down on his chair and clapping his hands.

"Ooh ooh! Ee ee!" agreed Chim-Chim, the evilest monkey.

"It can instantly corrode anything it touches," Cyber-Lenin explained. "Just like Communism itself, but condensed down into its purest and most evil form."

"Excellent!" Blofeld exclaimed. "With your power, you can destroy America from the inside. And when America falls, the world will be ours!"

"And finally we can defeat Aquaman!" Black Manta added. Everyone just stared at him. "I'll get back to mopping the floors."

* * * *

"Man, I love beer," Buck the Marine said as he drank his domestic. "I don't think there is anything I like more than beer... oh wait, killin' for'ners. I like that better; doesn't make me want to pee as much."

"So where are you shipping off to tomorrow?" Rumsfeld asked as he drank his double whiskey sour.

"I dunno," Buck answered. "Some other country where people will speak gibberish and shoot at me with AK-47s. I'll kill 'em all and shout, 'Ooh-rah!' Another day, another dollar."

"Eighty-five cents," Rumsfeld corrected him.

"What?!"

"The rich needed more tax cuts; sorry, Buck."

"So they reduced all us Marines' salaries?"

"No, just yours."

"Dangit. Why always me? I'm so mad I could kill! Kill foreign people, that is!"

"That's the spirit," Rumsfeld told him, patting him on the back.

"You can't have your dog in here!" shouted the bartender.

"Then make him leave," Rumsfeld answered.

The bartender looked at Chomps, the world's angriest dog, who had found the bar stool he hated the most and was now tearing it apart. "Hey! Dog!"

Very slowly, Chomps turned his head to look at the bartender with a steady glare.

"Uh... never mind," said the bartender.

Chomps slowly looked back at his bar stool and continued mutilating it.

"What's that out the window?" Buck asked.

Rumsfeld looked out to see a light in the sky that projected the image of two hands ready to strangle. "That's the Strangle-Signal!" Rumsfeld exclaimed. "Come, Chomps, to the Strangle-Mobile!"

"See you later, Rummy!" Buck called to him.

"Have fun killin' for'ners," Rumsfeld answered.

"I always do," Buck said, taking another sip of his beer.

Rumsfeld and Chomps jumped into the Buick and sped off toward the White House. Before they could get there, though, they were blocked by protestors.

"Rarr!" Rumsfeld exclaimed. "They are the smelliest, most incoherent protestors yet!"

The crowd held up signs such as "Yay Dictators! Boo Bush!" and "No Blood for Liberation!" and chanted slogans such as, "Blood lied, Hitler is Oil."

"Skibberdy-wa-gibber doo!" shouted a hippy at Rumsfeld, communicating nothing more than that he needed a strangling. Rumsfeld was happy to oblige.

Chomps started to growl, beginning to fill with anger as he looked at all the hippies. "There's too many for you to mangle," Rumsfeld told him, "and Lord knows I'd just ruin my hands with arthritis if I tried strangling them all. We need to get to the White House and find out what riled up this many dimwits at this late an hour. The only way to do that is plow right through them."

Rumsfeld pressed the pedal to the metal and ran straight through the protestors. Soon hippies and placards were flying everywhere while he was inundated with the smell of patchouli oil. Eventually Rumsfeld crashed through the gates of the White House.

"Going to be spending a long time cleaning hippies off my Buick," Rumsfeld grumbled as he and Chomps ran into the White House.

"Glad to see you," Bush exclaimed as he saw Rumsfeld. "We were hoping the Rumsfeld Strangler would come, but at least you're here, Rummy."

"There are hippies everywhere," Rumsfeld said angrily.

"Yeah, they just started protesting out of nowhere!"

Out of the shadows emerged the dark figure of Karl Rove. "An ancient evil has come," he uttered. "If left unchecked, it can destroy the Republican party, as prophesied by the ancient tome *The Dark Book of Punditry*."

"That's bad!" Bush exclaimed.

"So do we know what we're up against?" Rumsfeld asked.

Clancy, dressed in his usual black tie, black suit, and black sunglasses, came forward and opened a briefcase. "We have some idea. Just earlier today, this was a supermarket full of merchandise, but look at it now." He handed a photo to Bush.

"People are in line for bread!" Bush said. "I've never heard of such a thing!"

"The only thing that could destroy a business so quickly is Pure Commie Evil," Condoleezza Rice exclaimed. "But the existence of such a thing was only theoretical. You'd need a host of pure evil to contain it."

"True," Clancy answered, "and we think we know who that host is. According to some second hand information from my cousin Barry, the body of Lenin has been floating around the black market for some time. Then, according to a gossip column in the *Idaho Statesman* newspaper, Lenin ended up in a wax museum in Norway. Finally, according to this transient I ran into last week, former KGB agents seized the body and revived Lenin using cybernetic technology."

"How sure was this transient?" Bush asked.

"Very sure," Clancy answered, "and somewhat drunk."

"Man, I thought after we captured the supervillain Chemical Ali we were in the clear," Bush said, "but now we have to deal with the threat of Cyber-Lenin. We'll need the best on this: Get me Aquaman!"

"We can't find Aquaman," Condi told him. "We tried contacting him with the Aquaphone, but all we got was his Aqua-answering machine. I guess he's busy battling the evil forces of the sea elsewhere."

"Dangit!" Bush exclaimed. "I guess we'll have to go to the second tier superheroes. Get Superman!"

"I'm afraid he's fallen in with the left-wing Hollywood crowd and doesn't like making judgments of good and evil," Condi informed Bush. "Also, there seems to be a strong association between him and a writer for the Daily Planet who is always writing negative articles about you and your big campaign contributor, Lex Luthor."

"Criminy!" Bush yelled. "Well, what about Batman?"

"You accidentally ran him over on a campaign stop in Gotham, remember?" Condi told him.

"Oh yeah. Well, if you run around at night in a dark costume, it was bound to happen sometime. I hope more superheroes learn to wear reflectors. Is Spiderman available?"

"He was one of the first to go when Giuliani started cleaning up New York," Condi answered. "He was always leaving webs everywhere."

"The Green Lantern?"

"Turned yellow."

"The Hulk?"

"Learned to express his anger through song."

"The Flash?"

"Ran away at the first sign of danger."

"The X-Men?"

"Remember? We decided mutants were a threat to society, so we rounded them all up with the help of large robots."

"Do we have the large robots, then?"

"They're rusting in some warehouse in Minnesota."

White House Press Secretary Scott McClellan came into the room. "I heard something was going on."

"Good, you're here," Bush said. "We need you to defeat Cyber-Lenin. If you need a weapon, you can have this letter opener—the point is somewhat sharp. Also, if you want a cape, you can borrow some drapes. Just make sure they get back before Laura finds out."

"Why do *I* have to fight Cyber-Lenin?" Scott complained.

Bush rolled his eyes. "Do you have something better to do right now?" Bush asked with annoyance. "Now come up with a cool superhero name and get to it."

"Bah!" Rumsfeld exclaimed. "Back in my day we didn't need any superheroes to handle our problems. If a supervillain tried to take over the world, or a portal opened up out of which aliens swarmed, we just picked up some rocks and sticks and beat the crap out of them."

"Fine, Rummy, you can try things your way," Bush said. "Just take Super Scott with you as back up. Oh, and tell your dog to stop ripping apart my desk."

"He must not like it," Rumsfeld answered.

"But it was picked out by *Queer Eye for the Straight Guy*," Bush said. "I'm the straight guy, by the way."

"Come on, Chomps, we have a Commie to kill," Rumsfeld told the dog. He then turned to Scott. "You too, Tubby."

"Alright," Scott answered, "but I better get overtime for this."

* * * *

Having made their way back through the hippy protestors, Rumsfeld, Scott, and Chomps drove around the city looking for Cyber-Lenin.

"So what's the plan?" Scott asked, fixing his floral-pattern cape.

"We find him, we strangle him," Rumsfeld answered.

Chomps looked at Scott and growled.

"I don't think your dog likes me," Scott stated a bit nervously.

"Is he ripping you apart?" Rumsfeld asked.

"No."

"Then he's still deciding." Rumsfeld looked around. "All the businesses here are either shut down or out of merchandise. And the cars are small and fuel efficient. We must be close to the corrosive effects of the Pure Commie Evil."

"What should I do?" Scott asked.

"See that McDonald's over there?" Rumsfeld asked.

"Yeah."

"Go get me a Big Mac meal with a Coke," Rumsfeld told him as he stopped the car and got out. "I get hungry after killin'."

Scott ran off to the McDonald's while Rumsfeld and Chomps started walking. "Plan is," Rumsfeld told Chomps, "I strangle him while you rip off his limbs."

Chomps growled angrily in approval.

They traced the destructive effect of Pure Commie Evil until they found themselves down an alleyway. There stood a glowing, red robotic figure. "You must be the Rumsfeld Strangler," he laughed. "I knew I'd run into you. Well, I'll destroy you, and your angry dog, too."

"We'll see about that!" Rumsfeld shouted. "Rarr!" Rumsfeld ran forward and tried to get his hands around Cyber-Lenin's neck, but it was protected by metal and bulletproof glass. Soon, Rumsfeld had to let go, as his hands started to burn.

Cyber-Lenin threw a punch, sending Rumsfeld flying backward. "Soon you will learn the power of Pure Commie Evil," Cyber-Lenin said, "and it will be the last lesson you learn, Rumsfeld Strangler."

Cyber-Lenin fired a red beam at Rumsfeld, but then Chomps leaped at him, his mouth agape and ready to bite. The beam hit him instead, sending the dog flying backward. He hit a wall and then fell unmoving to the ground. "Chomps!" Rumsfeld exclaimed with worry. He then turned his rage to Cyber-Lenin. "Rarr!"

He threw a punch at his enemy, but Cyber-Lenin caught it in his metal hand and backhanded Rumsfeld, sending him smashing through the brick wall behind him. Dazed and injured, Rumsfeld tried to get up, but Cyber-Lenin was soon standing over him. Rumsfeld looked again to Chomps, but he lay there motionless.

"It is over for you, Rumsfeld Strangler," Cyber-Lenin said, his hands charging with red Pure Commie Evil as they prepared to release the fatal blow. "Say goodbye to your precious country, as it will not be here much longer either. Muh ha ha ha!"

* * * *

Is this it for the Rumsfeld Strangler? Is Chomps now in Doggie Heaven (or in Hippie Hell, biting hippies for all eternity)? Will the Republican party and America fall against Pure Commie Evil? Will Black Manta ever get to defeat Aquaman?

Find out in ***The Rumsfeld Strangler vs. Cyber-Lenin Part II****.*

August 25, 2003

The Rumsfeld Strangler vs. Cyber-Lenin Part II

Cyber-Lenin's hands pulsed with red Commie power, and Rumsfeld braced for the death blow. Somehow he always knew he would go out this way—killed by a cybernetic Communist.

Suddenly he heard a voice. "I got your Big Mac, Rumsfeld," Scott McClellan called out. "So did you find Cyber-Lenin?... Oh, there he is."

Cyber-Lenin turned to look at Scott. "Quick, do something, Tubby!" Rumsfeld yelled.

"Er... uh..." Scott muttered as he looked at the McDonald's food in his hands. Finally, he threw a Coke at Cyber-Lenin.

"Arggh!" Cyber-Lenin screamed. "Your capitalist confection burns like acid!"

"Quick, let's get out of here!" Rumsfeld yelled as he ran over to pick up Chomps. Both he and Scott ran for the Buick as red beams of Pure Commie Evil flew at them. Rumsfeld put Chomps in the back of his Buick and then quickly sped off as Scott jumped in.

"I think we lost him," Scott said. "Boy, it sure was lucky I was there in time to... ergh... ack..."

"That was my Coke!" Rumsfeld yelled as he strangled Scott with one hand and steered with the other.

"Sorry! You can have my Sprite!" Scott answered.

"Bah!" Rumsfeld exclaimed. "How is Chomps doing?"

Chomps barely moved and whimpered weakly. "He doesn't look so well," Scott answered.

"We'll head to Condoleezza Rice's secret lab and have him looked at," Rumsfeld said, anger marking his face. "Then we'll send that Cyber-Commie into the ashbin of history."

"Yeah, we'll learn him good," Scott said, trying to sound tough. "So... you still want your Big Mac?"

* * * *

Bush stayed in his office practicing with a katana. "Do you think if I train really hard, I can be like you one day?" Bush asked Kôtôichi.

"No, you're an idiot," Ichi answered. "But keep bothering me, and I'll gouge your eyes out."

Distracted, Bush accidentally cut the wall. "Aww, not again."

Laura Bush ran into the room. "George! Are you playing with your sword in the Oval Office again?"

"No," Bush answered and then realized he was still holding a katana. "I took this from Kôtôichi, who was being bad and swinging his sword around. You can never trust the Yakuza."

"No katanas in the Oval Office," Laura said, taking away his sword. She looked at the windows. "Is one of my drapes missing?"

Suddenly they could hear the sounds of motorcycles. Outside the office was a biker gang driving around the White House. "It's the Hell's Democrats!" Bush exclaimed. "There's Big Fat Teddy K, the Dean, Dick the Knife, and By the Way I Served in Vietnam."

Suddenly a pipe hit Bush and sent him rolling back into his office. "Don't forget Tom Smashle!" Tom Daschle said, brandishing a pipe. Soon the rest of the Hell's Democrats entered the Oval Office following Tom Daschle. Laura ran to Bush's side and helped him up.

"You're going to be in so much trouble for driving motorcycles in the White House," Laura said sternly.

"Yeah!" Bush exclaimed. "Ichi, kill them all."

Ichi laughed. "Kill who? I don't see anyone."

"Hey, I said I'd get you that thirty ryo," Bush yelled at him.

"Know what, I think I'm going deaf, too," Ichi responded.

"You limey bastard!" Bush yelled. "Fine, I'll have to take care of this myself." He looked at Laura. "Give me my whoopin' hat."

"Your cowboy hat is at the dry cleaner's because you spilled grape juice on it," Laura informed him.

"Dagnabbit, now I'm going to have to fight hatless!" Bush exclaimed. He approached Daschle with his dukes up, but Daschle grabbed Bush and tossed him across the room.

"Suddenly we Democrats feel so powerful!" Daschle exclaimed, laughing his weasel laugh. "And now we will take over the White House and do what you never did—find Saddam Hussein!"

"And then we'll surrender to him!" Kerry added.

"And we'll only use military action if the UN or French tell us to!" Dean laughed.

"But first we'll crush you! Wha ha ha ha!" Big Fat Teddy K said.

"Help me, Laura; they're going to hurt me!" Bush exclaimed.

Laura rolled her eyes. "I guess I have to do everything." She sunk into a praying mantis fighting stance and then sent Daschle flying out of the room with a series of kicks and punches.

"Kill the librarian!" Daschle yelled.

Kerry swung a chain at her, but she caught it and used the leverage to send him flying into Bush's desk.

"Ah! That injured me!" Kerry yelled. "Just like I could have been injured while I served in Vietnam!"

Dean held up a bat. "I'm going to knock you out of power just like I would have left Saddam in!" He swung at Laura, but she ducked underneath his swing and swept out Dean's feet.

"Grerawerr!" Big Fat Teddy K growled as he charged Laura. She flipped out of the way, and Teddy K went head first into the wall.

"Time to die, 'publican!" Dick the Knife screeched as he charged Laura from behind. With a flash of a sword, the knife was cut from Gephardt's hand. "Ahh!" he screamed, clutching his wound. "That's my hand for reaching into the pockets of taxpayers!"

"Hey, you helped her for free!" Bush yelled at Kôtôichi.

Ichi laughed. "I didn't see me do anything," Ichi said, resheathing his sword. He then sniffed the air. "I smell patchouli oil. The hippies are flooding into the White House."

"We need to get out of here," Laura said, fixing her hair.

"To the helimocopter!" Bush yelled.

* * * *

"Let's see," Buck said as he looked through his pack, "got my knife for killin', got my rifle for killin', got my bullets for killin', got my grenades for killin', got my MREs so I can keep fed and kill, got my postcards to send home about my killin', and I got my ballpoint pen to use to write about killin', and on rare occasions, for the act of killin' itself. I guess I'm ready to be deployed."

He walked through the military base, but suddenly a glowing red figure appeared in the air, shooting down beams of red.

"I don't know what that is," Buck said, "but it looks foreign to me!" Buck took out his M-16, chambered a round, and opened fire.

"Muh ha ha ha!" Cyber-Lenin laughed. "Your pathetic weapons cannot harm me. Now face Pure Commie Evil!"

A red beam hit Buck's M-16, turning it into a cheap imitation AK-47. "Dang it! This ain't good for killin'!" Buck yelled as he ran for cover from more shots of Cyber-Lenin's Pure Commie Evil.

Soon, Cyber-Lenin had flown away, and all of the high-tech American equipment had been turned into cheap, Russian surplus. "Now us Marines will never get deployed!" Buck exclaimed. "And without us killin' for'ners, they'll multiply like rabbits! God help us all!"

* * * *

"Come on, Chomps, get angry at something," Rumsfeld yelled.

Chomps just whimpered.

"I'm afraid the Pure Commie Evil has infected his body," Condoleezza Rice informed him. "It's made his white blood cells angry—very angry—so he has a high fever. I don't think he'll make it."

"I'm sorry, Rumsfeld," Scott said. "We can get you a new dog... and then psychologically scar him so he'll be just like Chomps."

"I don't want a new dog!" Rumsfeld yelled. "I want Chomps back to his old angry self! What can we do to get the Pure Commie Evil out of him?"

"Any operation would only risk infecting others, such as ourselves," Condi said, "but if you destroy the carrier of this Pure Commie Evil, I think the infection will fade away."

"So I need to kill Cyber-Lenin," Rumsfeld stated, brimming with anger.

"Yeah, but he's too powerful," Scott said. "I just saw on the news he took out a military base. Why don't we just hide down in this underground lab where it's safe and we have cable and free sodas?"

"The sodas are not free!" Condi yelled. "There's a cup right next to the fridge where you need to put fifty cents. It's very clearly marked!"

Bush, Laura, and Kôtôichi now walked into the lab. "The Democrats have the White House," Bush said somberly.

"You little pansy!" Rumsfeld shouted. "How could you let the whiny little Donks take power?"

"Well, they were big and mean," Bush answered defensively, "and they yelled at me... and I didn't have my hat."

"We need something with which to destroy Cyber-Lenin!" Rumsfeld demanded.

"I have something," Condi said. A door on the wall opened up, revealing a cybernetic suit. "It's only a prototype. It was made by the lowest bidder, who then used the cheapest parts that would work to greatly increase their profit margin. When the prototype was finished, the corporation laid off hundreds of workers to raise their stock value... i.e., this suit is the product of pure capitalism."

"So let's have someone put it on and fight Cyber-Lenin," Bush said.

Condi looked at him sternly. "We can't have just anyone use it. For it to work properly, the user has to perfectly represent the chaotic rage that is capitalism. That's why... Hey! Where's the suit? And where is Rumsfeld?"

"I guess I better go with him," Scott said with a look of resolve as he put back on his floral pattern cape and placed his letter opener in his belt. He then ran out of the lab. "Super Scott away!"

Bush shook his head. "The new guy is such a dork."

Laura just looked on in disbelief. "Tell me those were not my drapes."

* * * *

Can Uninhibited Capitalism defeat Pure Commie Evil? Can Bush get his White House back from the Hell's Democrats? Will Buck ever get to kill more foreigners? Will Chomps survive the night? Will Scott defeat evil with his letter opener? And why is a librarian versed in multiple forms of martial arts?

Find out these answers and less in the final installment, ***The Rumsfeld Strangler vs. Cyber-Lenin Part III****.*

August 27, 2003

The Rumsfeld Strangler vs. Cyber-Lenin Part III

"We hold this press conference to announce that the Democrats control the government," Hillary Clinton said as the Hell's Democrats biker gang drove around the White House lawn. "No one can stop us!"

"No one?" asked a reporter.

"No one!" Hillary responded.

"We, the elite media, hail the rise of the Democrats to power; should the stupid people in fly-over country do the same?" asked another reporter.

"That question is tough but fair," Hillary responded. "All who are against us are intolerant and will be placed in tolerance camps to learn the error of their ways, such as supporting wars because of 'national security' or 'morals' instead of the only reason for wars—a poorly defined concept of multilateralism."

"Me likey Democrats!" shouted one reporter.

"Another intelligent question," Hillary answered. "You reporters sure are nice."

"Isn't the Pure Commie Evil of Cyber-Lenin the only reason you've come to power?" FOX News reporter Melinda Hawkish challenged. "And aren't your plans to turn America into a weakened quasi-Europe?"

"Blasphemer!" Hillary shouted along with the other reporters, all fingers pointed at Melinda. "Right wing bias! She must be silenced to restore order!"

"But I am fair and balanced!" Melinda protested before a gorilla-like union thug grabbed her. "I'll kill you all!" she shouted just as her mouth was being covered up.

"Now that it's just us professional, unbiased media types," Lefty Stevens of CNN said to Hillary, "I'd like to ask you how you plan to celebrate your seizure of power, which experts I shall not name agree is a great thing."

"We've decided that the monuments on the Mall must go!" Hillary declared. "One celebrates the first Republican president, whom we declare evil! The other is an obvious phallic symbol and must be destroyed. Later today we will demolish them both and replace them with new monuments. One will be a monument to gun confiscations, and the joys of powerlessness. The other a monument to taxation, and how lovely it is for us smarter people in government to take your money at the point of the aforementioned confiscated guns. Another monument will be a celebration of hippies and all poorly informed, nigh-retarded political activists. Finally, there will be a shrine to the almighty abortion at which we can all bow and worship, praying for the end of the scourge of babies once and for all!"

The reporters all applauded while the union thug dragged Melinda away. As he neared an alleyway, someone blocked him.

"That ain't the way you treat a lady," Buck the Marine said angrily.

"Me like union. Me like Democrats. Me smash!" the union thug yelled.

"We'll see what my fists have to say about that," Buck said, knocking out the union thug with a swift punch. "Ooh-rah!" He then looked at Melinda. "Are you alright? You aren't one of those feminist chicks who don't like being saved, are ya?"

"No. Thanks, Buck," Melinda said.

"There's big trouble about," Buck stated. "A crazy, flying, robot Commie destroyed my weaponry."

"Weaponry or not, we have to stop Hillary Clinton and the Hell's Democrats," Melinda responded. "They want to blow up the Washington Monument and the Lincoln Memorial."

Buck growled angrily. "Not in *my* America."

* * * *

"DC is a parasitic entity," Cyber-Lenin mused to himself as he flew over the landscape. "I need a place of real industry to corrupt with my Pure Commie Evil." He spied some factories near a port. "Perfect," he laughed evilly as he landed.

He charged up with Pure Commie Evil, ready to destroy, but suddenly a blast hit Cyber-Lenin, knocking him off his feet. He turned to see behind him Robo-Rumsfeld, armored in a suit of Uninhibited Capitalism that glowed red, white, and blue.

"Curse you, Rumsfeld Strangler!" Cyber-Lenin yelled. "Your effects of capitalism befoul me!"

"Then why don't you cry to your mommy, Commie?" Rumsfeld said as he threw a punch, knocking Cyber-Lenin through a nearby wall. Cyber-Lenin countered with a red blast of Pure Commie Evil, stunning Rumsfeld, and then charged Rumsfeld, knocking him down.

"You will soon discover that nothing—nothing!—is more powerful than Pure Commie Evil!" Cyber-Lenin shouted, preparing to blast Rumsfeld again.

Rumsfeld rolled out of the way and jumped to his feet. "Whatever, Mecha-Pinko." He then came at Cyber-Lenin with a series of capitalism-powered punches, knocking Cyber-Lenin backward. Rumsfeld let loose a red, white, and blue blast of Uninhibited Capitalism. Cyber-Lenin tried to block it with a shield of Pure Commie Evil, but it powered through and struck him to the ground.

"No! This can't be!" Cyber-Lenin shouted. "Nothing can defeat Pure Commie Evil! It's the most powerful thing known to man!"

"The most powerful thing known to man is a pissed-off American," Rumsfeld said, preparing to finish off his nemesis.

"We will finish this later!" Cyber-Lenin vowed, flying away over the ocean.

Suddenly a large tail came out of the water and knocked Cyber-Lenin back to earth. "No escape for you!" said a booming voice. There, riding a whale, was a man with green pants and an orange shirt.

"Aquaman!" Rumsfeld exclaimed. "The homo crime fighter of the sea!"

"I'm not gay!" Aquaman responded. "I just like flamboyant clothing."

Distracted, Rumsfeld was knocked down with a blast of Pure Commie Evil. "If I can't escape," Cyber-Lenin announced, "I will destroy us all." He took out a glowing, red orb. "This is a Commie Bombie. It will destroy everything within a mile radius with its Pure Commie Evil." Cyber-Lenin moved to press the trigger, but suddenly he screamed in pain as something struck his hand. The Commie Bombie rolled harmlessly into the sea, while Cyber-Lenin pulled a letter opener out of his hand.

"Someone call for a White House Press Secretary?" Scott McClellan said proudly, his floral-pattern cape flapping in the wind.

"Could you have been any later?" Rumsfeld asked angrily as he got to his feet. He looked at Cyber-Lenin, who stood up, too. "Time to cross you off my blacklist," Rumsfeld snarled. "You've made a lot of mistakes, Lenin. You fell for the evil of Communism, you killed millions with your Soviet Union, and you dared to stand against America. But your worst and last mistake was HURTING MY DOG! RARRRRRRR!" Rumsfeld's rage fueled the capitalistic energy in his suit into a chaotic fury. It charged up around him and then blasted forward at Cyber-Lenin, sending him flying into the air, where he exploded into a display of fireworks. A little red beard softly floated to earth.

"Let's see them preserve that body," Rumsfeld laughed.

"We fought him like real superheroes!" Scott exclaimed.

"Yeah," Rumsfeld answered, "and now we get to go to a bar where you'll treat me to a beer."

"Can I come too?" Aquaman asked.

"It's not that kind of bar," Rumsfeld answered. "Why don't you go sleep with the fishes."

* * * *

"Are you sure you know how to rewire explosives?" Melinda asked.

"If it involves killerin', I knows it," Buck answered.

"Quick, the ceremony is about to start!" Melinda warned.

"And now, to destroy the evil monuments!" Hillary said, preparing to activate the detonator as crowds of cheering hippies watched. When she hit the button, though, the crowds of hippies exploded instead. "What?" Hillary exclaimed as she and the Hell's Democrats looked on in shock.

"Decided it was time to put an end to your... uh... being Democrats," Buck said, stepping forward as the mist of red settled.

"Tom Smashle, stop him!" Hillary ordered. Senator Daschle charged Buck, but he responded with a slap to Daschle's face, which sent Daschle running back crying.

"I feel weak and whiny again," Daschle said.

"The Pure Commie Evil must have worn off," Hillary said. "That means Cyber-Lenin is dead! We have to escape."

She and the Hell's Democrats began to flee, but suddenly they heard the click-clack of claws against pavement. There before them stood a four-legged figure. Two bloodshot eyes stared at them. A row of jagged teeth shined in the light. A growl emanated from the creature, and its whole body shook with rage.

"That dog looks angry," Hillary said.

"Very angry," Daschle added.

* * * *

"George W. Bush has returned to power," the anchorwoman announced. "When asked how it felt to return, Bush beat the crap out of the reporter just for the heck of it and then yelled, 'Yee-haw!' while firing his guns into the air. Everything in the White House is now back to normal, except for one set of drapes that is reportedly missing.

"In other news, Senator Hillary Clinton, Senator Tom Daschle, Senator John Kerry, Representative Dick Gephardt, and Governor Howard Dean are all missing and presumed mauled by a very angry dog."

"Also, in Maryland, police have found the remains of what they believe to be Vladimir Lenin. They relate the homicide to the infamous DC serial murderer the Rumsfeld Strangler. At the scene was found a note reading, 'I'm Donald Rumsfeld. I blew up this guy.' Penciled in the corner of the note is, 'I'm Scott McClellan. I helped.' Police believe this means the Rumsfeld Strangler has an accomplice, someone they have dubbed 'Chokehold-lad.' He is believed to have a semi-sharp letter opener and should be considered dangerous. While there are no witnesses to either of them, profilers say that the Rumsfeld Strangler is probably an overweight seventeen year-old Filipino girl with a wooden leg, while Chokehold-lad is most likely a pudgy white man in his mid-thirties with a thankless job in public speaking."

Ernst Blofeld watched the TV quietly. Finally, the silence was broken.

"You know," Black Manta said, "if we had only defeated Aqua—"

"Don't even say it!" Blofeld shouted. "The Rumsfeld Strangler may have won this time, but we'll eventually do away with him and destroy America. Muh ha ha ha!"

"And Aquaman," Black Manta added. "Don't forget about Aquaman."

"Fine, and we'll defeat Aquaman, too," Blofeld said and then turned to the rest of the Legion of Doom. "So who wants to go to T.G.I. Friday's?"

THE END

September 03, 2003

It's All About the Jesus

"With the constant killings and terrorist attacks in Iraq, will you now admit that it's become a Vietnam-like quagmire?" CNN reporter Lefty Stevens asked.

"No," Condoleezza Rice answered firmly. "It's like post-war Germany."

"Vietnam," Stevens insisted.

"Post war Germany!" Condi answered back angrily.

"Vietnam."

"Post war Germany!!"

"Quagmire! Admit it!"

"I'll kill you!" Condi screamed, jumping onto the reporter and pummeling him.

"You started the press conference without me," Rumsfeld stated as he walked up to the podium.

Condi dropped the reporter. "You're late."

"I arrive when I damn well feel like it," Rumsfeld grunted. He then looked at the reporters. "So what do you want?"

"Do you think that you sent too few troops to Iraq?" asked a reporter.

"Are you questioning my military strategy?" Rumsfeld demanded angrily.

"Well, uh..."

"You, a brainless reporter, think you know more about how many troops a conflict takes than the Secretary of War?"

"I just—"

"It's tiring, me carrying a gun this heavy," Rumsfeld stated, pulling out his Luger. "Maybe I should lighten it."

"No no!" the reporter shouted. "Question withdrawn!"

"Anyone else want to waste my time?" Rumsfeld asked as he put away his gun.

"What are your plans for settling Iraq, and afterwards?" asked another reporter.

"We will civilize Iraq, killing all the terrorists and Baath party members and whoever else strikes our fancy. Then we will begin forcefully converting everyone to Christianity. This will coincide with our attacks on other Middle Eastern countries."

"Convert everyone to Christianity?" asked one confused reporter.

"What? Did you think this war was all about oil?" Rumsfeld scoffed. "We, the West, have always been bitter about losing the Crusades. Unlike the silly Muslims, we've been able to keep our resentment quiet. See, back then, we were backward in comparison to the Muslims and wholly outmatched, but now we have laser-guided cruise missiles, while they just have rocks and sticks. Thus, the Crusades can finally be completed, and the Holy Land will return to Christian hands."

"You can't force religion on people!" a reporter exclaimed.

"Actually, studies show that torture and threat of death are quite effective methods of religious conversion," Condi added.

"So you're going to convert everyone in the Middle East?"

"Either that or kill them," Rumsfeld said. "Except for those Jews; they're some tough bastards."

"What about freedom of religion?" asked an exasperated reporter.

"That's only for Americans," Rumsfeld answered. "It is the administration's position that only Americans have God-given rights, He having forsaken all other countries."

"So you're going to take over all of the Middle East?"

"No; rulership will be handed to the Pope in the spirit of the Crusades. Then history books will have to be rewritten to say that, while the Crusades started out rough, they were eventually successful due to the Bush administration."

"And his plucky National Security Advisor," Condi chimed in.

"The American people won't stand for this!" one reporter asserted.

"According to polling data, the American people don't care what we do militarily as long as bad people die and their prime-time television doesn't get interrupted with news breaks. Also, while the American people support other religious views, they wish Muslim women would wear more revealing clothing."

"Isn't this the worst fear of the Muslims in the Middle East?"

"Yes," Rumsfeld chuckled. "And everyone thought they were nuts in thinking we wanted to conquer them all. Well, they're still nuts, but they were right."

"Wouldn't Jesus be against torture and murder in His name?"

"Well, Jesus isn't running the show; I am!" Rumsfeld answered angrily. "This is a matter of honor for the western world. We're not satisfied just being economically, militarily, and hygienically superior to the Islamic extremists; we want to say we won the Crusades, too."

"We have to get going now," Condi told the reporters. "We need to get fitted for our suits of armor and then pick out our swords for severing the heads of the unbelievers."

"Did you hear Bush still wants to wear his cowboy hat with his armor?" Rumsfeld grumbled. "What a jackass."

"We still have a lot more questions about this!" insisted a reporter.

Rumsfeld drew a broadsword. "This press conference is over unless you wish me to smite thee!"

The reporters all fled the room in terror.

"Man, they're gullible," Condi laughed. "Now they'll all be distracted by this while we steal us some oil."

Rumsfeld looked a little sullen. "Really did want to smite someone, though."

September 08, 2003

The Fall Guy

"Now that I've made the case for Iraq getting eighty-seven billion dollars, we need to find ways to get that money embezzled back to us through dummy corporations," President Bush said.

"Don't worry," Dick Cheney stated. "I've got it all set up."

"I'm afraid that someone might find out, though," Condoleezza Rice said. "I think we need a fall guy."

"But where are we going to find someone to be the fall guy?" Bush mused aloud.

"Can we go over some notes before the next press conference?" White House Press Secretary Scott McClellan asked as he entered the room.

"Scott! Great to see you!" Bush exclaimed.

Scott stopped for a second and looked at Bush with suspicion. "Why are you being nice to me all of a sudden?"

"Because you're a valued part of the team," Bush answered.

"Really?"

"Yeah, now get over here and stop being such a douche bag," Bush ordered. "I need you to sign this paper before the next press conference. It... uh..."

"It verifies that you are going to be truthful and honest in the press conference," Condi said.

"But Bush always yells at me when I'm truthful and honest," Scott said.

"Change of policy," Bush said, handing over the document. Scott started to look it over, but Bush slapped him on the head. "Don't read it; just sign it!"

* * * *

"Is it fair to ask for eighty-seven billion dollars for Iraq when the economy is in a recession?" asked a reporter.

"The economy is not in a recession," Scott responded, "and we have to do whatever it takes to get the job done right."

"I did some investigation," said another reporter, "and the money all seems to be going to corporations in your name."

"What?" Scott exclaimed. "That's ridiculous."

"And they aren't even real corporations," the reporter continued. "They just seem to be ways for you to take that money and keep it from the needy Iraqi people."

"That's crazy," Scott said adamantly. "I don't own any corporations, and I would never do such a thing."

"Why you take money from me and my family?" asked a little Iraqi girl in broken English. "I am sick and hungry."

"I didn't take your money, little girl," Scott pleaded. "Honest."

"Boo!" all the reporters yelled.

"You're not supposed to boo at a press conference!" Scott said in frustration.

"Boo!"

* * * *

"You wouldn't believe what I was charged with at the press conference today," Scott said, walking into the Oval Office. "They said..." Then Scott noticed the room was filled with canvas bags with dollars signs on them. "You took the Iraqi billions!" Scott accused, pointing a finger at Bush.

"That's crazy," Bush answered. "That's so crazy I should have you locked away in an asylum where you can't tell anyone anything incriminating about me."

Laura then came into the room. "What's this commotion all about?"

"Nothing, dear," Bush answered.

"He embezzled billions of dollars that were supposed to help the Iraqis and then framed me for it!" Scott stated angrily.

"George, is this true?" Laura asked sternly.

"I was going to buy you something nice with it," Bush answered meekly.

"You give all that money back to the Iraqis, and you apologize to Mr. McClellan this instant!"

"I'm sorry, Scott," Bush said. "But I was going to quietly pardon you at the end of my term—honest!"

"Well, that's better," Laura said. "Now you be less mischievous in the future." She then left the room.

Bush glared at Scott angrily. "Squealer."

September 15, 2003

Autocide Bomber

"Wow! You got a neat place here in Israel!" Bush exclaimed, playing around with things in Ariel Sharon's office. "What's this?"

"It's an Uzi; don't touch that!" Sharon chided him.

"So I hear you have a lot of Jews here in Israel. Is that true?"

"Well, back in 1947—"

"Hey, who's this?" Bush called out.

"That's a guy named Uzi; don't touch him!"

"I heard Jesus was born near here," Bush said. "Do you still see Him around? If you do, can you ask Him about having the Democrats smote? I hear He has contacts to get that done."

"No, I haven't seen Jesus," Sharon said impatiently. "Aren't you here to talk about the suicide bombings?"

"The what now?"

"Don't you watch the news?"

"No, that's what I have advisors for," motioning to Colin Powell and Donald Rumsfeld. "I brought my wussiest advisor and my most violent and bloodthirsty advisor."

"Which one is which?" Sharon asked.

"I dunno; ask them a question."

"What do you think we should do about the terrorists who target our children for murder?" Sharon inquired.

"Well, we need to talk to them and get to the root causes—" Powell started to say.

"Kill them all!" Rumsfeld yelled. "They will be peaceful when they are dead!"

"I like the second one's attitude," Sharon whispered to Bush, "but what's with his dog?"

Chomps, the world's angriest dog, ripped a piece out of the drywall and began chewing it apart.

"That's just Chomps," Bush explained. "He's a little mentally unstable, but he's pretty famous, too. He's been in three different episodes of *When Animals Attack*."

Suddenly they could hear ululation. "What's that?" Bush asked.

"I think it's a suicide bomber," Sharon answered.

They all looked out the window and saw a crazed man running toward the building. He stopped at a car and then exploded.

"My Buick!" Rumsfeld cried.

"It was just a rental," Bush said.

"But it's the principle of the thing!" Rumsfeld asserted. "It's time to exile Arafat... to hell!"

"I think we shouldn't be so hasty—" Powell started to say.

"Rarr!" Rumsfeld yelled, picking Powell up and throwing him out the window. He then charged out of the building, Chomps following him.

"Should we go help Colin Powell?" Sharon asked.

"No, Rumsfeld throws him out the window all the time; he's used to it, Sharon."

"SHARE-*OWN*," Sharon corrected him, "it's a long 'o.'"

"Whatever."

* * * *

"This is Melinda Hawkish reporting from the Gaza Strip. A celebration has erupted, with many Palestinians cheering the mindless destruction of the Secretary of Defense's rental car and dancing around like crazed monkeys.

"Wait, some figure seems to be joining the crowd... a figure and his dog. Now there's blood everywhere, the celebration ending with an attack so violent you'd think a Palestinian was involved. Luckily, we brought a tarp, so my blouse will be protected from the splash damage."

* * * *

"So, did we kill the American Secretary of Defense?" Arafat asked.

"No, we only got his car," answered one of his men.

"P'lo!" Arafat exclaimed, slapping his head. "What should we do?"

"Kill the Jews!" answered one of his advisors.

"Jooooos! Keeeel!" answered another advisor.

"There seems to be a man charging us," said one guard, "much like a suicide bomber... except without the bomb or the suicide."

"Rarr!" Rumsfeld yelled as he and Chomps busted through the wall. "You destroyed my car. Now you die!"

Rumsfeld and Chomps then began to lose their footing.

"I covered the floor in baby wipes," Arafat laughed evilly. "Don't... wipe out! Muh ha ha ha!"

Both Rumsfeld and Chomps tumbled to the ground. This made them angry.

Very angry.

"Rarr!" Rumsfeld screamed.

"Gerawer!" Chomps growled.

The force of their combined anger caused the entire room to burst into flames, burning up the baby wipes. Chomps leapt at the guards, his maw open expectantly, while Rumsfeld grabbed Arafat.

"Don't kill me!" Arafat pleaded.

Rumsfeld calmed down a bit. "Though you blew up my Buick, I guess there are others who deserve to kill you more."

* * * *

"Now, to finally exile Arafat, we will launch him out of this cannon," Sharon announced before the gathered Israelis. With a cheer, the cannon was fired, and Arafat went tumbling through the air.

"I'll be back!" he vowed before disappearing into the distance.

"So, you think this will bring peace to the Middle East?" Bush asked.

Sharon shrugged his shoulders. "I just wanted to see Arafat fired out of a cannon."

"We all did," Bush said with a smile as he patted Sharon on his back. "We all did."

September 17, 2003

Buck the Marine and the Jolly Rancher Bandits

"Why are you filming the GIs helping school children?" CNN's Lefty Stevens asked FOX News's Melinda Hawkish. "There's no story there."

"I think people would be interested in how war and destruction have improved the lives of the Iraqis," Melinda answered.

"Bah! Only stories of failure are newsworthy," Stevens answered. Nearby he saw a troop fall to the ground, and he and his cameraman quickly rushed over to film him. "Yet another troop has fallen in this burgeoning quagmire," Stevens narrated.

"I'm alright," said Private Gomer, standing up. "I just done tripped on a rock."

"Blast it!" Stevens exclaimed. "Well, scream for us if you are more seriously wounded."

"Alrighty."

"What's wrong with those people?" Buck the Marine asked Melinda.

"They're just CNN; don't mind them," Melinda answered. "So are you ready to show us what you've done here?"

"Well... uh... I don't know if you're dressed properly," Buck said. "You might offend the Muslims."

"But I wore a veil," Melinda protested.

"Yeah... uh... but not much else."

"Well it's so darn hot here!" Melinda answered.

Some Iraqi men walking buy shouted something in Arabic while smiling and whistling at Melinda.

"The Iraqis are so nice," Melinda smiled. "Anyway, Buck, tell our viewers what you have done for the Iraqi children."

"Well, since we got a break 'tween killin's, we helped them little Iraqi kids by fixing up their school and building them a playground with swings and a teeter-totter and one of them twirly things to make them kids dizzy."

"We love big American!" shouted one of the kids.

"We love candy, too!" said another.

Buck laughed and tossed the kids some Jolly Ranchers. "We got tons of these candies here," Buck explained to Melinda. "These Jolly Ranchers are like the only things that won't melt in the 120-degree weather. Frankly, I'm sick of the dang things, but the kids can't seem to get enough of them."

"More candy!" demanded another kid.

Buck laughed. "Don't worry, little for'ners, we have plenty more... Ow! One of them kids bit me!"

"Quagmire!" Stevens yelled as his cameraman filmed.

"Calm down, kids," Buck told everyone, "there is plenty of candy for everyone."

"Can I be a big Marine like you, American?" one of the children asked.

"Aww," Buck answered, "America will make sure you can be anything you want. Now you kids go play in your playground, but be careful; life is not all candy and biting Buck. There are still evil for'ners afoot. And what do you do to evil for'ners?"

"Kill them!" all the Iraqi kids shouted in unison.

A tear almost came to Buck's eye. "That's some good kids."

* * * *

"Since the big American says I can be anything I want," said an Iraqi boy as he sat on one end of the teeter-totter, "I'm going to own a big corporation. I'm then going to downsize everyone to drive up the value of my stock."

"I'm going to become an actress," said the Iraqi girl on the other end of the teeter-totter, "and I'm going to use my fame to speak out about politics even though I'm an idiot."

Suddenly Baathist thugs came up and knocked the kids off the teeter-totter. Then they blew it up. "That is what happens to everything made by the American invaders!" yelled one of the Baath party members.

The children started crying. "We'll tell the big American, and he'll stab you with his knife!" one yelled.

"Muh ha ha ha! No one can stop us!" the thugs laughed as they ran away.

* * * *

"They blew up the teeter-totter!" Buck exclaimed, barely containing his anger.

"There's three others," one soldier said.

"But that was the best one!"

The kids nodded in agreement.

Private Gomer came by, rubbing his head. "Someone done hit me on the head."

"But you were supposed to guard the supply of Jolly Ranchers!" Buck said. He ran to the Jolly Rancher silo. It was empty.

"What was your one job, Private Gomer?" Buck asked angrily.

"To guard the Jolly Ranchers," Private Gomer answered, looking at his feet.

"And what happened to the Jolly Ranchers?"

"They got stolen," Private Gomer answered. "I'm sorry."

"You apologize to them little for'ner kids," Buck told him.

The kids started crying. "No more candy?" asked one tearful youth.

"We'll see about that," Buck answered.

"A teeter-totter destroyed and their candy gone, this war has quickly descended into and unending quagmire," Lefty Stevens narrated in front of a camera.

"I'll avenge that teeter-totter and get back that candy, or I'm not Buck the Marine," Buck swore. "There are more things I distribute than candy." He dramatically chambered a round into his rifle, ejecting the round that was already chambered. "Oh yeah."

* * * *

"Now I can film a Marine in action and show how well things are going here," Melinda said, following Buck with a camera.

"Bah!" Stevens answered. "We're going to film him being yet another casualty, proving how horribly this occupation is going."

"Quiet, you two," Buck said, slowly moving across the landscape. "I sense foreignness in the air."

There was a sudden ambush, and just as suddenly, Buck ended it with fire from his M-16. "Ooh-rah!"

"Yay America!" Melinda yelled.

"Boo!" Lefty Stevens called out.

"The scent of watermelon-flavored Jolly Ranchers is unmistakable," Buck said. "They went into that cave over yonder."

Buck entered the cave, followed by the two reporters and their cameramen. He was soon attacked, but the resistance was nothing for an experienced Marine. He killed the enemy so quickly he didn't even feel the need to shout "Ooh-rah!" in triumph.

"When is he going to get killed?" Stevens exclaimed with exasperation.

Soon they came to a large room. Buck crept in carefully, but suddenly a light came on, and he was surrounded by evil Baathists. "Time to film his death," a voice called out. At the front of the room stood Christiane Amanpour.

"It's the war slut!" Melinda yelled.

"Funny words coming from a reporter wearing a bikini," Amanpour answered.

"And a veil," Melinda said defensively.

"What are you doing here?" Buck demanded.

A new figure came to stand by Amanpour—one with a bushy mustache. It was Saddam Hussein! "She has agreed to help me get back into power to show what a failure the Bush administration is," Saddam said. "Then she gets the exclusive. First, though, we kill one more American do-gooder!"

"Wow! So this is how objective journalists do things!" Stevens exclaimed as he backed away to film the action.

"We're surrounded!" Melinda said. "Do you know what to do?"

"According to the Marine killin' manual," Buck answered, "when surrounded, you kill everyone... in a circle."

Buck dropped to the ground as he tossed grenades to each side. While the enemy fighters were confused by the explosions, Buck began picking them off with his M-16 as they fired uselessly at him. Buck then set his sights on Saddam.

"You're going to be known as Saddam Who-dead!" Buck yelled as he charged the former dictator.

"Uh-oh!" Saddam yelled as he ducked into a secret passageway. Once Buck got there, all he could see was the flame of an advanced propulsion system.

"Danged Baathists and their rocket cars," Buck grumbled. He then turned to Amanpour. "You got some answering to do, little lady. Conspiring with the enemy, trying to get a Marine killed—why, that has to be one of the least ethical things the left-wing media has done in... well... two or three days."

"More like eight hours," Melinda stated. "You need to watch more news."

"Don't have time with all my killin' duties," Buck answered.

"I was just trying to tell the truth," Amanpour said, "without being intimidated by the Bush administration." She then looked at Melinda Hawkish. "Or FOX News."

"I never tried to intimidate you!" Melinda yelled angrily. "I'll strangle you for saying that!"

Amanpour shrieked and ran away.

Buck now located the stockpile of stolen Jolly Ranchers. "That will make the kids happy." He then turned to Lefty Stevens. "I hope you learned something about being a more ethical journalist."

"I haven't learned anything," Stevens asserted. "That's why I work for CNN."

* * * *

"Yay big American!" the Iraqi children shouted. "Yay candy!"

"Big American kill all bad people!" said one child proudly.

"Time to get to rebuilding that teeter-totter," Buck said, picking up some tools.

"So how does it make you feel to see all these happy children?" Melinda asked, holding out her microphone toward Buck.

"Seeing their joyous smiles makes me a happy Marine," Buck said. "So happy... well... so happy I want to kill evil people." He thought for a moment. "Oh wait, I always want to kill evil people. Ooh-rah!"

September 22, 2003

Visit from the Parents

"Well, place looks just like I remember her," Bush Sr. said, taking a look around while he entered the White House.

"I remember it being tidier," Barbara Bush said and then looked at Laura. "You need to keep it clean in here to give a good impression to the tourists."

"It *is* clean," Laura asserted angrily, "and they haven't had tours of the White House in a while because of 9-11."

"Maybe they just told you it was because of 9-11," Barbara said, "but I'll bet it was really because people were getting embarrassed about the appearance of the White House."

Laura looked to her husband to do something. "Mom and Dad, it's great to see you two!" Dubya exclaimed. "I gotta show you the new HDTV; they didn't have that during your term."

"Very nice. We can watch a baseball game," Bush Sr. said.

"And that will give me time to show you how to properly decorate," Barbara told Laura.

Laura just steamed silently.

"We need to talk," Scott McClellan said, approaching Dubya.

"Who's this dork?" Bush Sr. asked.

"That's my new White House Press Secretary," Dubya told him. "I sure miss Ari, because this guy is such a dweeb."

"I'm standing right here," Scott said angrily.

"I know," Dubya answered, rolling his eyes. "What do you want?"

"There are allegations that you've been funneling money away from lunches for underprivileged school children to help fund baby seal clubbing."

"Man, I was hoping that story wouldn't break for a couple more months," Dubya said. "Just give the press the standard line."

"Standard line?" Scott repeated, confused.

"Yeah, the standard line."

"What's that?"

Bush groaned. He then fetched a handgun from a nearby drawer. "If the press keeps on asking questions, threaten to murder them all."

"Threaten to murder them all?" Scott said with surprise as he took the gun.

"There; you got it," Dubya declared and then handed Scott an extra magazine. "Here, you'll need more ammo to back up your threat."

"I'm not actually supposed to kill them, am I?"

"Do I have to explain everything to you?" Dubya asked angrily. "Now shoo! I'm talking to my parents."

"I don't think that throw rug goes with the room," Barbara told Laura.

"Thanks for your opinion," Laura said, holding back her anger. She then looked at Dubya. "Can we talk for a moment, honey?"

"Sure, dear," Dubya answered, the two of them moving out of earshot of his parents.

"Your mother won't stop criticizing me," Laura said sternly.

"Well, maybe she has a point about you not being a very good wife," Dubya offered.

Laura thought about that for a moment and then responded.

"Ahh! My groin! I need that from time to time!" Dubya yelled as he collapsed to the ground. He then recovered and stood back up. "Come on, Laura; I know you're smart enough to know not to ask me for advice."

"I don't want your advice; I want you to try and do something about it."

"Okay," Dubya said and walked back toward his parents.

"So where are my grandkids?" Barbara asked.

"Heck if I know," Dubya answered, shrugging his shoulders.

"They're at college right now," Laura said.

Condoleezza Rice now approached. "Something important has come up."

"Is this your maid?" Bush Sr. asked.

"No, she's my National Security Advisor," Dubya told him. "She's really smart."

"Having a black woman on your staff—that's very forward-thinking of you, son," Bush Sr. praised Dubya.

"You never told me you were black," Dubya said to Condi with surprise.

"Don't worry, I know how to talk to her, son," Bush Sr. remarked. He then turned to Condi. "So what's the dealio, sistah-girl?"

Condi took a deep breath and unclenched her fist. "Crazed General Wesley Clark is causing trouble on the West Coast," she said. "As part of his campaign, he's attacking everyone with his army of cybernetic ninja monkeys."

They turned on a TV. There stood Clark, riding atop a tank. "Muh ha ha ha!" he laughed as destruction rained about him. "Soon I will have the nomination. Then the White House will be mine! And then the world! Muh ha ha ha!"

"I don't think that cape is standard military issue," Dubya remarked.

"Should we do something?" Condi asked.

"Bah; the West Coast is like hundreds of miles away," Dubya said.

"It's just standard Democratic primary antics," Bush Sr. commented. "It'll all stop when it's decided who's got the nomination." He then looked at his son. "Could we talk privately for a moment?"

Dubya led his father to the Oval Office. "I'm glad you followed in your father's footsteps, boy," Bush Sr. said, "but I hoped things would have been easier for you. Instead, you've got all this terrorism to deal with."

"I'm handling it," Dubya assured him. "I have a good staff."

"Great. You know, a father always wants things to be better for his son. What I'm saying is that I want you to be a two-termer and not make the same mistakes as your old man. So... are you going to get Saddam?"

"He's out of power, and we're hunting him down."

"And are you also taking care of the economy?"

"We've cut taxes, and things are improving."

"That's a good boy," Bush Sr. said, patting Dubya on the head.

"Thanks for explaining to me how everything I do is wrong," Laura said with a forced smile as she entered the room with Barbara.

Suddenly Condi came running into the room, followed by Kôtôichi. "The White House is under attack by terrorists!" she exclaimed.

"Awww!" Bush moaned. "And when my parents are visiting."

"Who's that guy?" Bush Sr. asked, looking at Ichi.

"He's a blind samurai we hired as a Secret Service agent because of the People with Disabilities Act."

"Back when I was president, we had enough money to hire better protection than a blind Chinaman," Bush Sr. remarked.

"I'm Japanese," Ichi shot back harshly.

"He's really good," Dubya assured his father, "but I think we'll need more help for this." Dubya picked up the phone. "Agent Smith, we're under attack. Get the Secret Service to handle it."

"I'm afraid right now is our union-mandated fifteen-minute break," Agent Smith answered. "If we do work while it's supposed to be break time, we'll get in big trouble with the union."

"Why did the Secret Service have to unionize?" Dubya grumbled as he slammed down the phone. "Ichi-san, will you help us?"

"Five ryo," he answered.

"But you took all my ryo yesterday in that dice game!" Dubya exclaimed.

"I have some Spanish doubloons in my purse if that helps," Barbara said.

"Offer accepted," Ichi remarked, drawing the sword from his cane.

"Instead of just relying on a blind swordsman, I also stored some automatic rifles in here for just such an incident," Laura said, opening a closet that was full of weaponry.

"Wow! You even have a spare cowboy hat," Dubya said, taking the hat and putting it on.

Barbara took a rifle. "You really should have coated these in oil a bit more before you stored them."

"That's important for gun care," Condi remarked.

"Don't you get on my case, too!" Laura shouted angrily as she chambered a round into her M-16.

Kôtôichi listened carefully. "The terrorists are almost upon us."

Father and son stood next to each other holding rifles. "Bring it on."

* * * *

"What an eventful past couple of hours," Bush Sr. remarked.

"Quite a battle it was," Dubya said. "One for the record books."

"I'll need to get my sword sharpened," Ichi commented.

"And it sure was a surprise to find out who was behind the terrorist attack all along," Barbara said.

"That *was* surprising," Condi remarked.

"And it's interesting how events came together to bring a better understanding between Barbara and me so that now we're best friends," Laura said.

"That *was* quite interesting," Dubya commented.

"And I didn't know you could disco dance like that, son," Bush Sr. said to Dubya.

"When the honor of Outer Mongolia is at stake, there is little I can't do," Dubya stated firmly.

"I'm also glad how all this taught me the true meaning of International Talk Like a Pirate Day," Condi said. "To think I had been so obsessed with just the commercialism of that holiday."

"I think we all learned many important things from those highly eventful past couple hours," Bush declared. "More than we can just casually remark about right now."

Scott came running up toward them, covered in blood. "Well, I killed all of the press."

"What?!" Dubya exclaimed in horror. "You were just supposed to threaten them!"

Scott started laughing. "I'm just covered in paint. I thought I'd play a joke on you like you do on me so we'd be like friends and all."

"I'LL MURDER YOU FOR TRICKING ME!" Dubya screamed, grabbing Scott by the throat and shaking him. "I'M THE @%*& PRESIDENT! YOU DON'T DO THIS TO ME!"

Bush Sr. chuckled. "That's my boy!"

September 24, 2003

UN Negotiations

"Rarr! I'll kill you!" Rumsfeld yelled as his fingers reached for Jacques Chirac's neck. They came up a few inches short.

"See, the chain is just as long as we agreed in the negotiations to set up this meeting," Bush assured the Frenchman. "He'll just be able to threaten you, not kill you."

"I won't be chained up forever!" Rumsfeld growled. "Then your neck is mine!"

"You never said the dog suspended above me would be so angry," Chirac protested, looking very scared at the dog hanging above him who was doing his best to try and bite Chirac.

"We did say the Rottweiler of Damocles, who would represent what it's like to have the threat of terrorism hanging over your head, would be angry," Bush told him.

"But not the angriest dog in the world."

"You never said he couldn't be," Bush retorted.

Chomps snarled and snapped his jaws in the air just above Chirac's head.

"Why do I have to sit in a highchair?" Gerhard Schroeder demanded.

"The negotiations said we get to choose the seating," Bush answered.

"But I don't want to sit in a highchair," Schroeder cried, banging his highchair, "and negotiations said I get a sippy cup! Where's my sippy cup?!"

"Condi, get him his sippy cup," Bush said with annoyance. Condoleezza Rice handed the cup to Schroeder, who snatched it greedily and began drinking his apple juice.

"I don't think we're going to get anywhere with these absurd demands you put on these discussions," Kofi Annan said. "If we are going to—"

He was interrupted as his head was grabbed by Bush and slammed into the table.

"Please stop doing that," Kofi said, holding his aching head.

"Negotiations said I can do that up to eighteen times during the meeting," Bush asserted, "so expect fifteen more of those."

"But you already did it five times."

"Three times," Bush responded. "If you don't believe me, ask the independent ref."

"Three times," said the independent ref.

"The independent ref looks a lot like Dick Cheney in disguise," Kofi said.

"According to negotiations, we are allowed to bring Cheney disguised as someone."

"Why did you have to bring Rumsfeld, though?" Kofi asked. "All he does is try to strangle everyone."

"Rarr! I'll strangle you for saying that!" Rumsfeld shouted, reaching for Kofi's neck but coming just short.

"Rumsfeld knows a lot about the war," Bush explained, "and his opinion on who needs a strangling is helpful."

"I think we should just beat the crap out of all these people," said a man with a guitar wearing a cowboy hat.

"And who is he, again?" Chirac asked.

"We negotiated that we would be able to bring a country western singer to this meeting," Bush said.

"I thought it was going to be one of the Dixie Chicks," Chirac grumbled.

"I have the beginnings of a song," the country western singer said and then began playing his guitar.

I don't like these people at the UN.
In fact, they really suck.
If I see them on the street outside,
I'll hit them with my pickup truck.
Yee-haw!

Bush and Condi applauded. "That was great," Bush said. "Now let's get down to business."

"We have some terms—" Kofi began to say but found his face meeting hard wood again.

"That's three times," said the independent ref.

"Actually, I have some terms," Bush stated. "If you people of the UN don't want to be completely irrelevant and wanna be allowed to help the US in Iraq, you'll need to each write a thousand-word essay on why America is so great and read it publicly. It must then be followed by a song and dance number."

"That's absurd!" Chirac shouted, jumping to his feet and thus putting his head right into Chomps's mouth.

"Uh-oh!" Bush yelled. "Chomps is swallowing Chirac whole! We have to stop him... eventually."

"Rarr!" Rumsfeld shouted, leaping at Kofi. This time, he lassoed Kofi's neck with his shoelaces and began strangling him.

"That wily Rumsfeld," Condi remarked.

"Waah! My sippy cup!" Schroeder cried as the country & western singer took his cup away. The singer then punched Schroeder, shutting him up.

"Dang!" Bush exclaimed. "This UN meeting is going about as poorly as... well... as I expected. Condi, let's just go across the street and get a burger."

"I don't think there's a burger place across the street," Condi said.

"If we walk around, we'll find one eventually," Bush remarked as he left the room.

September 29, 2003

Rumsfeld Carefully Considering His Resignation

"Murder! Kill! Destroy!" Rumsfeld screamed.

"We haven't asked a question yet," said one reporter.

"If your questions are any good, that should have answered them," Rumsfeld responded.

"Democratic presidential candidate Howard Dean has asked for your resignation," stated another reporter. "How do you respond?"

"I'm thinking it over," Rumsfeld said calmly.

"I've heard you threw Howard Dean through a plate-glass window."

"I think better when I'm throwing people through plate-glass windows," Rumsfeld responded irately, not liking being challenged.

"Kinda like how I think better when I pace," offered one reporter helpfully.

"Rarr!" Rumsfeld yelled, grabbing the reporter by the neck. "No one was talking to you!" He soon let go of the reporter and calmed himself. "There is no reason for me to resign because some whiny Democrat asked me to," Rumsfeld asserted. "Things are going very well in Iraq. Soon all Iraqis will be dead."

Condoleezza Rice whispered in his ear.

"I mean, all Iraqis will have democracy and freedom," Rumsfeld said, rolling his eyes.

"What do you think of General Wesley Clark?" asked a reporter.

"He can't make up his mind on whether he would have supported the war in Iraq," Rumsfeld stated, "but I've made up my mind on whether I'll strangle him next time I see him."

"And what have you decided?" inquired another reporter.

Rumsfeld pulled out his Luger and shot the man. "Ask a dumb question, get a dum-dum answer," Rumsfeld quipped as he put his gun back into its holster.

"Do you think the Iraqis will be able to sustain themselves with their oil revenues?"

"Of course not," Rumsfeld said, "since all their oil has mysteriously disappeared."

Condoleezza Rice whispered in his ear again.

"Oh... that won't happen until tomorrow," Rumsfeld said, a bit flustered. He then looked at all the reporters sternly. "And it will be a big shock for everyone!"

All the reporters nodded in fear.

"On second thought, you people know too much," Rumsfeld said ominously. "I'm going to need to strangle you all."

"But the viewers at home have already heard!" protested one reporter.

"No one watches these things," Rumsfeld said with a smile as his hands eagerly tensed for a strangling.

October 01, 2003

Boldly Going Where No White House Press Secretary Has Gone Before

"There was a leak about a CIA operative!" Bush said angrily. "Nothing enrages me more than leaks!" Bush turned to the man next to him who wore a black suit, tie, and sunglasses. "You're my intelligence guy, right, Clancy?"

"I can neither confirm nor deny that."

"You're kind of annoying," Bush grumbled. "Do you have any idea where the leak came from?"

"The what? I'm not sure what you're talking about?" Clancy said.

"It's all over the news!" Bush shouted.

"I don't read the news."

"What do you know, then?"

"Classified stuff."

"Like what?"

Clancy chuckled. "I can't tell you."

"Dangit!" Bush yelled. "What about you, Rumsfeld? You know who the leaker is?"

"If I did, wouldn't there be someone lying strangled on the ground?" Rumsfeld answered gruffly.

"True," Bush admitted. Bush then looked under the conference table. "What about you, Chinese guy with surveillance equipment hiding under the table? You seem to keep tabs on everything. You know who did the leaking?"

"No speak English," the Chinese man answered, shrugging his shoulders.

"Fair enough," Bush answered, "but I will not rest until I find out who is behind this leak! Nothing will keep me from my goal! I swear on the name of my dear departed father that—hey, what's this?" Bush picked up a newspaper. "General Wesley Clark is planning on going faster than the speed of light! If he beats us to that, we'll lose the woman vote!"

Karl Rove emerged from the shadows. "I think you have become distracted by something shiny and are not making sense, President Bush."

"I'm *more* than not making sense, Rover!" Bush declared. He turned to Condoleezza Rice. "How close are we to going faster than the speed of light?"

"According to our knowledgeable scientists," Rice answered, "that's impossible."

"Then fire them and get me some unknowledgeable scientists!" Bush demanded. "We'll show that Weasely Clark who can go warp speed!"

* * * *

Bush looked at the large orb-like device that was attached to a slingshot. "So what's the chance of this going faster than light?" Bush asked.

"According to our statistician," Condi answered, "the chance of this working cannot be expressed as an actual number but instead only as an infinitesimal."

"I feel fate is with us, though," Bush said confidently. "So are you ready, Scott?"

"To report on this event?" asked Scott McClellan.

"No, you're going to ride it and confirm that it goes faster than light speed. We'll shine a flashlight at the same time, and you see if you can beat it."

"Why me?"

"Why me?" Bush answered back mockingly as he shoved Scott into the transporter. "Be a team player for once, Skippy."

"Why is it aimed at a wall?" Scott asked, a bit scared.

"Because the wall was built recently," Bush explained with annoyance. "If you go faster than light, you'll go back in time, and thus you'll fly forward before the wall was built. If you don't go faster than light, you'll just hit the wall. This makes the outcome obvious."

"I dunno—" Scott started to say but was cut off as Bush shut the door on the transporter.

"Fire this baby!" Bush yelled.

The slingshot was released, and the transporter slammed right into the wall.

"That didn't look like it went faster than light at all," Bush commented.

"No, I guess not," Condi answered.

"I'm very hurt," said a weak voice from inside the transporter.

"Want to try again?" Condi asked.

"I'm bored of this now," Bush declared. "What were we doing before?"

"Finding the leaker."

"Oh yeah," Bush said walking off. "I bet it was the pizza boy. I can't tell Stevie anything classified without the whole pizza joint finding out."

"Help me..."

October 06, 2003

Total Recall 2—This Time It's Personal

"Dah!" Arnold Schwarzenegger yelled as he picked up his desk and snapped it in two.

"You have to calm down," President Bush told him. "You have to expect these kinds of attacks from evil people like Gray Davis."

"Women have boobies, and I like to touch them!" Arnold shouted. "Why is that wrong?"

"Hey, I don't make the laws," Bush said defensively but then thought for a moment. "Well, I do sign them."

"And I no like Hitler!" Arnold said angrily. "Nazis are puny! I crush them! I am Ah-nuld!"

"We all know that; I wouldn't worry about it."

"By the way, thank you for coming to support me, President Bush person," Arnold stated more calmly. "You are very wise."

"Well thanks," Bush answered, "but I actually came down here to visit Disneyland." Bush's hands shot up into the air. "Pirates of the Caribbean!"

On TV, Cruz Bustamante was giving a press conference. "It is disturbing to me that Arnold gropes women while praising Hitler," Bustamante told the press, trying to look serious and concerned.

"Dah!" Arnold screamed, crushing the TV with his fists. "I will kill that fat bald man! I will kill Davis, too. They are puny! I will crush them! I am Ah-nuld!"

"Hey, the election is tomorrow," Bush told Arnold. "I'll tell you the same thing I told Rumsfeld: Wait until the polls close to go on a murderous rampage."

"You are a smart politician," Arnold said, "but I must go by what I know, and that is that the solution to all problems is bloody vengeance!"

* * * *

"I myself would never grope women," Bustamante continued. "Why, even now, I make sure to get written permission before touching my wife. Also, I never praise Hitler on a daily basis."

A large figure in a black leather jacket and sunglasses appeared in front of the podium. "Are you Cruz Bustamante?" he asked in a low voice.

"Uh... yes."

"You will be terminated!" Arnold shouted, grabbing Bustamante and lifting him into the air. "See brick wall over there? He your new friend. You go meet him up close and personal." Arnold then threw Bustamante so hard that he became embedded in the brick wall.

"Arnold killed Cruz Bustamante!" shouted a reporter.

Arnold turned to stare into a camera. "You are next, Davis!"

* * * *

"He's after us!" Gray Davis's aide exclaimed as he watched the TV.

"Bah!" Davis yelled. "We will hit him with so many allegations that he will be paralyzed! No one can stop me from finishing my incompetent term as governor! No one!"

"But putting out allegations that he supports Hitler!" the aide exclaimed. "That's so extreme it's almost a self-parody!"

"I say come up with even worse allegations!" Davis yelled. "Where are my loyal trolls from the *Los Angeles Times*?"

The slimy trolls emerged. "We are here to serve the Democratic party, master."

"Put out a story that an unnamed source witnessed Arnold having gay sex with Satan."

"Certainly, master."

"Wait, I have an even better one," Davis said. "Allege that part of his bodybuilding routine was to make an energy shake by putting a puppy in a blender."

"That's so evil and ridiculous no one will believe it!" the aide shouted.

"Silence!" Davis screamed. "Flying monkeys, take him away!"

"Noooooo!" the aide yelled as he was dragged off by the winged monkeys.

"We will go print your allegations, master," the trolls said as they left the office.

Davis then laughed evilly to himself until he was interrupted by the voice of his security officer over the intercom. "We're being assaulted by Arnold Schwarzenegger wielding a minigun!"

"That means a really small gun, right?" Davis asked.

The only response was the sound of automatic gunfire. Soon Davis's door was kicked in, and there stood Arnold. He tossed his minigun aside and said, “Instead of Gray Davis, you will now be known as Black & Blue Davis!”

“Ha!” Davis answered. “Everyone always underestimates me, but I’ll show you!” Davis then charged Arnold and threw a punch at him. It landed with no effect.

“Dah!” Arnold shouted as he punched Davis, sending him flying backward and smashing his desk apart. “You are puny, Davis! I crush you! I am Ah-nuld!” He approached the wounded Davis. “You said you wanted a debate? Well now you will get to debate St. Peter on whether you are allowed through the pearly gates.”

Davis held up a remote control. “If I can’t be the incompetent governor of California, no one can! Muh ha ha ha!”

As Davis hit the button, Arnold jumped out of the window, plunging three stories as the governor’s mansion exploded behind him.

Bush, wearing a Goofy hat, quickly ran over to help Arnold up off the ground. “So is Davis really gone for good?” Bush asked.

Arnold looked at the rubble of the governor’s mansion. “We will know for certain soon. I am Ah-nuld!”

TO BE CONTINUED TOMORROW AT A CALIFORNIA POLLING PLACE NEAR YOU!

October 08, 2003

Stabilizing Iraq

"Hey kids, I'd love to do my imitation again, but it ain't good for my equipment."

"Please, big American!" the Iraqi kids pleaded.

"Well, alright," Buck the Marine said. He then dropped his rifle, raised his hands, and shouted, *"J'ai une odeur comme le fromage!"*

The children all laughed and clapped their hands.

"Pick that rifle back up!" said a stern voice behind Buck.

He took his rifle and turned around to see Condoleezza Rice. "Hey, you're that National Security Advisor."

"Yes, and I'm now in charge of stabilization in Iraq and Afghanistan," Condi answered. "I've decided to take a hands-on approach." She turned to an Iraqi loitering nearby. "What are you doing?"

"Sitting on a barrel."

"Don't sit on that barrel!" She looked around. "Sit on that barrel over there."

"Okay."

Condi watched carefully as the Iraqi moved his sitting place to the other barrel. "Excellent."

"Do you really need to micromanage like that?" Buck asked.

"I will not be questioned!" Condi yelled. She then turned to one of the children. "How old are you?"

"Seven."

"That's old enough to make me coffee; get to it! And as for the rest of you kids, you need to start work on rebuilding that bridge over the river to the east."

"But we don't know—"

"I said go build a bridge!" Condi screamed and raised her hand to strike. The kids ran away in fear.

"Should I help the kids?" asked the loitering Iraqi.

"I told you to sit on that barrel, and you're going to stay on that barrel!" Condi yelled. She then composed herself and looked at Buck. "I cannot have a stabilized Iraq unless people do as I say unquestioningly. Now, I have a job for you, Buck. I hear there are still some terrorists left here, and I need you to deal with them."

"I will do my best, ma'am."

"I want them all dead by tomorrow morning. My carefully laid plans require all evil people in Iraq dead by tomorrow."

"Uh... okay, ma'am... uh... all of them?"

"I think I made that clear!" Condi said curtly. "You'll have help from the UN, by the way. I've brought with me the award-winning UN peacekeeper Chomps, the world's angriest dog."

Chomps, wearing his blue helmet, came running up to Condi's side, looking quite angry at everything. "This heat makes him grumpy," Condi explained.

Chomps started barking at the sun. He stopped after the light stung his eyes too much but then recovered and barked at the sun again.

"So just to be clear, ma'am, my job is to kill all terrorists in Iraq within twenty-four hours?" Buck asked dubiously.

"By tomorrow morning! You'd better not take twenty-four hours!" Condi warned.

Buck prepped his rifle. "Yes, ma'am!"

* * * *

"You're goin' to have to kill a lot of terrorists with your teeth," Buck told Chomps. "Because I don't think I have enough bullets."

Chomps savagely mangled a patch of sand that somehow angered him.

"Quiet, Chomps," Buck whispered. "I think I hear me some for'ners."

From a nearby cave, they could hear some voices.

"We must kill the American invaders!" said one man.

"We need to get all Americans and Jews out of the Middle East," said another. "Then we can once again be a true Islamic region and go back to just killing each other."

"That will be great," answered the first, "but did you just drop a small green pineapple?"

* * * *

"All them Islamic terrorists is goin' to be bad for your stomach," Buck told Chomps. "Why don't you chase that down with a pork chop."

He threw the piece of meat to Chomps, who ate it greedily.

"Well, I'm out of ammo, and my knife needs sharpenin'," Buck said. "Hopefully we got all them terrorists 'cause I'm startin' to get tired."

They trekked back to town just as the sun was rising. "Are all the terrorists dead?" was their greeting by Condi when they arrived.

"I think so," Buck answered. "Durin' the night, we went all around Iraq killin' anyone who was too foreign. There was a lot of them, but they's dead now. Usually killin' gets me pumped up, but I'm pretty tuckered out about now. So how is the rebuildin'?"

"Well, the school, the hospital, and the police station are behind schedule," Condi admitted, "but my palace is nearly done." She pointed to a giant palace that everyone was busy at work on. She then spotted something. "What is that? Syrians are getting in here! I thought you killed all the terrorists, Buck!"

"Well, I got all I could find here, but there's more that keep comin' in from Syria."

"Then you go into Syria, and you kill everyone thinking of coming into Iraq," Condi commanded. "There are some nice Jewish boys in Israel who can probably help you with that."

"Can't I get a nap first, and then kill all the bad people?" Buck asked. Chomps whimpered, being so tired that he barely looked angry.

Condi rolled her eyes. "Fine. Take a quick nap, and then invade Syria."

"Can I stop sitting on this barrel?" asked the Iraqi behind her.

"When I told you to sit on that barrel, I had a good reason!" Condi shot back. She then looked at the people working on her palace. "More gold inlays!"

October 13, 2003

The Demoncrat—Volume 1

"There is a disturbance in the Beltway," Karl Rove uttered ominously.

"What is it, Rover?" Bush asked as he practiced on a putting green in the Oval Office.

Karl Rove closed his eyes and tried to focus. "I cannot tell yet, but it does not bode well."

"I once thought I had a premonition," Bush said as he prepared for a putt, "but it was just bad shellfish." The golf ball rolled right by the hole's edge. "Dagnabbit!"

* * * *

The Democratic debate for the presidential nomination raged on as usual.

"I hate Bush!"

"I hate Bush more!"

"I wish I had some policy ideas... but I'm too busy hating Bush!"

"We hate Bush, too!" yelled the sympathetic crowd.

"Wesley Clark is not really a Democrat!"

"I am, too! You're a doody-head!"

"You take that back!"

Suddenly a vortex appeared at the center of the stage. From it emerged a giant figure in black armor with glowing red eyes. "I am O'Yama, Eater of Souls and registered Democrat!" he screamed, lighting bursting about him and the entire auditorium shaking at the sound of his voice. "I will plunge the world into eternal darkness, raining blood upon the land, all funded by taxing the top one percent, who are not paying their fair share!"

The audience applauded.

"I'm sorry," said the moderator, "but you can't just materialize in the debate like this."

"Your soul is mine!" O'Yama yelled, and a beam issued forth from his fingertips. Soon the moderator was reduced to nothing but a skeleton.

"Well, I welcome any Democrat to the debate," Senator Joe Lieberman said, "but I'm not sure that eternal darkness is the direction we want to take the country in."

"Quiet, moderate fool!" O'Yama screeched, launching a fireball at Lieberman. It exploded the Senator right off the stage. "I will wreak death, vengeance, and a progressive agenda upon the world, and no one can stop me! And I have been a Democrat since before time began... unlike a certain General in our midst."

"Hey! That's a cheap shot!" Wesley Clark protested.

"Quiet, or suffer for all eternity!" O'Yama threatened. "Only I can defeat George Bush! And when I do, his soul will be mine!"

There was a standing ovation in response as O'Yama's evil laughter echoed throughout the chamber.

* * * *

"Bush! Bush!" White House Press Secretary Scott McClellan yelled as he ran into the Oval Office. "There's a new Democrat who's entered the race for the presidency!"

"Who is it now?" Bush asked with annoyance.

"An evil demon which vows to destroy the world and eat your soul!"

Bush jumped out of his chair in surprise. "But Hillary promised she wouldn't run for the presidency!"

"He speaks of O'Yama, Eater of Souls," Kôtôichi, Bush's blind samurai Secret Service agent, uttered. "An ancient evil."

"That sounds bad," Bush declared.

Scott turned on the TV to a news station. "O'Yama, having just entered the race, is already polling as the front-runner," said the anchorman. "Apparently Democrats are warming up to him because of his left-leaning politics and how his vow to slaughter all humanity doesn't leave him as vulnerable to attacks about being weak on national security."

The screen then showed O'Yama, his eyes glowing red with evil, giving a speech before a crowd of reporters. "When I am president, the oceans will boil, the cities will be destroyed in fire, and there will be universal health care!"

"What?!" Bush exclaimed as he watched the television. "A universal health care plan could be harmful!"

"Why have you waited until now to enter the race?" a reporter asked O'Yama.

"Long ago, I was imprisoned within the void," O'Yama explained. "But the collective hatred for Bush has given me strength to break the seal and once again spread my evil and leftist politics across the world. In a way, you can say the Democratic faithful drafted me."

The O'Yama supporters in attendance cheered while the ancient demon laughed a spine-chilling laugh, and the clouds above him darkened and lightning struck around him.

The TV then showed a reporter interviewing an O'Yama supporter. "Does his being an evil demon concern you?"

"At least he's better than Bush," the young man answered, "who's like Hitler because of... stuff and uh... Bush lies like when... he said... things... Go O'Yama!"

"Sounds like the Democratic base of barely coherent idiots is behind him," Karl Rove said as he emerged from the shadows.

"So do you think he'll have a chance of beating Howard Dean in New Hampshire?" Bush asked.

"We cannot wait to find out!" Ichi exclaimed. "You must slay him now!"

"Hey, I'm not slaying anyone," Bush stated. "Best not to attack any of the Democrats until the primary is over. Isn't that right, Rover?"

"The destruction of the world could go against our partisan goals," Karl Rove said. "Perhaps this problem should be handled now."

"Fine," Bush said. "I'll get my .45, and then it's one dead ancient demon."

"No man-made weapon can defeat O'Yama," Ichi said. "You must find a hidden cave in the mountains of Japan and obtain the enchanted katana known as Crat-Cutter. Only with that can you send O'Yama back to the void."

"Okay, Scott, go fetch me that sword," Bush ordered.

"It can only be wielded by the leader of the free world," Ichi said. "You must go yourself, Bush-san."

"Fine," Bush moaned. "Every time I'm getting ready to settle in for a restful weekend, I have to go on some mystic quest to Japan."

* * * *

"Why do I have to carry everything?" Scott asked as he trekked in the snow behind Bush.

"Because you're the sherpa," Bush answered, poking Scott in the belly with his walking stick.

"Stop doing that!" Scott yelled. "And who is answering press questions while I'm gone?"

"I told Rumsfeld to cover for you."

* * * *

"Rarr!" Rumsfeld yelled as he strangled a reporter.

* * * *

"Are you sure that's a wise decision?" Scott asked.

Bush rolled his eyes. "When was the last time I made a wise decision?" He surveyed the landscape. "Now where is this hidden cave?"

"Well... it's hidden," Scott answered. "Kôtôichi said destiny would lead us to it."

"But how long is that going to take?" Bush complained. "What if a yeti or a Wampa gets us first? And do you see any steakhouses nearby? Because I'm hungry."

"I'm pretty sure we're in the middle of nowhere," Scott answered.

Bush looked around. "Aieeee! Snow monkey!" he exclaimed and then dove to the ground.

"That's just a rock," Scott said and then noticed Bush was gone. "Where are—" he started to say but then fell down a hole. Once he got off the ground, he saw Bush sitting there looking quite annoyed.

"Just our luck to stumble into some sort of... hidden cave," Bush grumbled. "Now we'll never find that steakhouse we were questing for."

"We're looking for the Crat-Cutter, remember?" Scott said.

Bush slapped his forehead. "Oh yeah; ancient magical sword." He then noticed an old Asian man with a long, white beard standing nearby. "Who are you?"

"I am the keeper of the sword you seek," the old man responded.

"Cool," Bush said and then held out his hands. "Gimme gimme gimme!"

"Before you can take the sword," the old man stated, "you must pass a series of tests that will try your strength, your will, and your wit."

Bush considered this. "Ben Franklin says I get the sword now," Bush said, holding out a one hundred dollar bill.

The old man snatched the bill in the blink of an eye. "You have passed the tests," he pronounced and then bowed as he handed the ancient sword to Bush.

"Sweet!" Bush exclaimed as he accepted the sword.

"Well, that could have gone a lot worse," Scott declared as he began to look for an exit to the cave.

"Yeppers," Bush answered as he put the sword in his belt. "Here's your wallet back, by the way."

* * * *

"Another debate between the Democrats seeking the presidential nomination is scheduled for a week from today," the anchorman said. "Pundits are expecting attacks against O'Yama, since he is now the front-runner in the polls. O'Yama is expected to respond by destroying the city with giant hailstones."

"Should be an exciting debate," said the anchorwoman. "And now we go live to Iraq to hear from Iraqis exactly how they are affected by the accusations against Kobe Bryant..."

TO BE CONCLUDED...

October 15, 2003

The Demoncrat—Volume 2

At his campaign headquarters, O'Yama, Eater of Souls and Democratic presidential candidate, sat at his throne and contemplated the destruction he would soon unleash across the world. A lone figure then entered his chambers.

"Announce yourself!" O'Yama demanded, standing to his full height of over nine feet (not counting the horns that protruded from his dark helm).

"I'm Terry McAuliffe, the DNC Chairman," McAuliffe said. "I just want to see if you're a team player unlike a certain Governor Howard Dean whom I won't mention."

"Ask your questions quickly before I become annoyed," O'Yama answered, his voice subdued but still threatening.

"So... what's your view on abortion?"

O'Yama clenched his fist and held it up in a threatening manner. "I'm for the killing of all things!"

"Supports a woman's right to choose," McAuliffe said to himself as he wrote on a notepad. He looked back at O'Yama. "What are your views on the war in Iraq?"

O'Yama chuckled, his laughter so cold as to chill one's soul. "Saddam's torture of his citizens pleased me. I would not have stopped him."

"Against Bush's unilateral action in Iraq," McAuliffe said as he continued to write in his notepad. "So what do you think of affirmative action?"

O'Yama's eyes glowed a fiery red, and then he stated in a ferocious voice, "Mend it; don't end it."

"Great, great," McAuliffe said smiling. "Now, one more question: Under that evil-looking armor you have on... you wouldn't happen to be a minority, would you?"

"I have grown weary of you," O'Yama announced. He then shot a fireball from his hands which knocked McAuliffe backward, sending the man crashing through a window. McAuliffe fell three stories to the pavement below.

Helping McAuliffe to his feet were Bill and Hillary Clinton. "So how'd it go?" Bill Clinton asked.

McAuliffe brushed off his suit. "I think we can work with him."

* * * *

Bush raised his sword into the air. "By the power of Grayskull... I... have... the... POWER!!"

"I don't think it works that way," Scott McClellan commented.

"Maybe it works this way," Bush said and then smacked Scott in the face with the flat of the sword.

"Ow!" Scott yelled. "Why do you keep doing that?"

Bush rolled his eyes. "Because you yelping in pain is funny; do I need to write you a thesis or something?" Bush looked at his enchanted sword, the Crat-Cutter. "Maybe I can unlock its secrets if I hold it higher." He prepared to power up. "Thundercats... HO!!!" he yelled as he plunged the sword skyward, accidentally stabbing the ceiling.

"George!" Laura Bush yelled. "What did I say about using swords in the house?"

Bush quickly concealed the sword behind him. "Uh... be really careful when I do it."

"No, I said never in the house, and you know that," Laura said sternly. "If you're going to play samurai, you do it in the backyard under the supervision of that nice Asian man."

"But Kôtôichi's blind."

"And yet he doesn't cut up the house with his sword."

"Alright," Bush answered and then looked at Scott. "You better go take over your press duties from Rumsfeld."

"Okay, but I'd just like you to know, Bush," Scott said sincerely, "that I have faith in you and that you can save the world from the wrath of O'Yama."

"Thanks, that means a lot," Bush answered. "And I have something to tell you, too." He then whacked Scott in the face again with the flat of his sword.

"Ow!" Scott yelled and then ran off.

"I think I'm taking that sword away from you," Laura said, approaching Bush.

"Stop, foolish woman," Karl Rove uttered as he emerged from the shadows. "Bush must train to use that sword to slay the evil demon O'Yama, or the world will be destroyed, thus causing the Republicans to lose Congress and the White House."

"Fine," Laura grumbled as she walked away. "I'll get some ice ready to put his finger in when we rush George to the hospital to have it reattached."

"Your training begins now," Kôtôichi announced, standing by the door to the backyard.

"Talk to you later, Rover," Bush said. "I'm going to be a samurai."

"May the ancients of the Republican party guide you to victory," Karl Rove said before disappearing back into the shadows.

Bush went out into the yard with Ichi. He swung the sword around. "How are you going to tell if I'm doing it right if you can't see?" Bush asked.

"From the sound of your sword swing, Bush-san, I can tell you are holding it backwards," Ichi said. "Remember: blade faces the enemy."

Bush rotated the sword in his hands. "This katana is complicated," Bush complained. "So how do I use its magical powers?"

"The magic comes from your heart," Ichi answered. "The sword will strike true if you wield it with honor, truth, and justice."

"Can I wear a cowboy hat when I do it?" Bush asked excitedly.

Ichi sighed. "Yes, you can wear a cowboy hat."

"Yee-haw!" Bush exclaimed. "I'm gonna give that O'Yama a samurai-sword slaying... Texas style!"

* * * *

"No more breathing for you!" Rumsfeld yelled as he squeezed the neck of a reporter.

"You can stop strangling people," Scott told Rumsfeld. "I'm taking back the press conferences."

"Fine," Rumsfeld said, releasing the reporter. "My arthritis is starting to act up."

"Any questions from anyone not strangled?" Scott asked as he took the podium.

"How do you respond to reports that Bush went on some mystic quest to Japan?"

Scott gave a forced chuckled. "Why is it every time Bush disappears without notice for a few days it's assumed he's on some 'mystic quest'?"

"People are saying he's gained a legendary sword in Japan that will help him slay the Democratic presidential hopeful O'Yama, Eater of Souls," said another reporter.

"How can you jump to conclusions like that?" Scott responded. "How do you know he didn't go to India to get a magic spear to slay John Edwards?"

"Well, O'Yama is the frontrunner, and thus Bush would have more motivation to slay him."

Scott shook his head. "You people always assume the most partisan reasons for everything."

"So why has Bush been seen practicing with a katana on the White House lawn?" asked one reporter.

Scott shrugged his shoulders. "He always practices with various Asian weapons; that doesn't mean anything."

"So in the upcoming debate, can you guarantee that Bush will not slay any of the ten presidential hopefuls?"

"I think I've made things clear on that issue," Scott answered, visibly sweating. "Doesn't anyone want to talk about the 'quagmire' in Iraq?"

* * * *

"There are some new rules for this debate," the moderator said. "We're going to be stricter about opening and closing remarks lengths, please no applause or other interruptions from the audience during the debate, and no eating the soul of the moderator." The moderator took a careful glance at O'Yama. "I'm not trying to single anyone out, but those are the rules. We'll now start with the opening remarks, and by random draw, the first one will be from Representative Dennis Kucinich."

"Thank you," Kucinich said. "I'd just like to say that I will be the candidate of peace. One of my first acts will be to make a Department of Peace that will stop wars and continue the fight against mind-controlling space lasers. In fact—"

"Quiet, impotent fool!" O'Yama screamed as he aimed his hand at Kucinich. Lightning then shot from O'Yama's fingertips, electrocuting Kucinich and dropping him to the ground.

"It's not your turn to speak, O'Yama," the moderator said gently. "We need to respect each other's time and not zap each other."

"You will not tell me what to do, insignificant bug!" O'Yama yelled, his eyes glowing with an even brighter fire as he once again aimed his hand and shot lightning from his fingertips, electrocuting Kucinich and dropping him to the ground.

"I'm sorry to say, but I guess this is what we can expect from O'Yama," John Kerry said. "I guess he's too afraid to let others speak."

"How dare you say that to me, you haughty, French-looking Senator from Massachusetts who by the way served in Vietnam?!" O'Yama shouted, his anger shaking the auditorium. "You will pay for your impudence!" He aimed his hand and shot lightning from his fingertips, electrocuting Kucinich and dropping him to the ground.

"I... cede... the rest... of my... time..." Kucinich uttered as he lay on the ground.

"O'Yama, you are next," the moderator said.

"Long I have waited in the void, dreaming up the destruction of the world and progressive policies that will curb the might of corporations. When elected, I will bring death, misery, and increased pay for teachers. Finally, the streets will run red with blood, evil will rule the day, and there will be an affordable prescription drug plan for the masses. Fire and lava will consume the land, all with the multilateral support of the UN. And not only will I undo the ruinous policies of George W. Bush, I WILL EAT HIS SOUL!"

The entire audience erupted into applause.

"Please, quiet," the moderator warned. "No applauding during the debate."

The applause stopped except for one person clapping slowly at the back of the room. Everyone turned to see a man in a cowboy hat.

"Nice speech, O'Yama," President Bush said. He then drew the Crat-Cutter. "Now I'm gonna cut you good!"

"Boo!" the Democratic audience yelled.

"You're worse than Hitler!" screeched one next to Bush.

"Would Hitler be nice enough to teach you some Japanese?" Bush asked the man. "This is called the 'kashira.'" He then struck the man in the head with the hilt of his sword.

"Foolish mortal!" O'Yama yelled. "How dare you try and stand up to my might. Witness my power." O'Yama now held out both hands, lightning shooting from all his fingertips, electrocuting Kucinich and dropping him to the ground.

"You can zap Dennis all you want," Bush responded, "but you won't intimidate me!"

"Then try handling this!" O'Yama said as he threw a fireball at Bush. With a swift swipe of his sword, Bush cut the fireball in two, setting people in the audience on fire on either side of the aisle.

"Ha ha! You set your own supporters on fire!" Bush mocked.

"We will settle this one on one!" O'Yama shouted, drawing a giant katana that glowed red.

Bush charged the stage and clashed with O'Yama, the other Democratic presidential candidates fleeing for cover. Bush was quick, but O'Yama was powerful. Bush blocked one of O'Yama's swings only to be knocked backward. Bush rolled back to his feet and persisted, coming at O'Yama with a quick series of swings. O'Yama easily deflected them and then attacked. Bush was too slow and took a cut to his side.

"Ow!" Bush yelled as he stumbled backward and fell onto his back. "Kôtôichi never told me swords hurt so much!"

O'Yama laughed evilly as he slowly approached the vulnerable Bush. "Now your soul will be mine!"

Bush began to panic, and he tried to remember what Kôtôichi had told him at the end of his training. *You are an idiot. You will probably lose. I am going to find a bomb shelter to hide in,* echoed in Bush's head. "Guess it's up to my Texas know-how," Bush said to himself.

O'Yama poised over Bush, holding his sword over his head to deliver the final blow. Before O'Yama could, though, Bush sent a quick kick to his groin.

"Arggh!" O'Yama yelled as he crumpled over in pain. "Why did I listen to my political advisor and not wear the codpiece to the debate?"

Bush sprung back to his feet and, with a quick swing, severed O'Yama's lowered head. Instantly O'Yama's body was consumed in a black flame as he disappeared back into the void.

"I saved the world!" Bush exclaimed as he waved his sword around and danced a jig.

The Democrats in the audience all booed.

"I'd like to be the first to condemn this blatantly partisan attack," Representative Richard Gephardt said.

"It was racist, too," declared Al Sharpton, "though I haven't figured out exactly why yet... but I will!"

"Warmonger!" yelled an audience member as the rest continued to boo.

Bush ceremoniously sheathed his sword. "Ah, shut up, you whiny little bitches."

October 20, 2003

Bush Haters of the World Unite!

"The meeting of Bush Haters is called to order," Michael Moore announced. "Jonathan Chait, please read the minutes from the last meeting."

"By unanimous vote, we declared that we hate Bush," Chait said as he read from the minutes that were made in hasty writing with a crayon. "Also, by unanimous vote, we declared that we are much smarter than the general populace. By majority vote, it was decided that people were much happier under Saddam than the occupying force led by Bush. We also determined that we will spend more time trying to resolve how Bush can be both extremely dumb, and evil and scheming and constantly outsmarting us at the same time. Still open to debate is whether Bush is worse than Hitler."

"I like Hitler! He kill Jooos!"

"Oh, I would like to welcome some new members to the Bush Haters club," Moore said. "But I need to remind our Islamic extremist friends that we refer to Jews here as 'neo-conservatives.' I think it's time to open the floor to general ranting. I'll start." Moore took a deep breath and fixed his hat. "I hate Bush!" he screamed, shaking the floor as he jumped up and down. "I'm too busy hating Bush to shave or bathe. And he drives me to eat excessively!"

"You could use some of your eating time to instead bathe," suggested someone in the audience.

"You shut up!" Moore responded.

"Bathing is overrated," Jacques Chirac said. "Anyway, I hate Bush, because he won't recognize the moral superiority of the French. He's always warring and liberating when the proper way to deal with foreign affairs is to be impotent and gripe about others."

Al Franken now stood up, his hair uncombed and his clothes disheveled. "Bush drove me to drink! I don't just hate him, but I hate the right-wing media, too, that keeps labeling me as 'deranged'! And I think the restraining order Alan Colmes put on me is overly harsh."

"Gerrwargh lies erghwaggy!" Senator Ted Kennedy stated, flailing his arms wildly. Everyone nodded in agreement with his wisdom.

"I think we need to raise the level of discourse," Chait stated. "There are a lot of perfectly rational reasons to dislike Bush, and..." Chait started getting tremors. "Who am I kidding?! I just hate Bush because of how he walks and... uh... stuff." Chait started punching a wall.

"We hate Bush because he has too many Secret Service agents guarding him!" shouted one of the Islamic extremists in the back.

"I hate Bush because he stole my pills!" yelled Helen Thomas.

A man with a bushy mustache stood up. "No one hates Bush more than me! I lost my job because of him."

"He only cares about the rich like me," Moore said firmly.

"And I lost two sons because of him," the man continued.

"If only Bush would help the poor get healthcare," Chait said.

"Yeah... it was a healthcare issue," the man said uneasily. "By the way, I need a place to crash since... uh... Ashcroft is after me with the Patriot Act since... uh... I said things about Bush... Yeah, that's the ticket!"

"What's your name?" Moore asked.

"Saddam Hu... I mean Ed."

Chait answered his cell phone. "What? There is an infiltrator in our group?!"

"Probably a Joooo!" yelled one of the Islamic extremists. "I mean neo-conservative!"

Moore looked to one of the most trusted members of the Bush Haters club. "Chomps, the world's angriest Bush hater, do you have any suspects?"

"Gerrrarh," Chomps answered.

"Maybe it's just the unidentified pills I took," Al Franken said, "but doesn't Chomps kinda look like a Rottweiler with a mustache glued on and wearing a Rastafarian hat?"

"And he's barely more coherent than Ted," Chait added.

"We can't just turn on each other for our odd appearances," Moore said. "Then again, those are kinda sharp, jagged-looking teeth he has, now that I can see them since he's curled his lips up. And the way he's staring at each of us with a thirst for blood is a bit unsettling."

"All this questioning of him seems to have made him angry," Chait said, "very angry."

"Uh-oh."

* * * *

Donald Rumsfeld sat on his back porch drinking whiskey. Suddenly Chomps ran up.

"There you are," Rumsfeld exclaimed. "I always wonder where you go running off to during the day; guess you have business of your own to handle. Now what's that in your mouth?"

Chomps dropped the item and panted happily.

"Looks like someone is missing an arm," Rumsfeld chuckled. "I guess that's why God gave us two."

October 22, 2003

When God Attacks

"General William Boykin, do you take back your statements about God and the current fight with terrorists?" asked a reporter.

"No. America is a Christian nation, and God has helped us all the way by putting Bush in office and giving us victory against the terrorists who worship a false god," General Boykin answered.

"And how can you be sure of that?"

"Because I say so!" answered a booming voice.

Everyone turned to see the giant figure of God, wearing a duster and the coolest cowboy hat ever. "America is truly a nation under Me," the Lord continued, "and I'm tired of dealing with all the others."

"Can You prove You're really God?" asked a skeptical reporter.

"Sure I can... SMITE! SMITE! SMITE!"

Reporters started dropping dead.

"I thought You were supposed to be benevolent!" exclaimed a panicked reporter.

"You're thinking of Jesus," God chuckled. "Now I'm going to get Old Testament on all the enemies of America!"

* * * *

"God has gone on a total rampage against terrorists," the anchorwoman reported. "His first action was to lift up the entire nation of Syria and then beat Saudi Arabia with it. We go now to a videotaped statement from Osama bin Laden."

"I thought Allah was on our side," said a frightened Osama, "but He's totally killing us all! He's even worse than America and the Jooooos!" Osama looked behind him. "Oh [bleep]! Here He comes!"

The videotape ended, and the anchorwoman came back on screen. "France has come out to condemn the unilateral action of the US, Britain, and the Lord Almighty. France was subsequently swallowed by the earth. The earth soon got very sick and spit France back out."

* * * *

"Oh no," Buck the Marine exclaimed. "I'm outta bullets, and there are still more terrorists to kill!"

"Hey, what's that falling from the sky?" asked another Marine. "Is it manna from heaven?"

"Better," Buck answered. "It's ammo! And hollow points, too! I guess God doesn't follow the Geneva Conventions. Ooh-rah!"

* * * *

"I think at this debate today, we Democrats should focus on policy issues instead of Bush hatred," Senator Lieberman said very slowly and boringly.

The crowd started booing and throwing things at Lieberman. "We want mindless Bush hatred!" shouted one of the people in the crowd.

Suddenly a giant figure crashed through the roof. "Oh no!" Gephardt squealed. "It's God, and He looks wrathful!"

"Bush will be president, for I have said so!" God announced. "And thus Democrats must be smoten!" Lightning and fireballs flew at all the Democrats. "Kill! Maim! Destroy! Make alive no longer!" God shouted while laughing maniacally.

"Religious extremist!" shouted a Democrat just before exploding into flames.

* * * *

"Do you condone God's partisan attacks?" a reporter asked.

"Well, I never planned to slaughter all the Democratic candidates," Bush answered, chuckling a bit, "but you're not going to get me to publicly disagree with God."

"Don't you think God is being a little harsh?" asked another reporter. "When terrorists pleaded to Him for mercy, He said He didn't understand their language and then crushed them under His foot."

"The glory of God is a mystery to all," Bush explained. "And thus He can both be omniscient and only speak and understand English." Bush thought for a moment. "Wow! I pronounced 'omniscient' correctly. That must mean..."

* * * *

"Wake up!" Condi commanded harshly.

"What?" Bush asked groggily.

"At important meetings about national security," Condi said angrily, "it's traditional to STAY AWAKE!"

Bush laid his head back down. "I'm following the Reagan tradition."

October 27, 2003

Mad... With Power!

"You are about to speak with North Korean dictator Kim Jong-Il," Karl Rove told President Bush, "and you need to take a hard stance with him."

"Hey, I know how to do deeplomosee, Rover," Bush answered. "I will be resolved in these talks."

Via a satellite connection, Kim Jong-Il appeared on screen.

"Ha ha! He's got poofy hair!" Bush exclaimed.

"You will not laugh at my poofy hair!" Kim yelled angrily. "You will fear me, for I am very intimidating! I have nukey boom-booms!"

"I'm supposed to believe you have the technology to make nucular weapons but not a comb?" Bush scoffed.

"You will treat me with respect! I very scary!"

"The only thing that makes me a little worried is your ability to control hoofed mammals I keep hearing about," Bush answered.

"The term 'Dear Leader' is meant to be affectionate," Rove whispered in Bush's ear. "It's not meant to imply that he can command deer."

"You will negotiate with me!" Kim demanded. "You will sign a non-aggression treaty!"

"But I like aggression!" Bush responded. "You're an evil, murderous dictator, and you better watch it or you're going to end up like Saddam and Osama—successfully hiding from us while occasionally sending out videotapes."

Kim smiled. "I like to be on TV!"

"You better like it!" Bush answered threateningly and then cut the communications. He turned to Rove. "I think I told him."

Rove sighed and faded into the shadows.

White House Press Secretary Scott McClellan came walking by. "What makes someone a crazy loon like Kim Jong-Il?" Bush asked him.

"Well, when someone is a dictator, they often become mad with power."

"That's a great idea!" Bush exclaimed. "I should become mad with power!"

"That wasn't what I—"

"With all this presidential power, think of the havoc I can cause," Bush said, reveling in the thought. "Quick, Scott, what's something you've always wanted?"

Scott thought for a moment. “A job where I’m respected by my boss.”

“That’s the gayest thing I ever heard, Tubby,” Bush laughed. “I guess I’ll have to think of my own thing to do with my unlimited power!”

Bush looked out the window. “Have those protestors outside the front gates killed!”

“Those are well-wishers,” Scott answered.

“Then have them thanked,” Bush said as he stared at them evilly. “Muh ha ha ha!”

“Uh... that’s not really evil laugh-worthy,” Scott told him.

“I know,” Bush responded, a bit disappointed. He then noticed something on his desk. “The red button!” He ran over and pushed it repeatedly. Then he noticed a little “Out of Order” sign on the side. “Dangit!”

“You alright?” Scott asked.

“I’m mad I can’t use my power,” Bush answered. “I know!” He walked out of his office while Scott followed. Bush then spotted someone. “You! You’re fired!”

“I’m just a tourist,” the man answered.

“What’s your name, and where do you work?” Bush demanded.

“Uh, Carl Johnson, and I work at a Wal-Mart in Memphis.”

Bush picked up a phone and quickly dialed a number. “I am the President of the United States, and I demand that Carl Johnson be fired... I don’t care if the number I dialed is invalid! I’m the president, and I’m mad... mad with power!”

Laura Bush came walking by. “What are you doing?” she asked.

Bush quickly hung up the phone. “Nothing, dear.”

“You’re not going mad with power, are you?” Laura asked suspiciously.

“No! Not at all!”

Laura stared at Bush sternly.

“Maybe a little.”

She continued to stare at him.

“It was all Scott’s idea!” Bush exclaimed, breaking down. “He’s a bad influence on me!”

“I wasn’t for any madness at all!” Scott responded.

“You two had better use your power sanely, or I’ll give you both a talking to you won’t forget,” Laura told them. “Now, there is a cabinet in the kitchen that needs fixing, so why don’t you two get ‘mad with power tools’ and take care of it.”

"Yes, dear."

"Yes, Mrs. Bush."

Laura walked off.

"Wait a second," Scott said to Bush. "Shouldn't you be handling important things like the economy and Iraq?"

"You're right, Scott," Bush answered. "You fix the cabinet while I handle all our problems, foreign and domestic."

"Okay, Mr. President," Scott said, running off to the kitchen.

"Moron," Bush chuckled to himself. "Time to watch *The Matrix Reloaded* on DVD again."

October 29, 2003

Die, Leakers, Die

"According to this leaked memo," the anchorwoman announced, "Rumsfeld is about to purchase a quart of milk, bananas, and a gallon of whiskey."

"That's my shopping list!" Rumsfeld screamed as he picked up the TV and smashed it on the ground. Chomps, the world's angriest dog, eagerly attacked the broken pieces. "Who is leaking my memos?"

Rumsfeld thought for a moment. "I have two options to end the leaks: find the leaker, or murder all reporters."

"Grrrrah!" Chomps growled, snapping at the air angrily.

"No," Rumsfeld answered. "Killing all reporters will take too long. We'll need to find that leaker and kill anyone who stands in our way. To the Buick!"

* * * *

Senator Daschle went flying out the front door of the Capitol building with Chomps running to fetch him. Rumsfeld then emerged, holding up Senator Leahy by the neck.

"I don't know anything! I swear!" Leahy cried. "I'm a member of Congress, for pete's sake; I couldn't find my butt with two hands and a flashlight!"

"Who is the leaker?" Rumsfeld demanded.

"I don't know! All I know is that I'm supposed to keep minorities from becoming judges! That's it!"

Rumsfeld dropped Leahy to the ground. "If I ever find out any different, I'll be back... and I'll kill you and all your constituency!"

The press then swarmed around Rumsfeld. "According to a recent leaked memo," said one reporter, "are you now admitting the war on terror is a failure?"

"I will answer that by strangling you to death," Rumsfeld responded. "Rarr!" He then grabbed the reporter by the neck. After a while, he dropped the reporter. "Any follow-up questions?"

The reporter didn't move.

Rumsfeld smiled smugly. "That's what I thought."

"Melinda Hawkish, FOX News," Melinda announced herself. "People are now concerned that we won't be waging the war on terror with the violence it deserves. Can you assuage their fears?"

Rumsfeld stared into the camera. "The terrorists will die! And whoever is leaking the memos will die! And whoever stands in my way will die! Murder, death, kill... remember those words!"

Rumsfeld then noticed a reporter holding a piece of paper and quickly snatched it. "That's the short story I wrote about a girl coming of age!" he exclaimed. "That was personal!" He gave it to Chomps to smell. "Find and kill whoever's touched it!"

Chomps immediately started savagely attacking the reporter. "I already know he handled it," Rumsfeld said, rolling his eyes.

* * * *

Bush watched as his office door was ripped off and then chewed to pieces.

"Hey!" Bush complained. "Your dog done ate my door!"

"We traced the leaks of my memos back to the White House," Rumsfeld responded as Chomps finished consuming the door.

"Well, I didn't have anything to do with it," Bush said. "I never even see your memos. I have some aides summarize all memos sent to me. Then I have another aide summarize all those summaries together. And then I don't read that."

"So where do my memos go?"

"Over there." Bush pointed to a wastebasket. It was clearly labeled, "Dispose of internal Rumsfeld memos here. DO NOT RAID."

Rumsfeld checked inside to find it empty. "Looks like it's been raided."

"Maybe we need to make the sign bigger," Bush suggested.

"Rarr!" Rumsfeld yelled as he kicked the wastebasket. Chomps then tore it apart.

"You need to learn to chill like me, Rummy," Bush said.

A voice came over his speakerphone. "We have a situation that could lead to nuclear war! Mr. President, you need to—"

"I'll get to it later," Bush answered. "I'm busy now." He went back to playing his Game Boy.

"The leaker is near," Rumsfeld told Chomps, his hands tensing in preparation for a strangling. "I can feel it."

As they left the office, Chomps's ears perked up. "You hear something, boy?" Rumsfeld followed Chomps until he could hear it too.

"Rumsfeld memos! Get your internal Rumsfeld memos!"

Rumsfeld and Chomps made their way outside and spotted a booth labeled "Rumsfeld Memos" manned by Bush's two daughters, Barbara and Jenna.

"I'll take a memo," said a reporter, walking up to the booth.

"It now comes with a free bullet," Rumsfeld said, pulling out his Luger and shooting the reporter.

"Uh-oh!" Barbara and Jenna exclaimed upon seeing Rumsfeld and his dog.

"You two have some 'splainin' to do," Rumsfeld said menacingly.

"Uh, we just felt like sitting down and thus sat at this booth," Jenna stated innocently. "Why? What does it say?"

"It says, 'Rumsfeld's internal memos—five for a dollar,'" Rumsfeld answered, seething with anger.

"It was all Jenna's idea!" Barbara exclaimed.

"Hey!"

Laura Bush then came walking by. "What's happening here?"

"Your two villainous daughters are selling my memos to the press," Rumsfeld told her, "and I'm going to strangle them."

"We're just trying to raise beer money... I mean money for school supplies," Jenna said.

"Well, you'd better give those memos back to Donald and apologize," Laura declared sternly.

They handed the box of memos to Rumsfeld. "Sorry, Mr. Rumsfeld."

Laura then led the two of them away. "Now you're going to get such a talking to that you'll wish you were strangled, by golly!"

Rumsfeld stood there holding his memos as Chomps tore apart the booth. "Aw, shucks; I wanted to murder someone. I know! Let's go to a local university and strangle some liberation protestors!"

"Grrrawerg!" Chomps growled in approval and anger.

* * * *

"The Rumsfeld Strangler has struck universities in the DC area," the anchorman announced, "leaving numerous hippies dead. Police do not plan to investigate too much, because we all hate stupid, smelly hippies. Now stay tuned to FOX News for more fair and balanced coverage."

November 03, 2003

George W. Bush in "Marked for Death"

"Honey, you need to take out the trash," Laura Bush told her husband, a bit irately.

"But I'm busy planning this country's economic future and fighting the war on terror."

"No you're not," Laura answered. "You're watching an *A-Team* marathon. Now take out the trash. Oh... and someone left a message for you on the front door."

"Fine," Bush said, getting off the couch and turning off the TV. He got the trash and took it outside and then found a message stuck to the front door by a dagger.

"Ooh! A message with a free dagger!" Bush exclaimed excitedly as he took the letter. "The best kind." The message was some weird symbol written in blood. "I wonder if this is a reminder from the blood bank," Bush mused aloud as he walked inside.

"Does this mean anything to you, Kôtôichi?" Bush asked as he handed the message to the blind samurai.

Ichi felt the writing. "This says you are marked for death by a deadly ninja assassin."

"*Deadly* ninja assassin?!" Bush exclaimed. "That's the worst kind of ninja assassin!"

"You are informed so that you may live the last hours of your life in constant fear," Kôtôichi added.

"It's working!" Bush shouted in a panic. "I *am* in fear! Oh man, I bet I know why this is happening, too. I should have listened to Karl Rove in Japan when he told me not give a wedgie to the leader of the Yakuza!" Bush grabbed Ichi by the collar. "You gotta tell me what to do, Ichi-san!"

"Three ryo, and I give you advice."

Bush searched his pocket for gold coins. "Here you go."

"My advice to you: make sure your will is up to date. Heh heh heh."

"That's not good advice!" Bush yelled angrily. "I want my ryo back!"

"No refunds!" Ichi said as he held his cane sword in a threatening manner.

"I really need to have less blind samurai in my administration," Bush grumbled to himself as he walked off. "You just can't trust them. Man, and I have this big speech about terrorism to give today, too. I can't back off from that, or it will embolden the terrorists... and the last thing the terrorists need is emboldening. This ninja assassin has to be the worst thing that's happened to me during this administration since the fourth time I got my tie stuck in the shredder."

Bush spotted one of his Secret Service agents. "Agent Smith, I need your help," Bush pleaded. "I'm targeted by a ninja for assassination, so I need extra protection."

"Sorry; can't help," Agent Smith answered. "It's a holiday today."

"What holiday?"

"Uh... the 'Don't Get Killed by a Ninja While Trying to Protect Bush' holiday."

"You made that up!"

"Union rules say I can make up holidays," Agent Smith answered as he went back to reading his paper.

"Stupid unionized Secret Service," Bush muttered and then spotted White House Press Secretary Scott McClellan. "Hey Scott, I need you to do something today."

"What?"

"I want you to give the speech on terrorism while wearing a cowboy hat just like I would, and this sign."

Scott looked at the sign. It read, "I am President Bush. If you want to assassinate the president, then kill me."

"Hey!" Scott exclaimed. "Have you been targeted by a deadly ninja assassin and are trying to set me up as a decoy?"

"No!" Bush said innocently. "Why? Would you have a problem with that?"

"I've already been shot far too many times on your behalf for just being a press secretary," Scott answered. "I'm not going to take a poison ninja throwing star for you."

"You don't know for certain they'll be poisoned!" Bush called to Scott as he walked off. "Guess I have to face this one alone," Bush said to himself. He approached Laura. "This may be the last time I see you, my dear wife. I have to go give a speech now, and I may not come back alive."

"Well, if you do come back alive," Laura answered, "make sure to pick up some milk along the way."

* * * *

"I have to give a speech about terrorism while a ninja is out for my head," Bush said to himself as he stood near the podium. "Things couldn't get any worse."

"I need to talk to you."

"Crap!" Bush yelled. "It's Senator Daschle. I don't have time to listen to your whines, Daschle; I'm trying not to get killed by a ninja."

"But it's important that I talk about how saddened I am by... ack... erk..."

Daschle fell to the ground twitching, and Bush noticed a poison dart in his neck. "Oh no!" Bush exclaimed. "President Bush has been assassinated by a ninja! So says I, weasely Democratic Senator Daschle. I guess that ninja can now go back to Japan while I go off to raise taxes and surrender in the war on terror."

The ninja hopped down from a tree. "You do not fool me, President Bush," the ninja said. "Now you die!" He drew his sword.

"A ninja sword!" Bush yelled. "Nothing can stop that!" Bush then ran off while the ninja pursued.

Bush was soon stopped by a reporter. "Hi. I'm from the *New York Times*. I was wondering what you have to say about your colossal failure in Iraq due to your poor planning."

"I don't have time to talk about that! A ninja is chasing me!" Bush said and then continued running.

"Ooh, I already have the headline," the reporter said, scribbling in his notepad. "'Bush Runs from War Record, Ninja.'"

"Think think think," Bush said to himself as he continued to flee. "Man, I have a hard enough time coming up with plans when a ninja isn't chasing me." He then spotted the ACLU headquarters ahead of him. "Aha!" He ran inside, and the ninja quickly came in after him, sword held above his head, ready to strike. Bush was hiding behind the door, though, and sneaked back out. He then whipped out his cell phone.

"Condi, do you have the coordinates of the ACLU headquarters ready for a missile strike?"

"I have it on the cruise missile version of speed dial," Condoleezza Rice answered.

"Hit it!"

Soon missiles came out of the sky and blew up the building, leaving nothing but rubble. "Ha!" Bush laughed. "Ain't nothing cruise missiles can't solve!"

"Aren't you concerned about collateral damage?" asked a nearby reporter.

"It's the weekend," Bush answered. "No one was in there."

"It's Tuesday morning," the reporter corrected him.

"Whatever," Bush said. "If the ACLU didn't want to get all blowed up, then... uh... they shouldn't have been harboring ninjas."

November 05, 2003

FOX & Friends Transcript—Interview with Donald Rumsfeld

...

E.D. Hill: I don't get it. Why doesn't Israel just kill all the Palestinians?

Brian Kilmeade: Well, apparently the UN is against that.

Steve Doocy: If you had to decide between being blown up by a suicide bomber and being whined to death by a representative from the UN, which would you choose?

Brian: Well, our next guest knows a lot about killing terrorists. Here is Secretary of Defense Donald Rumsfeld.

Donald Rumsfeld: To start off, I just want to say I'm here by the president's orders. I never wanted to be on some vacuous morning show.

E.D.: But we ask deep questions!

Rumsfeld: Whatever, blondie. Let's just get this show on the road.

Steve: As we all know, you're very busy with the War on Terror...

Rumsfeld: There are a lot of people alive who shouldn't be, and I'm trying to motivate this administration to do something about them despite the wishes of weaker, whiny countries.

Brian: We were just talking about the UN...

Rumsfeld: Don't even mention them to me!

Steve: Actually, since you've arrived in New York, a lot of the UN members have been found strangled to death. Would you know anything about that?

Rumsfeld: I know it's a good thing.

E.D.: Anyway, the reason you're here today is to talk about your work with kids.

Rumsfeld: Yes, the First Lady keeps nagging me to help kids. I say kids these days are a hopeless cause, but I'll see if I can improve them.

Brian: And you're trying to make them better prepared for the threats we face today.

Rumsfeld: Can I explain this?

Brian: I was just trying to help you along...

Rumsfeld: Shut up! As I was saying, kids these days are weak, and our enemies prey upon weakness. These days if a child falls down and scrapes his knee, he starts crying like some fruit, and that emboldens terrorists.

Brian: But kids were tougher back when you were young.

Rumsfeld: I'm sorry, Mr. Kilmeade, do I get to explain this, or do you?

Brian: Well... uh... I'm just following the teleprompter...

(gunshot)

Rumsfeld: There; no more distractions.

E.D.: But the teleprompter is where all my intelligent questions come from!

Rumsfeld: Zip it, blondie! Back to the topic, when I was a kid, we didn't whine and cry like common Democrats. Why, one day when I was six, I took an arrow to the shoulder, killed the Hun who shot it with a wood ax, and then went back to playing hopscotch—all without shedding one tear.

Brian: What happened to the Huns?

Rumsfeld: We killed them all. They interrupted one of my little league games, and we were fed up. I still have the blood-stained bat.

Steve: So what's your batting average with regard to Hun heads? (laughs)

Rumsfeld: You find this funny?

Steve: Well, I—

Rumsfeld: You make another idiotic joke in my presence, and I will kill you. Do you understand?

Steve: Yes, sir.

Rumsfeld: Continuing, the point is that kids were tough in my days but are weak today and are in danger of becoming another generation of hippies... just like the terrorists want. And since you can't strangle to death a whole generation—or so I'm told—I'm trying to steer young kids toward becoming rugged individualists with my school program called "Stop Crying or I'll Beat You."

E.D.: Now, some teachers have complained about your program, describing it as nothing but a bunch of yelling and hitting.

Rumsfeld: The teachers are fools! They coddle children and make them weak!

Brian: One child says you almost strangled her to death.

Rumsfeld: And I'll bet she's smarter for it! Kids need to learn to have a strong backbone and be self-reliant.

E.D.: Now, with my children—

Rumsfeld: I don't care about your stupid children.

E.D.: This is a good story...

Rumsfeld: You may think I'm too old-fashioned to hit a woman, but you can find out for sure by continuing to talk.

Steve: I think it's time to take some phone calls.

Rumsfeld: Oh, yay! Let's hear the opinions of people with nothing better to do during the day than call in to a TV show.

Steve: All the way from Baghdad, Iraq, we have Buck on the line.

Buck: I would just like to ask Mr. Secretary when we in the military can expect to go where there are more for'ners to kill who ain't hiding. Uh... ya know... a more target-rich environment?

Rumsfeld: It is my plan to soon have the US military roaming the entire Middle East, killing everyone who looks like they are in need of it.

Buck: Ooh-rah!

Rumsfeld: Don't "ooh-rah" too soon. That's not going to happen while Bush is still listening to that fruit we have for a Secretary of State.

Brian: You're talking about Colin Powell?

Rumsfeld: That's the fruit.

Steve: Next on the line we have Susan from Chicago, Illinois. What's your question for Secretary Rumsfeld?

Susan: I was just wondering if he thinks he's made a mistake in not having enough troops in Iraq?

Rumsfeld: And why in the world would I think I've made a mistake?

Susan: Well... uh... it just seems that—

Rumsfeld: I'm sorry; what's your occupation, Susan?

Susan: I... uh... work in a department store—

Rumsfeld: And suddenly you know all about military strategy, then? I will kill you for your impudence! Where in Chicago does she live?

Steve: I don't know exactly...

Rumsfeld: Maybe I can go to the back room and trace the call.

Brian: And there goes Secretary Rumsfeld...

Steve: I guess the interview is over.

E.D.: You know, I agree with a lot of his policies, but I think he's a bit too gruff.

Brian: Fighting Huns when you are a kid can do that to you.

Steve: I'll bet inside him there's a cute little puppy, though... which he swallowed whole this morning. (laughs)

Rumsfeld: I WARNED YOU! RARR!

Steve: I thought he was out of the studio! Oh sh—!

November 10, 2003

Stop Those Saudis!

"Did you know I was actually behind 9/11? Fascinating. I didn't even suspect that."

"You need to stop reading these left-wing conspiracy newsletters," Karl Rove said, snatching the paper away from President Bush. "You are too easily influenced."

"So I shouldn't join that protest against our illegal occupation of Iraq?" Bush asked.

"No!" Rove shouted. "You need to focus. The economy is improving, thus we need to make sure the American public is on your side in the war on terror. If we can do this, then victory and prosperity are ours. Otherwise, a Democrat will become president, and terror will reign, as foreseen by the elders."

"Don't worry, Rover," Bush said. "I just gave this great speech on bringing democracy to the Middle East. Who could be angered by that?"

* * * *

"I am very angered by this!" shouted the evil Saudi king. "We can't have those meddling Americans bringing democracy to the Middle East. That will mean peace and prosperity for our people. That will also mean they won't be focusing anymore on blowing up Jews, Americans, and each other, and instead will realize how tyrannical our rule is. This cannot happen. How can we stop these ideas from spreading?"

"We can blame everything on the Jews," offered an aide.

"But we need *new* ideas now!"

"Uh... we can blame everything on the Episcopalians."

"Not good enough!" the evil Saudi king said. "We need to go into Iraq and make sure their democracy fails. If the Americans fail, the Iraqis will fail, and then the people of the Middle East will remain poor and ignorant while we continue to prosper. Muh ha ha ha!"

* * * *

"Yes, it was an odd set of circumstances," Condoleezza Rice said. "First Dick Cheney died of a heart attack—no one saw that coming—and then, soon after I was elected vice president in 2004, Bush died by sticking a fork into an electric socket. People became so enamored by my rule that they declared me empress, and of course I had to accept. Now, everyone, let's pause for a moment to worship me and behold my beauty."

"Uh... am I interrupting something?" Buck the Marine asked, looking a bit confused.

Condi quickly sat down behind her desk. "No, I was just... uh... planning the future of Iraq. You're Buck, right? Buck the Marine?"

"Yes, ma'am." Buck looked around Condi's office and noticed all the marble statues and gold artifacts. "You sure have a nice office here in Iraq."

"Riches help me think," Condi answered curtly. "Anyway, tomorrow is an important day for Iraq. A council is convening to work on the new constitution. Our intelligence suggests that people will be trying to disrupt this meeting."

"Why?" Buck asked. "Who could be wanting to harm these poor Iraqis and us Americans who are trying to help everyone?" Buck then thought for a moment. "Oh yeah, for'ners, just like I kill all the time." Buck squinted his eyes menacingly. "I done hates for'ners."

"Good, because I want you to find whoever is plotting against us and kill them," Condi said. "You will have the help of the world's angriest UN peacekeeper, Chomps." A Rottweiler wearing a blue UN helmet entered the room and immediately started attacking a marble statue. "Bad dog!"

* * * *

"Well, this is the building where the meeting will be taking place," Buck narrated. "So what's your anger sense telling you, Chomps?"

Chomps started growling and then ran off. Buck quickly followed. Behind the building they found three people standing around a cart. "What are you people doing?" Buck demanded.

"We are but street vendors," answered one, "and are not involved in any terrorist activities whatsoever."

Chomps growled and gnashed his teeth.

"Chomps seems to think you're up to something foreign," Buck accused them.

"Perhaps," answered one of the men. "So I would keep looking at us and not look behind you."

"I am going to keep my eyes on you," Buck said threateningly. "'Cause I don't trust you. In fact, I think you might be for'ners! So I'm—"

Chomps started barking wildly at something behind Buck. Buck turned around to see two terrorists sneaking up on him with AK-47s in hand. He quickly fired at them with his M-16 as they fired back. He shot one, but a bullet hit his rifle. Chomps jumped at the remaining one, mouth agape, while Buck dropped to the ground and drew his .45, shooting the three men around the cart, who had now drawn guns as well. Six more terrorists came running at Buck and Chomps, each firing an AK-47. Suddenly they all fell to the ground, revealing a woman standing behind them dressed in black, wearing sunglasses and holding a Beretta in each hand.

"Is that you, Dr. Rice?" Buck asked, standing up. Chomps coughed up a hand.

"Yes, I thought you might need some help," Condi answered. "I always wanted to shoot people with dual Berettas."

"I didn't need no woman's help," Buck said. "And why are you dressed like some S&M queen?"

"It's my Halloween costume," Condi answered. "I'm Trinity from *The Matrix*."

"I don't watch sci-fi," Buck answered. "The future is an undiscovered country... an undiscovered *foreign* country."

"Whatever," Condi answered, rolling her eyes. "The important thing is that the terrorists have been stopped. I wonder who they were."

"Well I know one type of for'ner that dies like that," Buck answered. "Saudis!"

"If there is some sort of Saudi plot, we'll have to deal with it later," Condi said. "The meeting is starting soon."

Chomps started savagely attacking one of the wheels of the cart. "Something about that cart is making Chomps angry," Buck said. He then pulled a tarp off the top of it and found a weird electronic device inside.

"It's a bomb!" Condi exclaimed.

Chomps immediately jumped up on the cart and swallowed the bomb whole.

"I don't think it's good for a dog to eat something like that," Buck remarked.

"As long as he doesn't vomit on the carpet in my office, I don't care," Condi said. "Now it's time to make a constitution."

* * * *

"You don't seem dressed for the occasion, Dr. Rice."

"I was just killing people and didn't have time to change," Condi said, taking off her sunglasses and sitting down. "So how do you like my draft of the constitution?"

"It's pretty good," one of the council said, "but I think it could do without all the swearing and the explicit sex scene."

"Fine, be a bunch of prudes," Condi sighed.

"Hey, does this say in really small writing that Condoleezza Rice will be queen?" asked one of the council who was looking at the draft constitution with a magnifying glass.

Condi smiled innocently. "That's just an ink smudge."

November 12, 2003

Strangle Rangel

"Ask your idiotic questions!" Rumsfeld yelled at the reporters impatiently.

"What do you think of General Abizaid's statement about using harsher measures in Iraq if attacks don't stop?"

"I agree with him fully. Anyone who attacks American troops must suffer and die in the worst possible way!" Rumsfeld shouted. "Baby Jesus will cry when He sees the torments we inflict upon our enemies! God will laugh, though; He's always liked vengeance. Next question."

"What do you prefer: Macs or PCs?"

Rumsfeld pulled out a .45 and unloaded it into the reporter. "You asked an inane question, and you are now dead; I hope that was a learning experience for you. Someone ask a question while I reload."

"Representative Charles Rangel has made a resolution asking for you to resign, sponsored by twenty-five other Democrats. How do you respond?"

"WHAT?!" Rumsfeld screamed in rage as he slapped a magazine into his 1911 and chambered a round. "He will soon be known as 'Charles Strangled.' They will all die! All of them! The Democrats' minority in the House is about to get much smaller!"

"How do you—"

"DEATH! No one questions me! No one!"

"In regards to—"

"MURDER!"

"What are you doing right now?"

"I'm putting on my strangling gloves," Rumsfeld answered as he put on a pair of black leather gloves.

"Is that to help you write your resignation? If it is... ack... erk..."

* * * *

"Representative Charles Rangel, you've made a resolution asking for the resignation of Secretary of Defense Donald Rumsfeld, correct?" asked a reporter.

"That is correct."

"And it was sponsored by twenty-five other Democrats?"

"True."

"All of whom were found strangled today?"

"That's what I hear."

"Now, DC police started to put some correlation between all those murders but then went on a lunch break. Do you think the murders are connected?"

"I don't know," Rangel answered. "I'm not some conspiracy theorist, but frankly I wouldn't be surprised if this was all acts of terrorism... terrorism Donald Rumsfeld failed to stop."

"It kind of sounds like you just barely survived being strangled yourself," commented another reporter.

"No, my voice has always been this annoyingly raspy," Rangel responded. "In fact, it's really helped me in the House, because people will end up agreeing with me just to get me to stop talking—my voice being quite similar to fingers being raked across a chalkboard. Even now, I can see you squirm as you listen to me."

"The bodies of the twenty-five Democrats were all found with notes saying, 'I, Donald Rumsfeld, am strangling these Democrats for their impudence in supporting that stupid resolution,'" stated a reporter.

"What's your point?" Rangel asked.

"Do you think the murders might be the work of the 'Rumsfeld Strangler' in retaliation for your resolution?"

"How would I know?" Rangel said with annoyance. "What am I? A forensic scientist? I'll let DC Homicide worry about that when they get back from their four-hour lunch. Also, I think this 'Rumsfeld Strangler' nonsense is a media invention."

"On each body was a list of the twenty-six Democrats who signed the resolution, with your name at the bottom of the list, and the ones already killed crossed off," said a reporter. "On the final body, all but your name was crossed off, and written in bold letters were the words, 'Charles Rangel is next.' Do you think you might be the next target?"

"How would I know how some deranged killer's mind works?" Rangel answered. "Shouldn't you reporters be investigating and figuring these things out?"

The reporters were all silent for a while. Finally one said, "We're actually very dumb."

"Fair enough," Rangel stated, "but I would like to stop focusing on this murder distraction and instead talk about Donald Rumsfeld's failure in Iraq to immediately convert a country that had been under a tyrannical dictatorship into a prospering democracy within a week's time."

"Melinda Hawkish from FOX News," spoke up Melinda. "I just wanted to ask, exactly how dumb are the people who keep electing you?"

"No specific studies have been done," Rangel answered, "but my constituents are, for the most part, quite moronic. I would like to remind everyone, though, that in a democracy, even the stupid deserve representation, and who better to represent the nigh-retarded than me?"

Melinda thought about that for a moment. "Well, that shut me up."

Donald Rumsfeld now slowly made his way through the crowd of reporters, his gloved hands held out in front of him, tensed for a strangling.

"Well, if it isn't the man of the hour," Rangel said. "I can tell from your homicidal expression that you're here to announce your resignation and offer an apology to the American people for your failure in Iraq. I would just like to say... ack... erk..."

November 14, 2003

FOX & Friends Transcript—Interview with Steve Irwin

...

Brian Kilmeade: We now join Melinda Hawkish straight from Baghdad. How are things going, Melinda?

Melinda Hawkish: Pretty good, Brian. The enemy is being slaughtered as we speak.

Steve Doocy: But we keep hearing how bad things are in Iraq.

Melinda: That's because most of the news reports leave out how much the scumbag terrorists are suffering. Those other channels like CNN leave out all the video we have of the enemies' brains getting blown out.

Steve: Let's see the clip.

Brian: Wow! That guy's head blew right apart.

Melinda: That's right, and that's what happens to dirty terrorists.

E.D. Hill: And you'll only see things like that right here on FOX News—Fair and Balanced.

Melinda: And the fair and balanced view is that America is kicking ass. Don't let any biased media tell you otherwise.

Brian: Thanks, Melinda.

Melinda: By the way, if you ever need someone to sit in for E.D., think of me when I'm back in the States. I promise not to get knocked up as much as her, either.

Steve: (laughs) You're quite the kidder, Melinda.

E.D.: Stay away from my job, bitch!

Brian: Anyway, our next guest has to deal with things almost as fearsome as terrorists. Let's welcome Steve Irwin, the Crocodile Hunter.

Steve Irwin: Hey, everybody, it's great to be here.

Steve: So are crocodiles as dumb as terrorists?

Irwin: No, they can be quite wily. You have to be careful when you deal with those crocs.

Brian: Now, you take quite a different approach to nature shows. Most before you only watched the animals from a distance and didn't disturb them, but you like to run up and tackle the animals and shake them around.

Irwin: You learn a lot about an animal by pissing it off.

E.D.: Do you ever get scared about being injured?

Irwin: No, because I have a special medical condition where I lack all common sense.

Steve: Sounds like you could be a liberal.

Irwin: Crikey! I hope not.

E.D.: Now, you brought some animals with you.

Irwin: That's right. In this cage my wife is bringing out is a king cobra.

Steve: Whoa! Careful where you hold that guy!

Irwin: Now this bugger is actually less venomous than a regular cobra, but he delivers more venom per bite. He could take down a—Crikey! He almost got me there.

Brian: You sure it's safe to have him out like this?

Irwin: I have him under control.

E.D.: Now there is something special about the cobra's hood, right?

Irwin: That's right. The king cobra can extend the ribs in its neck to make this hood to intimidate other animals. Also, if you grab the snake by the ends of its hood as I'm doing and shake it vigorously...

Steve: I don't think the snake likes that.

Irwin: That's right! There's nothing it hates more. Crikey! He's trying to kill me now! Isn't he beautiful?

Brian: He really wants to bite your face.

Irwin: Excellent observation. The king cobra is now trying to eat my face, not, mind you, because it's hungry, but instead because it figures that's the most painful way to kill me. That's how mad I made it! Isn't it beautiful?

E.D.: It sure is angry.

Irwin: Let's put him back in his cage.

Steve: Now this next guy looks less threatening.

Irwin: He can be a nasty little bugger, though. He's a ring-tailed lemur.

E.D.: And what's the significance of the rings on his tail?

Irwin: I don't know. But if I grab him by the tail and swing him over my head thusly...

Brian: Wow! You're really spinning that rodent around!

Irwin: Actually, it's a monkey. Now you can hear its squeal changing as it becomes angrier and angrier. Now I'll stop spinning him and set him down...

E.D.: He's just staring at you.

Irwin: That's the extremely rare lemur stare of death. Right now he's just absorbing how angry he is, but soon... Crikey! He's trying to kill me now! Isn't he beautiful?

Steve: He's really trying to claw and bite you. I've never seen a monkey that angry before.

E.D.: I have.

Irwin: He is so angry that he will not eat or sleep until I'm dead.

E.D.: Fascinating.

Irwin: Let's put him back in his cage. There you go, you angry little bugger. Now let's bring out the next animal.

Steve: Looks like you already swung this one over your head in the green room.

Irwin: No, this animal here is always angry. Actually, he was rated by the *Guinness Book of World Records* as the world's angriest dog.

Brian: That's a thick chain holding him.

Irwin: He shouldn't be able to chew through it until the segment's over.

E.D.: Wow! He's really chewing away at it. Now, my neighbor has a Rottweiler, and it's not this angry. What makes this dog so different?

Irwin: No one really knows. It might be a chemical imbalance in his brain or that he's just highly opinionated.

Steve: Whoa! Hey!

Irwin: Don't worry. He's only angry at your chair.

Brian: Look at him rip it apart.

Steve: So is he part of *Queer Eye for the Straight Guy*? (laughs) Whoa!

Irwin: Now he is angry at you. Probably didn't like that joke.

Steve: Everyone is a critic. Can you get him to... uh... stop trying to kill me?

Irwin: Hey! Chomps! What's that behind you, boy? What's that behind you?

Brian: Now, I've seen dogs chase their tails before, but it really looks like he wants to kill his.

Steve: He's stopped. Now what's he barking at?

Irwin: Looks like he doesn't like one of the stage lights.

Brian: Can we have that turned off?

E.D.: It looks like that calmed him down... or at least made him less angry. Now, you're going to host a FOX special, aren't you?

Irwin: Yes, we're going to find out what is the world's angriest animal, and Chomps here is one of the contestants. The others are Razor, the Eternally Agitated Wolverine, Squeakers, the Schizophrenic Tiger, Rumsfeld, the Enraged Secretary of Defense, and Wally, the Murderous Sloth.

Brian: Murderous Sloth?

Irwin: Very slow to move, but very quick to anger.

Steve: He's chewing through his chain again. Are we going to be alright?

Irwin: As long as you don't say the F-word.

E.D.: We're a family show, so you don't have to worry about that.

Irwin: I don't mean the four-letter one. I mean the one about cheese-eating surrender-monkeys.

Steve: You mean the French?

Irwin: Crikey! There he goes trying to kill everyone! Isn't he beautiful?

Brian: Can't you shoot him with a tranquilizer or something?

Irwin: Not at this stage of anger, I'm afraid. The only thing that will calm him down is mauling a hippy. I'll have my wife let him loose outside so he can find one and tucker himself out.

E.D.: Is that safe?

Irwin: Not for hippies.

Steve: There's one right out the window behind us.

E.D.: Look at the sign he's holding up! We're not right-wing! We're fair and balanced. I hope Chomps gets him.

Steve: Looks like he found him...

Irwin: Crikey!

Brian: I haven't seen that much blood splattered on a window in New York since Dinkins was mayor.

Steve: We'll have to get the window washer out there during the commercial break. Thanks for joining us, Steve.

Irwin: It was my pleasure.

November 17, 2003

Ah-nuld Takes Office

"Dah! I am governor now! I am Ah-nuld!"

"Yeah, congratulations on getting inaugurated and everything," President Bush said. "I was so afraid I was going to screw up my own inauguration and not get to be president."

"What are you doing here, puny president man? Don't you have work to do?"

"I'm just hangin', seein' how you're doin'," Bush answered. "I have lots of smart people back in Washington to keep things under control."

* * * *

"Now that Bush is gone," Rumsfeld said, "let's start nuking things. Let's start with Syria."

"Only if we can nuke Finland," Condi added.

"Deal. Does the UN advisor approve?"

Chomps barked in approval, causing his blue helmet to slip over his eyes, which indubitably made him angry.

"Now, I don't want to question the wisdom of the Secretary of Defense, National Security Advisor, and a psychotic Rottweiler," Colin Powell stated, "but I think going nuclear is a bit rash and should be contemplated a little longer."

Rumsfeld stared at Powell a moment. "Let's just cut to the chase: how much do you want to be bitch-slapped?"

* * * *

"I must improve the economy!" Arnold shouted. "It is too puny! And the debt is too big! I must make it puny!" Arnold then grabbed a write-up of the economy and held it vigorously. "You improve, economy, or I crush you! Dah!" Arnold then ripped the folder in two and started stabbing it with a ballpoint pen.

"Now, they don't let me in most of the meetings about the economy," Bush told him, "but I don't think that's how it works."

"How do you improve the economy, then?" Arnold asked. "Tell me, or I will crush you!"

"Well, you reduce taxes."

"And what if that doesn't work?"

Bush thought some. "Reduce taxes again."

"And if that doesn't work?"

Bush thought long and hard. "Reduce taxes again."

"But I also need money to reduce the debt! I am Ah-nuld!"

"Money, eh?" Bush mused aloud. "We could do a daring bank robbery... or, better yet, we could go to Vegas and rob a casino. We'll first need to hang out there and look inconspicuous as we case the joint."

"Your ideas are puny!" Arnold shouted. "I will crush them! Don't you have any good ideas for making money?"

"Well, you could always invade a country and steal its oil," Bush answered, "but you'll need a army for that..."

Arnold took out an M-60 from behind his desk. "I will do it myself. I am Ah-nuld!"

* * * *

"So the governor of California is invading us, eh?"

"Yeah, what's that all aboot, eh?"

"I dunno, but he just blew up the local gas station, eh."

"Maybe we should do something, eh?"

"I think we should hide... I'm so scared right now I almost forgot to say 'eh.'"

* * * *

"So is it true that Governor Schwarzenegger has gone on a violent rampage at the advice of the president?"

"It's not that uncommon for a new governor to go on a rampage of some sort," White House Press Secretary Scott McClellan answered.

"Yes it is," the reporter responded.

Scott paused for a moment. "Okay, I got nothing on this one. Anyone want to talk about Iraq?"

"Actually, my question is, why did we nuke Syria?" said another reporter.

"And you're not curious about why we nuked Finland?" Scott responded. The reporter thought about that. "No, not really."

November 19, 2003

O'Reilly Factor Transcript—Interview with Donald Rumsfeld

Bill O'Reilly: Next up on the Factor is Secretary of Defense Donald Rumsfeld.

Donald Rumsfeld: Where the hell are you? What is this?

O'Reilly: It's a satellite hook-up. Mr. Secretary—

Rumsfeld: Then how am I supposed to strangle you if you enrage me?

O'Reilly: (laughs) I guess you'll just have to come over here.

Rumsfeld: I will. Start your questions!

O'Reilly: So what is your opinion of how things are going in Iraq?

Rumsfeld: Excellent. Our enemies are being slaughtered in mass numbers.

O'Reilly: But there are many who don't like America.

Rumsfeld: And they will die! We will hunt them down and kill them like dogs. Actually, I was just on a dog hunt this morning.

O'Reilly: Fair enough. Now, some people say that you have botched the occupation, and—

Rumsfeld: They will die as well!

O'Reilly: But you have to admit that some people can perceive that things aren't going so well in Iraq—

Rumsfeld: And some people will be strangled by my own hands!

O'Reilly: Come on, Mr. Secretary. This is the No Spin Zone. Are we supposed to believe you can actually strangle everyone criticizing you?

Rumsfeld: Are you questioning me, you impudent fool?! I know where you live, which will soon be known as where you died!

O'Reilly: With all due respect, Mr. Secretary, you're just dodging the question now. Now, what about—

Rumsfeld: Each time you speak, you add that much more pain to your death.

O'Reilly: Hey, it's my show, and I get to talk, so—

Rumsfeld: You pompous prick! I will rip your guts out with my teeth, then—

O'Reilly: Cut his mike. Okay, now I get to talk, Mr. Secretary. A lot of people think you have not committed enough troops to Iraq, and I want a "no spin" response to that accusation. Put his mike back on.

Rumsfeld: ...it down your neck. Your blood will paint the entire—

O'Reilly: You're still not answering the question.

Rumsfeld: Sorry, could you repeat it?

O'Reilly: The question was about how people think you have failed in Iraq and—

Rumsfeld: And I said I'd kill them. What don't you understand?

O'Reilly: But that's not answering—

Rumsfeld: Why must I answer the concerns of people who will be dead?

O'Reilly: You're just repeating the same tired old lines. You can't possibly kill all of them when you didn't even successfully kill Steve Doocy. In fact—

Rumsfeld: I'll show you! Rarr!

O'Reilly: And apparently the Secretary has destroyed the satellite connection. Well, I guess he couldn't stand the No Spin Zone. On to our next topic: Why must our tax money go to NPR douche-bags who won't allow a fair discussion of my new book, *Who's Looking Out for You?* With us, we have some idiot from NPR.

NPR Idiot: Now, I'd just like to point out—

O'Reilly: Quiet! There's breaking news... Apparently, a group of about a hundred protestors has been found strangled to death. Police think it's the work of the so-called "Rumsfeld Strangler," as a note was found at the scene, reading, "I, Donald Rumsfeld, strangled these guys, and now I'm coming after Bill O'Reilly." Police are currently deciphering what that's supposed to mean, and we'll have more information as it becomes available. Now, back to the NPR Idiot... Hmm, he seems to have been strangled to death. I guess yet another person couldn't stand the No Spin Zone. Now for the most ridiculous item of the day... ack... erk...

November 24, 2003

Negotiating the Medicare Bill

"Who is the mysterious protestor sniper?" Bush said to himself as he aimed his rifle. "No one knows, for he strikes deadly and quietly."

"Are you sniping people again?" Laura Bush asked angrily.

"Just with rubber bullets," Bush answered defensively.

Laura picked up some of the bullets. "These look like copper-tipped."

"Uh... copper is a type of rubber."

"I'm taking your gun away," Laura said, snatching the rifle. "Now, you play nice."

"Now what am I going to do?" Bush moaned as Laura walked off.

Out of the shadows emerged the cloaked figure of Karl Rove. "You must focus on getting the Medicare bill passed. The Democrats want it to be an issue, and they must be denied. So speak the elders."

"Don't worry there, Rover," Bush answered. "I'm just about to negotiate with some Democrats. I'm sure I'll know how to sweet-talk them."

"Do not fail," Rove warned ominously as the shadows consumed him.

Senator Tom Daschle then entered Bush's office. "I know you wanted to talk to me, but I won't vote for this Medicare bill because of... uh... seniors and... uh... yadda yadda."

"I understand your concern," Bush said, approaching Daschle, "but you should hear what I have to say." He then started repeatedly bashing Daschle's head into the top of the desk. "Now, you vote for that bill, you slimy weasel! I'm a big man! I'll hurt you good!"

Suddenly, the wall gave way as Ted Kennedy came crashing through. "Grerawerr! You're trying to privatize Medicare! Me filibuster! Me destroy!"

"Oh no!" Bush exclaimed. "It's Big Fat Teddy K! And he's come to eat me!" Bush tossed Daschle out the window and hid under his desk.

"Grerawerr!" Big Fat Teddy K exclaimed as he swatted the desk aside with his massive arm.

Bush cowered in fear, but then he spotted Chomps out in the hallway. "Attack! Chomps! Attack!" Bush called out.

Chomps ran into the office and started savagely attacking one of the paintings on the wall. "Hey! I didn't like that painting either," Bush said, "but it was a present from my mother-in-law, and now's not the time for art criticism." Bush then rolled to his feet and started running before Big Fat Teddy K could stomp him.

Bush found his wife washing dishes in the kitchen. "Quick, Laura," Bush yelled, "I'm negotiating the Medicaid bill, and I need my shotgun."

"It's the Medi*care* bill, dear," Laura corrected him, "and you'd know where your shotgun is if you'd put it back on the shotgun rack after using it."

Bush heard the roar of Big Fat Teddy K and kept moving. He then ran into Scott McClellan. "Hey Scott," Bush said to him, "wave your arms in the air and say, 'I want to cut taxes.'"

"Why?"

"Just do it!"

Scott waved his arms in the air and said, "I want to cut taxes!"

"Grerawerr!" Big Fat Teddy K roared with rage upon seeing Scott.

"Eep." Scott ran off with Big Fat Teddy K in pursuit.

Bush let out a sigh of relief. "That was a close one."

Senator John Edwards then walked up to Bush. "I just want to tell you I'm not going to vote for that—"

Bush punched Edwards in the face.

"Okay, I'll vote for the bill!" Edwards said as he ran away crying.

Now Daschle came back, followed by some policemen. "That's the man who assaulted me!" Daschle yelled as he pointed at Bush.

"So what?" Bush answered. "I pardon myself. Plus, I reverse-pardon Daschle for the charge of indecency, since he's such a slimy weasel."

"You can't do that!" Daschle declared.

"That's for the courts to decide," one of the officers said as he slapped cuffs onto Daschle. "Now let's get you back to the federal penitentiary, you pervert."

As soon as Daschle was led away, Karl Rove materialized. "Have you handled the problem?"

"Negotiating is hard," Bush complained. "Want to play some Mario Kart, Rover?"

Rove vanished back into the darkness once again, just as if he had never been there.

"Man, that guy is no fun."

December 01, 2003

The Axis of Evil Strikes Back Part I

"A new day dawns," Buck the Marine said as he admired the sky, "and this date shall be carved in the tombstone of many a forner who crosses my path."

"Hey, Buck," called a voice from behind him. He turned to see President Bush.

"You back in Iraq again?" Buck exclaimed.

"Yeppers," Bush answered. "Had so much fun last time I thought I might stop by again. So what are we doing?"

"Contemplating the people we are going to kill today," Buck said. "Hey! Are you eating one of my MREs?"

"Just trying to be like one of the troops," Bush stated, "by helping myself to their stuff. Found some homemade cookies in one tent. Want some?"

"Isn't it dangerous for you to be out here?" Buck asked.

"That's what my Secret Service agents said," Bush replied, "so I didn't bring them with me... except for Kôtôichi since he's blind and doesn't know where the heck he is."

"I thought you said we were going to the Bahamas," Kôtôichi, the blind samurai, stated, "but I do not hear the waves."

"Maybe you're going deaf too, Blindy," Bush chuckled. He then leaned over to Buck and whispered, "That's my new nickname for him: Blindy." After another moment's thought, he leaned over to Buck again and added, "Because he's blind."

"Isn't your wife going to miss you?" Buck inquired.

"She's happy to have time to herself to do wifey stuff," Bush answered.

"Like what?"

"I dunno... clean stuff and uh... nag people."

* * * *

"And a last minute entry to the Demolition Derby: Laura Bush!"

* * * *

"Hey, look! Iraqi children!" Bush exclaimed.

"What are Iraqi children doing in the Bahamas?" Ichi asked.

"Tell us all about America, Mr. President man," said one of the children.

Bush sat down among the kids as Buck watched and Kôtôichi kept listening for the ocean. "In America, everyone is happy," Bush told the kids, "and the streets are paved with gold. And the kids get all the candy they ever want."

"Can we come to America some day?" one of the kids asked.

"No," Bush answered sharply, "we already have enough immigrants."

"Will Iraq be as great as America one day?" inquired another kid.

Bush just laughed. "You'll be lucky if your country isn't torn apart by religious extremists."

The kids all looked sad. Finally one asked, "Will you at least do something about the ninjas?"

"Of course," Bush said, patting the kid on the head. "Wait a second... what ninjas?"

All of a sudden, a ninja charged Bush, and the kids scattered. Bush rolled out of the way just in time for the sword to miss him. "Eek! Ninjas!" Bush yelled, ducking as throwing stars barely missed him.

"You said there would be no ninjas in the Bahamas," Ichi grumbled.

"I got 'em," Buck said. He then fired upon the ninjas with his M-16. They all deftly dodged the bullets. Buck then tossed aside his rifle and drew his KA-BAR. "Dodge this!" he yelled as he stabbed at a ninja. The ninja dodged it. "Dangit!" Buck exclaimed. "I shouldn't have told him to dodge that."

"Blindy! Do something!" Bush yelled, ducking from ninja blades.

Kôtôichi ran away.

"Good idea," Bush said, following.

"I hates retreating," Buck grumbled as he ran after them.

They soon found a cave to hide in. Buck took out his radio. "Base, this is Buck the Marine. We are under attack by ninjas... yeah, with swords and throwing stars and everything."

"Tell them about how they flip," Bush said.

"And they flip, too," Buck said into the radio.

"They are no ordinary ninjas," Ichi stated. "They are robot ninjas."

"How do you know that?" Bush asked.

"They kept shouting, 'We are robot ninjas! We are robot ninjas!' over and over," Ichi answered.

Bush shook his head. "Man, I'm a bad listener."

* * * *

“The meeting of the Axis of Evil is called to order,” Ernst Stavro Blofeld announced. “And once again, President Jacques Chirac is here as an observer.”

“We just want to know what the enemy is doing,” Chirac said, “so that we might better appease them and know which direction to run in is most cowardly.”

“We must stop the Americans in Iraq!” Saddam Hussein yelled. “They are very powerful, though. They killed my sons; even I wasn’t able to do that.”

“If the Americans are made to look as fools in Iraq,” Osama bin Laden stated, “then I can gain even more followers. Muh ha ha ha.”

“And France will replace them as a world power!” Chirac said. “Wha ha ha ha!”

“And I can enter the race for presidency and beat Bush!” Hillary Clinton exclaimed. “Bwa ha ha ha!”

“And I can take Disney World away from Japan!” Kim Jong-Il laughed. “Tee hee hee!”

“And Aquaman will be defenseless!” shouted Black Manta. “Gra ha ha ha!”

“Ooh ooh! Ee ee!” said Chim-Chim, the evilest monkey.

“Don’t worry,” Blofeld said. “We have plans for the Americans. Tell them, evil dictator of China.”

“I, evil dictator of China,” declared the evil dictator of China, “have flooded Iraq with our robots ninjas. Soon their forces will fall. But we must keep any of this from being traced back to China, or we’ll be considered as vile in Americans’ eyes as France is.”

“Then you shouldn’t have put ‘Made in China’ on all the robots’ parts,” Blofeld commented.

“We take pride in our workmanship!” the evil dictator of China shot back.

“Do you think this will be enough to stop the Americans?” Saddam asked.

“To be sure,” the evil dictator of China said, “we have more help.”

Suddenly a portrait of Chairman Mao floated into the room. “It is I, the haunted portrait of Chairman Mao!” it said, its eyes glowing red with

Commie evil. "I shall help lead the forces, and they will fall to my Commie evil!"

"We must make sure the Americans do not find out of our plans," Osama bin Laden stated. "I bet they have spies about."

Saddam turned to his compatriot at his side. "Have you seen anyone suspicious, Chomps, the world's angriest Baathist party member?"

Chomps shook his head no.

"Maybe it's just me," Osama said, "but Chomps looks a lot like a Rottweiler with a fake mustache and a beret."

"I will not have anyone questioning Chomps!" Saddam responded angrily. "He has been a loyal Baathist party member since earlier this morning." Saddam then added more quietly, "Plus, it makes him angry... very angry."

* * * *

"So that's their dastardly plan!" Condoleezza Rice exclaimed.

"See! The mustache cam worked just like the guy at Radio Shack said it would," stated Clancy, the intelligence guy.

"How did you find out about this meeting, anyway?" Condi asked.

"Well, we found this Muslim cleric who claimed to be blind," Clancy explained, "so we held up a number of fingers, and he answered how many there were incorrectly. So his story held up... so far. But we didn't trust him. So we roughed him up until he finally admitted he wasn't blind. We then did the 'how many fingers am I holding up' test again, but he failed. Ends up he was lying about not being blind just to get us to stop beating him. Now we knew this guy didn't have any scruples. So we took some jumper cables—"

"Is this story going somewhere?" Rumsfeld demanded angrily.

"To cut to the chase," Clancy said, "we found a flyer for the meeting at the Safeway."

"But how are we going to deal with the robot ninjas?" Condi asked. "We'll have to operate carefully."

"Carefully my ass!" Rumsfeld exclaimed. "Let's just kill them all!" He grabbed the microphone that was connected to Chomps. "Hippies! Hippies!"

* * * *

"Something seems wrong with your Baathist party member," Blofeld stated, watching Chomps snarl and snap at the air in fury. Suddenly, his mustache fell off.

"Oh no!" Saddam exclaimed. "Terminal Mustache Disease!"

As Chomps became even wilder, his beret finally fell off.

"*Sacre bleu!*" Chirac yelled. "It is angry American dog Chomps!" Chomps then leapt over and grabbed Chirac by the head. He shook the Frenchman vigorously while everyone else fled.

* * * *

"So the Axis of Evil is behind the robot ninjas, eh?" Bush asked through the satellite hookup from Iraq. "And we have to deal with the haunted portrait of Chairman Mao. Anyone remember how they defeated the haunted painting in *Ghostbusters 2*? Because I really don't feel like watching that again."

"Sorry, but our intelligence does not encompass the climaxes of special effects-laden comedy sequels," Clancy answered. "What we do know is that the Axis of Evil is working overtime to make America fail."

"But I like America!" Bush exclaimed. "It's my favorite country! We need to do something."

"Extreme measures will be required," Condi advised.

"I know the most extreme," Bush said firmly. "Get me Robo-Patton!"

TO BE CONTINUED...

December 03, 2003

The Axis of Evil Strikes Back Part II

"I don't know about using a haunted robot," Rumsfeld grumbled. "Back in my day we did all of our killing with rocks and sharpened sticks."

Condoleezza Rice rolled her eyes. "Well, in the present day, we fight wars using androids possessed by the spirits of long-dead generals." She looked over the giant robot laden with ivory accents. "Such power. He can stick his hand into another man's face and turn it into a pile of goo. Hopefully he won't go on an insane killing spree this time, though." She hit some buttons on a console and reactivated Robo-Patton. "Robo-Patton," Condi called out, "your objectives are to follow your orders and only kill whoever falls under your mission parameters. Please repeat your objectives."

"My objectives are to follow my orders," Robo-Patton responded in a deep synthesized voice, "and only kill whoever falls under my mission parameters... and whomever else I feel like killing."

Condi shrugged her shoulders. "Close enough."

* * * *

"All these rumors about Iraq and the president being stuck in some sort of 'robot ninja' quagmire are unfounded," White House Press Secretary Scott McClellan told the press.

"So is he actually in Iraq?" asked a reporter.

"No... uh... he's resting in the White House," Scott answered.

"Then why won't he come out?"

"He... uh... um... thought he saw a bear and decided to stay inside where it is safe. Any more questions?"

There was a pause while the press thought things over. "Is that a giant robot standing behind you?"

"Oh yeah; I forgot to mention Robo-Patton," Scott said, slapping his head. "He'll now be leading the troops in Iraq to fight the robot-nin... I mean terrorists."

"Isn't this the same robot who went on an insane killing spree in Berkeley?" asked a skeptical reporter.

"Yeah... uh... but he's changed now... or something," Scott answered.

"Robo-Patton, do you think the war in Iraq is an unnecessary quagmire?" a reporter asked the robot.

"Quagmire does not compute," Robo-Patton answered. "Your question has bothered me." Robo-Patton then let loose a mighty slap that took the reporter's head clean off. "All your questions annoy me." Robo-Patton's arms turned into Gatling guns. He opened fire, killing the entire press corp.

Scott stared at the carnage in shock. "Uh-oh."

Rumsfeld and Condi now walked in. "Did you see how quickly he killed them all?" Condi asked smiling.

"Beats my record," Rumsfeld said.

"Uh... aren't there laws against killing reporters?" Scott asked, looking warily at Robo-Patton, who still scanned with his glowing blue eyes for more enemies to annihilate.

"'Aren't there laws against killing reporters?'" Rumsfeld mimicked in a high-pitched voice. "Aren't you Mr. Goody-Two-Shoes?"

"I desire more destruction," Robo-Patton announced.

Condi smiled. "I think you're ready for Iraq."

* * * *

"Kôtôichi," Bush whispered, "do you see any robot ninjas out there?"

Ichi groaned. "All I can see is your idiocy."

"Those robot ninjas don't play fair," Buck complained. "They won't get shot or stabbed or nothing."

"And now we're stuck hiding in some cave like some common bin Laden," Bush added. He then peered out of the cave entrance. Not seeing anything, he threw out a rock. It was immediately struck mid-air by a throwing star.

"I think they're still out there," Bush whispered.

Suddenly they could hear rapid gunfire and explosions. "What's that?" Bush exclaimed.

"Sounds like..." Buck's eyes lit up. "War!" He ran out of the cave.

"Careful, Buck!" Bush called out. The sounds of violence died down. "You out there, Buck?" Bush asked.

"Yeah, and there's a robotic World War II general out here," Buck answered.

Bush came out of the cave. "Eisenhower?" he asked excitedly. He then saw the robot. "Aww... it's just Robo-Patton."

"Who is your third friend?" Robo-Patton demanded. "He looks Japanese."

"The Japanese are our allies now," Bush explained. "Instead of being obsessed with warmongering, they're now obsessed with excessively violent, porn-filled cartoons."

"Is this true?" Robo-Patton asked.

Ichi shrugged his shoulders. "I've never seen one."

"So are you here to save me?" Bush asked Robo-Patton.

"I am not programmed to save," he answered. "I am only programmed to kill."

"Well, it will be an honor to work with you," Buck stated. "My grandpappy, Jebediah the Marine, always talked about how you led America to killin' many a for'ner."

"But there are still foreigners left to kill," Robo-Patton answered. "My mission is to find and destroy the robot ninjas."

"Ninjas always have secret hideout," Ichi stated. "If we can find it and destroy it, then the ninjas will be defeated."

"I hate secret hideouts," Bush grumbled. "They're the hardest hideouts to find."

* * * *

"Know who I blame, Mohammed?"

"I dunno, Mohammed; who do you blame?"

"The Jooos!"

"Me too! But know what? I know this guy from Pakistan who sometimes blames the Hindus."

"What? Doesn't he know about the Jooos?"

Suddenly a giant figure crashed through the ceiling of the terrorist hideout.

"Ahh! It's imperialist, American robot general!" yelled another one, who was probably named Mohammed.

In under a second, all the terrorists in the room were killed with Gatling guns, except for one whom Robo-Patton grabbed by the neck.

Bush, Buck, and Ichi now entered the building. "Dang, that's some mighty for'ner killin'!" Buck exclaimed.

"Where is the robot ninja hideout?" Robo-Patton demanded to the terrorist.

"It's to the north!" the terrorist squealed.

"You are of no more use to me," Robo-Patton said and then threw the terrorist up into the air. Next he launched a missile, blowing the man to bits.

"I always wanted to do that," Buck said, "but I thought it was against the Geneva Conventions."

Robo-Patton headed out of the building. "The Geneva Conventions does not compute."

* * * *

Unseen, two red, glowing eyes watched the group as they left the terrorist hideout.

"Yes, capitalist fools; head right into my trap. Soon you will be begging for death! Muh ha ha ha!"

"Ee ee ee!" added Chim-Chim, the evilest monkey.

TO BE CONCLUDED...

December 08, 2003

The Axis of Evil Strikes Back Part III

"What's going on in here?" White House Press Secretary Scott McClellan demanded as he watched the ruckus in the White House.

"Kegger party," Dick Cheney answered. "What's it look like, dingus?"

"Is this appropriate while the president is in danger?" Scott asked.

"Who invited the dweeb?" inquired an obviously drunk Donald Rumsfeld.

"Not me," answered Condi as she threw back a Jell-O shot. "Skippy, don't you have some idiotic questions from the press to answer?"

"I think we all have jobs to do... such as—" Scott started to say but was interrupted by a thrown beer bottle.

* * * *

"Ninjas can't dodge buckshot, can they?" Bush asked as he inspected his shotgun by looking down the barrel.

"So say the ancient texts," Kôtôichi answered.

"How could you know?" Bush chuckled. "You couldn't have read them, Blindy."

In the blink of an eye, Ichi's sword was drawn and resheathed. Then Bush's tie fell off.

"Man, my tie budget has doubled since hiring you," Bush complained.

"Shouldn't we call an entire force to take out the robot ninjas?" Buck the Marine asked.

"The press will call me a wimp if I can't handle a bunch of robot ninjas by myself," Bush answered, "except for the help of one Marine... and a blind samurai... Oh! And a robot fueled by the soul of a dead general."

"All must die," Robo-Patton said in his deep, heavily synthesized voice.

"That's the spirit!" Bush exclaimed.

"We are near the ninja hideout," Ichi said. "I feel much ninja-ness about."

"Sometimes I wonder if you're just full of it, Ichi," Bush stated irately.

"Ha ha! You would never know," Ichi chuckled.

"I bet they're in that foreboding building ahead," Buck said.

"Let's kill the sonafabitches!" Robo-Patton yelled as he charged forward.

"You're the strategerist," Bush said, following the robot.

The four of them entered the building but didn't see anything. Suddenly bright lights came on, nearly blinding everyone except Ichi. "Is it the ninjas?" Buck asked.

"Worse," Bush answered, "it's the press."

"You said there would be evidence of a quagmire here," said one of the reporters.

"Patience, my useful idiots," answered the haunted portrait of Chairman Mao.

Now the robot ninjas surrounded Bush, Buck, Ichi and Robo-Patton. "That's some good quagmire!" exclaimed one of the reporters filming the event.

"Man, this couldn't get any worse," Bush sighed. Suddenly he felt a bite on his shoulder. "Ahh!" he screamed. "It's Chim-Chim, the evilest monkey! Get him off! Get him off!" He looked at Buck. "What do I do when there is a monkey on my back?"

"I think you're supposed to stop, drop and roll," Buck answered.

Bush dropped to the floor and rolled. "Robo-Patton, you take care of the ninjas," he ordered. "Buck, you kill the press. Ichi, you stab the monkey on my back."

"I don't know if I'm supposed to kill the press," Buck answered.

The ninjas attacked, but Robo-Patton opened on them with his Gatling guns. "Kill! Kill! Kill!" Robo-Patton yelled.

"Foolish American robot general!" the portrait of Chairman Mao shouted. Beams of pure Commie evil then shot out of his eyes, knocking Robo-Patton down.

"Yay! More quagmire!" yelled one of the press.

"I hate art!" Buck exclaimed, firing at the portrait.

Mao just laughed. "Your puny weapons are no match for Commie evil! Kill, ninjas! Kill!"

Ichi pried Chim-Chim off Bush with his cane. Bush then grabbed Chim-Chim and threw him. "Ee ee!" Chim-Chim yelled as he flew out the window.

"What's our status?" Bush asked.

"Robo-Patton can't fight back while that Mayo guy is keeping him down," Buck answered.

Bush flicked the cap off of a Sharpie with his thumb. "He's mine!"

* * * *

"So is there any way to spin this as a quagmire?" asked the anchorman.

"I'm afraid not," answered CNN's Lefty Stevens. "Bush and Robo-Patton soundly defeated all the ninjas. As much as I tried, I can't spin this as a defeat for him."

"But there could be more quagmire in the future, right?" the anchorman asked hopefully.

"Maybe," Stevens answered, not too assuringly.

Bush turned off the TV. "Hooray!" he exclaimed. "Evil is defeated once again!" He then looked around the White House. "What happened here?"

"Teenagers broke in and vandalized the place," Cheney answered.

Bush shook his fist in the air. "Teenagers!"

Laura now entered the room holding a trophy. "Well, this place is going to need a good cleaning, by golly."

"Hey honey," Bush said, "did you keep yourself busy while I was gone?"

"I did a few things here and there."

"Hey, that's a nice trophy you have there," Bush remarked.

"It's... uh... for winning the pecan pie-baking contest," Laura answered.

"Then why does it say 'Ultimate Fighting Championship' on it?" Bush inquired.

"Well, you know how they like to hype those pie-baking contests, by golly," Laura answered with a nervous smile.

Bush nodded his head knowingly. "They're nothing but politics; that's why I stay out of them."

"We have communications from Robo-Patton," Condi stated.

"Are you busy leading the troops in Iraq?" Bush asked Robo-Patton.

"No. I've decided to finally do as I've always said and storm right into China."

"That was MacArthur who wanted to do that," Bush told him.

"Whatever," Robo-Patton shot back. "Now leave me be as I weave a path of destruction."

"Okay. Have fun." Bush turned off the radio.

"He's going to slaughter countless people in his insane pursuit," Condi stated. "What should we do?"

Bush looked at his watch. "Well, it's about lunchtime—let's order pizza. What toppings does everyone want?"

"I like sausage," Scott said.

"You *would* like sausage," Bush chuckled. Everyone else laughed too.

"I hate you guys," Scott grumbled.

* * * *

The mood at the meeting of the Axis of Evil was dire.

"Ooh ooh! Ee ee!" Chim-Chim swore in revenge.

"Bush may have defeated us this time," the haunted portrait of Chairman Mao said, "but he has not seen the last of us! Muh ha ha ha!"

Everyone else laughed evilly, too, but then Saddam finally asked Mao, "Did someone draw glasses, a mustache, and buckteeth on you?"

"There is no reason to draw attention to it!"

THE END

December 15, 2003

Ace in the Hole

Rumsfeld entered the Oval Office, a solemn look on his face. "Mr. President, I want to warn you that first reports aren't always accurate but..."

Bush jumped up, knocking over his desk in the process. "We caught Saddam, didn't we?"

"We got the bastard!" Rumsfeld answered, smiling. "Found him hiding in a hole!"

"I always said we should look in holes!" Bush exclaimed. Both of them danced around the office.

Daschle now entered. "I just want to say that I'm very saddened by how... Hey! Why are you two so happy?"

"We caught Saddam, you slimy weasel!" Bush shouted with glee.

"Oh @#$%!" Daschle exclaimed.

"I know!" Bush yelled to Rumsfeld. "Let's beat up Daschle in celebration!"

Rumsfeld grabbed Daschle from behind while Bush prepared to punch him. Laura Bush then walked into the room. "Why are you two beating up Daschle in a celebratory manner?" she demanded.

"We caught Saddam!" Bush answered.

"Well, golly, isn't that good news," Laura said smiling, "but isn't there something better to do now than pummel Daschle... such as question Saddam?"

"You're right dear," Bush said, thinking things over. "Off to Iraq once more!"

* * * *

"There was no reason to bring a turkey, dear," Laura told Bush.

"No, it's tradition," Bush protested. "When you come to Iraq, you bring a turkey. That's what we did last time."

"That's because it was Thanksgiving."

"But... uh... oh..." Bush handed the turkey over to the guard. "Here's a turkey. Where's Saddam?"

"He's waiting inside," the guard said. Bush, Laura, and Rumsfeld quickly hurried inside the cell. There stood Saddam, staring back at them defiantly.

"I well tell you fools nothing!" he shouted.

"Rummy, you can ask the first question," Bush said.

Rumsfeld lunged at Saddam. "I'll strangle you! Rarr!" The guards held Rumsfeld back.

"For pete's sake!" Laura exclaimed.

"I guess he'll be the bad cop," Bush remarked and then looked at Saddam. "Now you answer my questions, or we'll unrestrain Rumsfeld. What are your ties to Al Qaeda?"

"I tell you nothing, American pig dog!" Saddam shouted back boldly.

"Have you been leading the insurgents?"

"You will get no answers from me, American dog pig!" Saddam snarled.

"Where are your WMDs?"

"You will learn nothing from me, pig American dog!"

"If two cars are eighty miles apart and heading towards each other, one going fourty miles per hour and the other fifty miles per hour, how long until they pass?"

"I will never tell you, dog American pig!"

"We'll see how strong your resolve is!" Bush yelled and then yanked on Saddam's mustache.

"Okay! I talk!" Saddam screamed. "They pass each other in around fifty minutes!"

"Fifty three and a third minutes, you evil dictator!" Bush shouted. "But if you show me your work, I'll give you partial credit!"

"Bah! I spit at your partial credit!"

"This is getting us nowhere!" Rumsfeld objected. "Let's just skip to the discussion of what we do with his corpse."

"But I'm not dead," Saddam objected.

Bush backhanded Saddam. "Shut up!"

"I say we cut him into four pieces and place each piece at the four corners of the world as a warning to others," Rumsfeld offered.

"I say we give him a taste of his own medicine," Bush said, "and bury him in a mass grave... a mass grave of one!"

"You will do nothing to me, Junior Bush!" Saddam yelled. "I curse you to be a one-termer like your father!"

"You take that back!" Bush exclaimed, lunging at Saddam as the guards tried to restrain him.

"I think we should let the Iraqis deal with him," Laura said. "They're the ones who have been most harmed by him."

"But that mean man tried to kill my daddy!" Bush objected. "I want to murder him dead myself."

"You have to put others' needs above your own, dear," Laura said.

Saddam made a whipping sound.

"That's enough out of you!" Bush said. "Maybe we could just exile him to France."

"Please, no!" Saddam pleaded. "That place smells like cheese and feces! Be merciful, younger Bush!"

"I think that's for the Iraqi people to decide," Laura stated.

"As always, dear, you're very smart and don't smell like a monkey," Bush said and then looked at Saddam, "unlike certain evil dictators I know." He turned back to Rumsfeld and Laura. "Since that's decided, let's get something to eat. I hear they just opened a new McDonald's franchise down the street. It's like a regular McDonald's in America, but to adapt to the local culture, everyone working there has a bushy mustache."

* * * *

"I'm sure you have a lot of questions about the Medicare bill," White House Press Secretary Scott McClellan said, "so let's get started."

"All of our questions are about the capture of Saddam Hussein, actually," stated one reporter.

"Well, we hope to find him soon, but it's a large country, and locating him could take time," Scott answered.

"But you did locate him," a reporter said. "Bush is over there questioning him now."

"What?!" Scott exclaimed, confused. "We caught him?"

"Yeah, on Saturday."

"So how are we going to execute him," asked FOX News reporter Melinda Hawkish, "and will the video of his execution have audio so we can hear his screams?"

"I had to hear about this from the press?! That bastard!" Scott exclaimed, ignoring the question.

"So you know less than us?" asked a reporter.

"If that's possible, yes," Scott said irately.

"So what do you think is the president's stance on this?"

Scott rolled his eyes. "I think he's happy... so happy he didn't think to tell his press secretary. Do we have any non-Saddam questions that I might be able to answer?"

"I have some about the Barney Christmas video," said a reporter.

"Super," Scott answered and then grumbled to himself, "let's talk about that stupid terrier."

"My favorite part was when Barney was playing cards with Ari Fleischer," giggled one reporter. "I miss him."

"Shut up."